PURO BORDER

PURO BORDER

Dispatches, Snapshots & Graffiti from La Frontera

EDITED BY

LUIS HUMBERTO CROSTHWAITE
JOHN WILLIAM BYRD
BOBBY BYRD

with JESSICA POWERS

Cinco Puntos Press
El Paso, Texas

Cover illustration: "$26" — *oil on canvas.* Copyright © 2002 by Francisco Delgado.

Book and cover design: J.B. Bryan

This book is funded in part by generous support from Fideicomiso Para La Cultura

Printed in Canada.

FIRST EDITION
10 9 8 7 6 5 4 3 2 1

Library of Congress Cataloging-in-Publication Data

Puro border : dispatches, snapshots, and graffiti / edited by Bobby Byrd, John William Byrd, and Luis Humberto Crosthwaite.— 1st ed.
    p. cm.
  ISBN 0-938317-59-8 (pbk.)
1. Mexican-American Border Region—Miscellanea. 2. Mexican-American Border Region—Social conditions. 3. Mexican-American Border Region—Description and travel. 4. United States—Relations—Mexico. 5. Mexico—Relations—United States. I. Byrd, Bobby, 1942-
II. Byrd, John William, 1973- III. Crosthwaite, Luis Humberto, 1962-
  F787 .P87 2002
  972'.1—DC21

                    2002006098

CINCO PUNTOS PRESS
El Paso, Texas

Contents

Introduction

BOBBY BYRD

> *"Hell is darknesses; and the way to it is the cloud of Ignorance; hell itself is but condemned Ignorance, multiplied Ignorance. Ignorance is not onely the drousinesse, the sillinesse, but the wickednesse of the soule. The cruellest man alive could not sit at his feast unless he sat blindfold."* —JOHN DONNE

The Border as Parable

La frontera is like an alleyway, un callejón, which runs between a rich man's house and a poor man's house. Sometimes the alley is very big and wide, like a desert is big and wide. Other times, the alleyway is narrow, only stretching the 15 miles or so to a place like San Diego, which is one of the glorious rooms in the rich man's house.

The rich man's house, which is of course very big, has many other fabulous rooms like San Diego. In every one of those rooms live the children and the relatives and the servants of the rich man. The rich man and his family and even the servants have many needs. They eat a lot, they drink a lot, they climb mountains, they race cars and boats, they travel around the world—they really like to enjoy themselves.

The rich man doesn't have enough servants to cook all the food, to tend the fields, to clean the toilets, to sweep the floors, to cut the grass, to sew the clothes. Nor does he have enough strawberries to eat or oil to put into all his many automobiles and airplanes.

The rich man does not like to want. He says to his children, "I want what I want when I want it." That is one of his maxims of life. And thus that maxim becomes a way of living for everybody. Even the servants.

Lucky for the rich man that on the other side of the alley is the poor man's house. That house is crowded with the poor man's relatives who need work to make enough money to feed themselves and their families. This is their understanding, this is their law.

The poor man knows he has too many relatives in his house and he wishes they would go away and take their problems with them. So the poor man's relatives start going to the rich man's house because they can get work there and they can make more money than they can make if they stay where they are in the poor man's house. In the rich man's house they get jobs cooking the food, cleaning the toilets, sweeping the floors, cutting the grass, and sewing clothes. And they send their money back to their families in the poor man's house.

So the alley between the rich man's house and the poor man's house becomes an empty place through which poor people must pass to enter the rich man's house. It becomes a negative value, a vacuum defined by its emptiness. A place of passage.

This alleyway is a good deal for the rich man and his family. But it puts the rich man in a sticky situation. On the one hand, he doesn't want all the poor people simply walking across the alley and into his house. He thinks maybe they will. They are brown people, they don't speak English. He's afraid of what will happen. So he builds a fence. But, on the other hand, he needs those people coming across the alley, so he builds gates through which the poor people must pass. Thus, the rich man has this steady supply of poor people to work for him. And all he has to do is guard the alley that stands between him and all of those poor people.

But things are not always fun and games for the rich man. He has his problems too. It seems like a lot of the poor man's relatives are sneaking across the alley and jumping the fence into the rich man's backyard. The rich man says he is a Christian man and he believes in an angry God. He doesn't think that anybody should be coming into his house without an invitation. That's why he hires more police and brings more guns and helicopters to guard the alley and writes more laws to keep these people out.

But the poor people keep coming because they can get jobs and make more money in the rich man's house. The harder it is, the more desperate they become. Some of them even die crossing the alleyway. Others get caught and are sent back to the poor man's house. And still others pay smugglers to sneak them across the alley.

But they keep coming.

It seems to go on forever.

But there are easier ways to skin a cat.

Like, smuggling drugs is a good cat skinner.

Some poor people understand this. They want to make more money than they need, like the rich man has more money than he needs, and they see that it's not too difficult to cross the alley. So they start sneaking drugs across the alley and they sell the drugs to the rich man's children and his relatives and his servants who like the drugs very much.

The rich man is undone. Again, he remembers that he is a Christian man and he believes in an angry God. And he doesn't think that anybody should be smuggling drugs into his house and making all that filthy lucre. Especially without his say-so. So he hires even more police and brings more guns and helicopters and airplanes to guard the alley to keep these people out.

But the drugs keep coming because the rich man's children and his relatives and his servants keep buying the drugs.

They like the drugs very much.

So more police come. And more guns. And more helicopters. And the rich man writes more and more laws.

And it feels like it will go on forever.

Then 9/11 happens and…

INTRODUCTION

The Border as Somebody Else's Business

When paseño poet Ricardo Sánchez died of cancer in 1995, the obituary department of the *New York Times* called me up to talk about Ricardo. The obit-man had that New Yorker attitude that grates against my heart. You know the type—sardonic, cynical, hipper-than-thou, baby. I repressed my hostility because I wanted the *Times* to officially consecrate Ricardo. I wanted them to tell the larger world about this ex-con poet who had roughed up the status quo of poetry with his righteous anger and his bilingual smartass puns. It would make his wife Teresa happy, his children proud. Besides, Ricardo, who perhaps was still paddling his little boat angrily across the River Styx, might hear a faint murmur of his obituary in the ether.

At the end of the interview, I asked the guy when the obituary would appear.

"Well," he said, "I don't know if we're going to do it yet."

"Why not?"

"Because we haven't decided yet if Sánchez was a good poet or not."

That pissed me off. That wasn't his decision. It was ours! But of course Ricardo's obituary was at this arrogant fool's mercy. It made me feel dirty, but I cajoled the obit-man, and the *Times* eventually announced that pachuco poet Ricardo Sánchez was dead.

I remembered all of this while I was sitting in an auditorium in El Paso looking down at stage lights and television crews. I usually don't spend my time this way, but the Medusa of U.S. media—the conglomerated witch with those gluttonous snakes, Time/CNN/AOL/ABC, entwined atop her frightening visage[1]—had gathered us there to celebrate the media's recognition of the U.S./Mexico border as a real place in the national consciousness. Called *La Frontera: A Day on the Border,* the event was billed as a "Town Hall Meeting." Each of the snakes on Medusa's head, their forked tongues working overtime, had their own job to do:

- *TIME* had anointed the frontera in its TIME-speak as "Amexica: The New Frontier" and had published a special Border section in its June 11, 2001 issue, snapshooting the miles between Brownsville to Tijuana
- CNN was doing the same thing with its week-long coverage of la nueva frontera
- ABC's Peter Jennings was endangering his helmet of hair in Laredo
- *and* AOL, that discombobulated contraption of dollar-technocracy, was making the "sights and sounds of the border come alive on an interactive, geo-cultural map that could be found at the Keyword: "LATINO."

Plus, the gavachos[2] on stage announced to us, AOL was broadcasting us live on AOL throughout the world. Just by being there in the auditorium, we were inside a real live

---

1 Don't look in her eyes, good buddy!
2 Gavacho is from 18th century French, a product of the reign of Maximilian, and it means foreigner. There's some discussion along the border whether it means any foreigner, or only those interlopers of Anglo heritage. Usually, fronterizos consider the term gavacho slightly less pejorative than gringo.

interactive chatroom accessible to everybody except God and Beelzebub. Everybody, that is, who was paying AOL $19.95 a month.

Holy shit. We haven't had so much media attention since the FBI trotted over to Juárez with their shovels.[3] Oh well. I should have been thinking about what Marshall McLuhan taught us way back in the 60s: "The medium is the message." But I wasn't thinking about anything. Like everybody else, I was fascinated by the attention.

Medusa's job for the afternoon was to feed the locals some intellectual stimulus. It was a two-course meal. The first course was a panel discussing political issues facing Border residents. Big Daddy called it "The Border in 2010: Do Washington and Mexico Want to Make the Border Disappear?" Well, of course, that's a stupid question. If you have lived in El Paso the last 20 years, you know for a fact that Washington doesn't want the border to disappear. If they did, then they would be radically liberalizing the drug laws and the immigration laws and tearing down fences and de-militarizing the border. Puro no-brainer.

But the panelists ignored the question's stupidity. Their job was to be serious and not to poke holes in the basic premise of the gathering. They were a mixture of state and federal bureaucrats and academics from both sides of the border. These folks came armed with data. They tussled back and forth. They explained the facts, they explained the immobility of government, they said life on the border might get worse before it got better, and they told us to vote.

Finally, the "Town Hall Meeting" opened the discussion up for questions from the audience. Somebody had had the bright idea to bus in the women activists from the colonias surrounding El Paso. These women got in line behind the microphones and took their turns speaking. One after the other, they asked for water to drink and to bathe in. They asked for a sewage system. They asked for parks for their kids to play in. They asked for jobs. They asked for streetlights and police protection. They asked for paved streets. They all spoke in Spanish, they spoke plainly and they spoke with passion. They were not ashamed of who they were.

This was not an intellectual exercise for them. They said that this place where they lived was supposed to be the United States of America, but it's just like Mexico. The leaders in Washington don't care, the leaders in Austin don't care, the leaders in Mexico City don't care. These women were speaking from immediate experience. They understood that, as far

---

3 In December 1999, 65 FBI agents swarmed across the border to Ciudad Juárez—in support of the Mexican federal police—to excavate the supposedly "hundreds" of bodies buried on a Mexican ranch by a drug cartel. National and international media descended upon El Paso and Juárez anticipating stacks of corpses to be found in the "killing fields" of Juárez. (They estimated that over 200 bodies would be found in the mass grave.) In the end, the bi-national search team found nine bodies. The embarrassed FBI and "parachute journalists" (they fly in, they fly out, they have no roots, they leave no sign) disappeared and let the story fizzle out. The "real" story, of course, was the media's thirst for a narco-traficante body count, while they ignored the more fundamental issues confronting the border—for instance, the brutal and unsolved murders of women in Juárez (over 200 at that time); the corruption of local and federal authorities in Mexico that allowed that to happen; and the slew of U.S. laws that exacerbate conditions in Juárez.

as Washington and Mexico City are concerned, the border will always be what it is right now—a guarded alleyway between the rich and the poor.

So much for that panel. It ended per the allotted time, the panelists disappeared backstage, and most of the people—including the women from the colonias, their anger vented for the moment—vacated the premises. Not me. I stayed around to witness a posse of hired cultural gunslingers file on stage to answer another frivolous question: "Culture and Society in the New Frontier: How Will It Change the U.S. and Mexico?" This discussion degenerated into the usual touchy-feely conversation about what it means to be "Latino/a in America today." Of course, nobody mentioned that being Latino/a means something totally different to the angry Mexicanas who were being bussed back to their colonias than it does to talking heads who have landed plush jobs in New York City.

I endured another hour.

Why? Because I'm slow. It took me most of that boring afternoon until I finally came to the obvious conclusion—the real purpose of the event was to advertise the media conglomerate that was putting on the show. Medusa with the snakes on her head had purchased and packaged us, and we hadn't felt a thing except the slow leak of energy from the room.

The Border as the Place Where We Live

On the border we talk about language all the time because our words cross back and forth the line as if there are no fences and armed guards and military helicopters and no drug laws and no such thing as "illegal immigration." No Washington, D.C. No Mexico, D.F. No rules. Linguistic adultery takes place every day of our lives, the syntaxes of Spanish and English are wet and infected with a viral illegality, and the infection has entered the brainstem, although the authorities refuse to announce to the world that the virus exists and that, indeed, it is contagious.[4]

We possess this cross-contamination of our language and our culture. It is like a biological weapon, an organism that grows into the shape of who we are and where we live. It feeds on words and sentences spoken in the streets and alleys of our cities and towns and pueblos on both side of the line, it feeds on the music and the sorrow and the bilingual puns and jokes, it feeds on the names of plants and animals in the vast wild spaces of la frontera, and it feeds on the histories of people who knew this land before the border ever existed.

The editors meant this book to be a collaboration by people from both sides of the border who understand this trans-border contamination. We wanted a fronterizo perspective—an ornery, bull-headed book that stands contrary to the super-processed media bites spit out by the conglomerates and to the blatant disrespect that we receive from Washington, D.C. and Mexico, D.F.

---

4 Cinco Puntos made an editorial decision a long time ago not to italicize Spanish words that appear in an English text. Because we live en la frontera, we want to assign equal value to the Spanish and English languages, an extension to our view that along the border these languages are partners in the way that all fronterizos, whether they live to the south or the north of the line, should be.

Still, no matter what we do or say, the miles of fences and the heavily armed police and the military helicopters and drug laws and "illegal immigration" exist in spades along the border. The federal governments of the U.S. and Mexico continue to make laws and policy that adversely affect our lives. They continue to ignore who we are and what we need. Thus, people here endure poverty and hardship because of this disregard, and it becomes harder and harder simply to go across to visit friends and relatives or to shop and eat on the other side.

We are restless, we are angry.

An Afterthought

Editing this book is a never-ending process. Every morning I pick up the paper and see something else that should be mentioned: activists demanding justice for the brutal and un-solved murders of more than 300 women in Juárez; a grotesque summer of death in the Arizona desert as immigrants trekked along the Devil's Highway of the Cabeza Prieta Wilderness; the drug-related wars in Tijuana and Juárez as rival factions battle for control of those cities' cartels in the wake of the deaths or arrests of their bosses; and hundreds of maquilas shutting down along the border in the wake of the U.S. recession and post-9/11 despondency, while the amoral transnational corporations flee for cheaper fields of labor. The exodus of jobs will leave hundreds of thousands of maquila workers unemployed, fur-ther exacerbating conditions on the Mexican side—an environment which Charles Bowden correctly identifies as "the laboratory of the future." A mad scientist is at work.

Still, we must put the lid on this book and twist it on tight.

The border is like any other almost ordinary place.

Not quite Mexico.

Not quite U.S.

And it's July here, and the last three days the skies have rained, a glorious and patient rain that will hopefully break a long drought and seep into the earth. The sages are bloom-ing pinkish-purple, the air tastes sweet, the tomato plants in my garden are drooping with delicious tomatoes, the birds and the insects are at work doing their jobs, Berta Alemán and her grandchildren are sitting on the front porch next door, and when the clouds clear away the sky will become blue, a rich metallic blue that is hard to comprehend unless you have lived here for a few years. Juan Hernández, our janitor at Cinco Puntos, woke up at four this morning in a colonia on the ragged foothills of the Sierra Juárez. His house, which he has been assembling from scrap lumber, had endured the rain. He was glad and proud. He kissed his wife and children goodbye; 30 minutes later a bus dropped him off near the El Paso Street Bridge. He crossed the Río Bravo,[5] and the sleepy agent looked at him. She swiped his laser card through the digital reader, and waved him through to the United States of America.

---

5 Which on his way home will magically become the Río Grande. Before 9/11, by the way, Juan used to cross at 5:30 or 6 a.m.

Juan is full of stories about "this side" and "that side." Sad stories. Happy stories. Always with a twist of funkiness. He's been in jail on both sides, and he knows what a gang will do if they catch you with a few bucks in your pockets. Juan grew up in Phoenix. English is his first language. He could take his family and go back if he wanted. It wouldn't be too hard. Not as hard as building that house on the bone-dry shoulders of the Sierra. Ask him why he stays in Juárez, and he just scrunches up his shoulders and smiles widely. "I don't know," he says. "This is my home."

Juan will probably never read much of this book, although he will be proud to see his name here. We will talk and he will tell me more stories.

Peronneau Breese goes against Juan's flow, living on the U.S. side and crossing to the Mexican side for work. Peronneau is a self-taught, world-class chef, a bilingual man who is equally at home on either side of the border. Peronneau's working day starts in El Paso where he is the teaching chef at Café Mayapan, a restaurant that serves as an incubator for unemployed workers (most of whom can't speak English) who want to enter the restaurant business. It's run by La Mujer Obrera, an activist organization dedicated to serving the needs of workers displaced by NAFTA. In the afternoons, Peronneau walks across the bridge and catches a cab to el Restaurante Aíleme, a wonderful restaurant that offers exquisite Mediterranean dinners with a taste of la frontera. There he serves the elite of Juárez, some of whom are probably paying their checks with drug-dirty money. Like Juan, Peronneau has stories about the border, but his stories extend into the weird history and social structure of El Paso and Juárez. He will tell you about Pancho Villa and Cormac McCarthy and Mexican governors and Catholic bishops and wild parties and delicious meals. He doesn't mind swinging the wrecking ball of iconoclasm, and his stories make me laugh and make me sad at the same time.

Peronneau fiercely loves his life here and he refuses to let people disparage it. He will read this book, and it will disappoint him because it deals so bluntly with difficult issues. He and I will probably argue about this book, but he will pour us each a martini derecho and tell me more stories.

Stories like Juan's and Peronneau's are like pieces of the fabric that bind me here to the border. The paradoxes, the surrealism. My love is irrational and maybe even foolish. My friend and fellow editor Luis Crosthwaite will explain that to you in his epilogue. But as a writer and a poet, I have a theory that fits inside my admittedly romantic vision of this place—it's here along the frontera, and the other likewise-disparaged and ignored places on our planet, that human beings will develop some type of compassionate understanding that can cope with this new century.

Here on the border they can no longer build walls high enough.

Eventually we will see what is truly happening.

We will make a full-hearted art and build a new syntax.

We will make angry politics and struggle.

And maybe we will seed the earth with our understanding.

Our Thank Yous

Cinco Puntos would like to thank the authors, photographers and artists who have permitted us to use their texts and images to put this anthology together. Working with this group of people has been an extraordinary privilege. This book is really theirs—our process was one of collaboration.

Beyond the names you read on the cover or in the table of contents are many others. These folks have contributed ideas, understanding and ambiente through conversations, emails, their passion for the border community, their questions and their interest in wanting to see this book published. Like us, they have watched in alarm as the border has become more and more militarized on the U.S. side and more and more destabilized on the Mexican side—the result of short-sighted lawmaking in both federal capitals, the huge influx of drug money, the so-called globalized economy with its migrant industries and the explosive growth of the population on the Mexican side. Throughout it all, to our collective amazement, the border remains the border, a remarkable place to live, with its two-headed culture, its resilient and interesting people, and its wild and vast landscapes.

Three people in particular have inspired our thinking about the border region. The first is Debbie Nathan. She is the writer who really introduced Cinco Puntos to the place where we live. In the late 1980s, we started reading her work in the *Village Voice* and discovered she lived here in El Paso. Soon afterwards, we began working with her on our first true border book, *Women and Other Aliens* (Cinco Puntos, 1991). Second is Charles Bowden. His chilling notion that Juárez and other communities along the border constitute "the laboratory of the future" lies at the heart of *Puro Border*. And the third is David Romo—writer, musician, research freak and grassroots arts-activist—who demonstrates that the creative and politically active imagination must be an essential ingredient of the cultural landscape if the border is to evolve beyond Bowden's apocalyptic vision.

Others with their writing, ideas and activism have likewise greatly influenced the process of this book—poet and novelist Benjamin Alire Sáenz; journalist John Ross who for years has sent his *México Bárbaro* communiqués from Mexico City and the jungles of Chiapas; photographer Julián Cardona; grassroots border scholar Enrique Madrid; artist Luis Jimenez; writer Luis Alberto Urrea; writer Miriam Davidson; journalist Diana Washington Valdez; storyteller Joe Hayes; and Esther Chavez Cano, director of the Casa Amiga Rape Crisis Center in Juárez.

And still others have offered information, support, encouragement, logistical help and ideas—Julieta García in Mexico City; George Kourous from the Interhemispheric Resources Council; Heather Courtney, director of the documentary *Los Trabajadores*; writer and border scholar Timothy Dunn; David Owen of Outward Bound in Redford, Texas; Bob Moore and Don Flores of the *El Paso Times*; sociologist and statistician Cheryl Howard, Ph.D., University of Texas at El Paso; writer and editor Becky Powers; Barbara Belejack, editor of the *Texas Observer*; Molly Molloy, librarian at New Mexico State University; and Evan Smith, editor of the *Texas Monthly*.

I especially want to thank translator Antonio Garza who stepped in at project's end and worked diligently and creatively in making sure that the translations of the Spanish texts do justice to the meanings and styles of the originals.

The Fideicomiso para la Cultura México / Estados Unidos in Mexico City gave Cinco Puntos a generous grant to research and support *Puro Border*, a grant without which we could not have published this book. Thanks to the Fideicomiso, with mil gracias to Beatriz E. Nava Rivera who was patient with my bad Spanish and poor bookkeeping from the beginning to the end and to Marcela Madariaga, who got the ball rolling.

But before we finally put the lid on this project, I must thank those in the immediate Cinco Puntos family who really got their hands dirty with *Puro Border*. Susannah Mississippi Byrd, my daughter, was to be the co-editor until she jumped ship to run the successful campaign of Mayor Ray Caballero in El Paso. Susie, who has continued to keep a watchful eye on the book from her new office atop city hall, came up with our title, *Puro Border*. Jessica Powers replaced Susie at Cinco Puntos. Besides performing most of the complex administrative duties required to put together an anthology, Jessica was a wonderful asset in our brainstorming sessions, providing insight and ideas as we wandered along. Besides, she's an excellent editor and a true book person. Then, there was our buddy Rus Bradburd, working for us as an intern in the winter and spring of 2002. Rus read and edited essays, made phone calls, commiserated with the editors, offered insight and generally served as a jack-of-all-trades while selling shoes on the side. And not to forget the two people who row the boat along, and when needed, bail it out—business manager Ed Holland and assistant business manager Mary Fountaine.

Finally, for a Cinco Puntos book to be finished, it must pass by the eyes and hands and heart of co-publisher Lee Merrill Byrd. She's the one who pulls all the strings together, does the final edit, interfaces with the designer (in this instance, our good friend Jeff Bryan in Albuquerque) and sends the book out the door. Some books are more difficult than others. *Puro Borde*r was the worst of the worst. Lee's the greatest, huh?

And working with my co-editors—one a remarkable son, the other a wonderful friend, both dedicated fronterizos—has been a true pleasure. With their collaboration, this book became a journey of the imagination.

—*Bobby Byrd*

The "Black Bridge" is the railroad bridge that links downtown Juárez with downtown El Paso. The bridge and the area of river in its vicinity was a favorite crossing point for illegal day laborers and migrants until "Operation Hold the Line" in the late 1990's. The infamous Black Bridge Gang controlled the bridge and the river on the Mexican side, charging tolls to those wishing to cross.

The Border is the Place Where We Live

*When I was a boy, Tijuana was a place of magic and wonder,
a place of dusty gardens laden with fruit, of pretty women,
dogs, food, music. Everywhere you looked, there
were secrets and astonishments. And everyone was laughing.*
—LUIS ALBERTO URREA

*On the border we talk about language all the time
because our words cross back and forth as if there
were no fences and armed guards, no military helicopters,
no drug laws and no such thing as "illegal immigration."
Linguistic adultery takes place every day of our lives;
the syntaxes of Spanish and English are wet and
infected with a viral illegality, and the infection
has entered our brainstems.*
—BOBBY BYRD

With the Smooth Rhythm of Her Eyelashes

Luis Humberto Crosthwaite

translated by Antonio Garza

A baby cries every day at four in the morning. This demanding child does not miss an opportunity to chastise her parents, especially when they're late to tend to her needs. Zombiefied, the father gets up to take the baby from the crib and puts her in the arms of her sleeping mother.

Thirty minutes later, groggy, in a daze, the father gets up to take the baby back to the crib.

The mother is pensive. She's worried about her daughter's future. She's already three months old and doesn't have a visa. She can't enter the United States like any other normal person. The father is also worried. Baseball season has started and the daughter needs to feel the thrill of watching the king of sports.

As if it were his morning civic duty, the father dials a phone number. He is notified that there is a 12-pesos-per-minute charge for the call. "I want to apply for a visa for my daughter." On the other end of the line, a woman speaks slowly, explaining each step in the process. The woman takes down the child's name, but the father is certain that he should tell her more. "She's not just a name, Miss, she's a person. You should see her sweet face, listen to her cry. Cough. Burp. It's amazing." Patiently, the woman listens to the man's rambling (at 12 pesos-per-minute). Then she tells the proud father not to forget Questions #33 and #34 when he fills out the application. They're the most important questions.

It's a solemn obligation (and a government requirement) that both parents appear at the administrative hearing for the conferring of the visas. But on the day of the appointment, the mother can't get permission to get off of work. The father is forced to attend alone. He carries his baby like an Olympic torch, and, unable to help himself, he shows her off to the hordes in the line. The hordes all certify that she is a beautiful, healthy baby.

The first stage in the process requires the filling out of the application.

The father is overjoyed in the discovery that they don't just require this little person's name, but also her eye color, hair color, complexion, religion, race, date of birth, blood type, names of parents and grandparents. The father waltzes to the edge of the earth as he fills in the blanks, until he abruptly arrives at Question #33.

It's not just one question but a whole series.

a.   *Have you ever been involved in a terrorist organization? Yes / No*

Who would answer yes to this question? Could there be honest terrorists? A truthful terrorist not wanting to jeopardize his entry visa?

b. *Have you crossed contraband into the United States? Yes / No*

Even though it's illegal to cross the border with agricultural products, as American customs laws clearly state, the father remembers one time when he brought two apples to a baseball game. In any case, there was no room for comments on the application.

c. *Have you ever been imprisoned for committing a crime? Yes / No*

The last thing America wants is people with prior convictions. The father remembers that one time…but that was a long time ago. In any case, these questions refer to the baby, and she's definitely done nothing wrong that he knows of.

d. *Have you ever assisted another person to enter the United States with false documents? Yes / No*

The father thinks this may be a trick question. False is an ambiguous adjective and with regards to the baby, no.

And that was just Question #33. Question #34 is much more simple.

a. *Are you entering the United States with the intent of participating in acts or intended acts of terrorism? Yes / No*

The father is shocked that it's even possible to participate in such organizations in the United States. The only thing on his mind is baseball. His wife just wants to hit the clothes and shoe sales.

The father looks at his little girl with her gray eyes, sweet smile, curly hair and angelic face. No. No. No, no, and no. The father releases his anger every time he checks off the No box. His daughter is not and will not ever be some kind of Patty Hearst. How could she ever possibly become one? Sadness fills him when he imagines baby Patty's dad answering a similar application. What would he have answered?

The father looks into his baby girl's eyes, looking for some indication. And his daughter opens her eyes with the smooth rhythm of her eyelashes.

There's no reason to ask such questions. There should be another application especially for cases such as these. They should be telling him, "You are the father of a beautiful baby girl, so you need to fill out Form 24B, not 25H."

Question #34 on Form 24B:

a. *Do you think that your daughter will fulfill all your hopes and dreams?*

b. *Do you think your daughter will one day marry a good-for-nothing punk?*

c. *Do you have reason to believe that your daughter will one day, when you least expect it, break your heart?*

These questions would be much more appropriate. And on any of these forms, no, no and no. No to it all.

The second step in the application process requires the father to have a brief interview with a consular agent.

"Are you her father?"

Yes.

"How about the mother?"

No, she's not here.

"Where is she?"

She's far away.

"How far?"

Very far.

"Occupation?"

The mother's?

"No, yours."

I write. Odd jobs from time to time. I write.

By sheer coincidence, this blond man also has a 3-month-old baby. He shows pictures of his baby son. As if accepting a challenge to duel, the father draws his own snapshots. Photo against photo. Two cardsharks pulling ace after ace from their sleeves. Baby: naked on the bed. Crying baby. Baby in need of diaper change. Bathing baby cries with shampoo in baby's eyes.

Question #35:

Do you think it's possible that someday your daughter will fall in love with the son of a consular agent? Yes / No

Life is full of uncertainty.

As a goodbye, the agent hands the father a sheet of paper that says "Congratulations! You have been approved for a Laser-Visa to enter the United States of America, the most powerful nation in the world."

The father goes home with visa in hand, and a heavy feeling bearing down on his heart. He, after all, got what he wished for.

OPEN LETTER TO MY RELATIVES

GARY PAUL NABHAN

from *Desert Legends: Restorying the Sonoran Borderlands,* 1994

As I write this for you, my cousins, all of you, I wonder if I might ever set the record straight. Snippets of your stories have already come back to me in their various versions, so I know what I am up against. On account of the ones I've heard already, I'm afraid I'm facing a stacked deck:

—How the only time my mother drove out to see me in the desert, she went limp upon arrival amid all that cactus and mesquite. She later told one cousin that she simply fainted from the relentless glare of the sun. But Aunt Rose heard that she had driven 160 miles without seeing another car, only to be told at my doorstep that we were all camping out that night—it was too hot to sleep within the adobe walls. She later swore to me that she saw a rattlesnake lurking just a few feet away from where the baby crawled around on the ground. Although she didn't crumple until she had swept the boy up into the bed of my truck, she herself never touched ground here again.

—How I nearly killed Aunt Linda on her only visit here, how I drove her three hours through a raging chubasco while water poured in through the cracked glass where a road-runner had collided with the windshield a few weeks before. When my old pickup crossed the arroyo at flash-flood stage, she claimed that water came in up to her knees—an impossibility, since there were ample opportunities for it to drain back down through the rusted-out floor of the cab.

—How, innumerable times when he was alive, my father had to wire money to perfect strangers in order to get me out of Mexican jails. And how, the night my father died, they could not reach me; the lightning raging that night knocked out all the telephone and telegraph lines running from El Norte clear into Sonora.

Since no one else is with us tonight, I'll admit to you that each of those stories contains tiny grains of truth. Trouble is, they've been tumbled smooth of any texture. It's not that they're outright lies. They simply reflect how our clan worries about one of its kin. One who has strayed from the fold.

"What went wrong with him?," they wonder. "When he was growing up among us, he seemed to just love being here, cuddling with 15 aunts and cousins on a couch, grinning from ear to ear. But if he still loves us, then why has he drifted so far from home? What in the world has he found that could be worth staying away from *us?* My God, he's been down in that desert nearly 20 years!"

You see, I have a problem with those stories that you, my cousins, tell. They lack any notion of what has driven me to the edge of what is familiar to you. That seemingly desolate frontier, or, as my neighbors call it, la frontera, is among the loves of my life. Have you ever wondered how I could love *land* as much as we have all loved our family?

Once my heart planted itself in the dry, salty earth called the Sonoran Desert, it sprouted roots that I don't think could have anchored themselves in any congested city. So even though I grew up in a clan as gregarious as ours, I now spend days on end talking only to spindly cactus and spiny shrubs. To you, they look like death on a stick—nothing like any living vegetable you know—but to me, this land is anything but barren because of them.

And this is why I have to set the record straight. I am not alone, on the bleak edge of the world. I have not been talking to myself or merely listening to an arid wind. There are voices here among these gray, armored, ancient plants. There are seldom-seen animals which have become my guides to water and to shelter and to other necessities I can hardly name. I now consider them, like you, to be my family. And so I spend a lot of time just listening to them, even when it seems to be no more than gibberish. It is just as I did when I was a kid, whenever we stayed with Aunt Fanny, who would refuse to speak English with me, preferring the language of the Old Country. I would listen not so much to particular words that were beyond my understanding but to the tone and timbre of her voice and to the dry and dusty places that it echoed.

Through Trials and Errors

Of course, I couldn't listen that well when I first got here. There were too many distractions, too much noise drifting in from everywhere else. And I was like the others when I first arrived. Green. A lush. Loose in my spending. Inattentive to the spottiness of pale but fertile soil, to the slightest changes in season, or to the local parlance by which they are announced. A rank beginner.

Oh, it has taken me two decades to develop some scars, wrinkles, and reserves in the right spots, to learn not to squander energy or water out of season, out of place. At first, all I could see was that the armor looked meaner, the grass less green, the women more sensuous, the culture more contagious, and the wilderness wilder on the other side.

We use that turn of phrase a lot down here: el otro lado. Two decades ago, the quest for what lies on that other side became my consuming passion. A half century ago, Graham Greene articulated what is so seductive about the lands and life across the border. It was when, I believe, he was crossing the international boundary into the Mexican deserts for the first time:

> "The border means more than a customs house, a passport officer, a man with a gun. Over there, everything is going to be different; life is never going to be quite the same again after your passport has been stamped and you find yourself speechless among the money-changers. The man seeking scenery imagines strange woods and unheard of mountains; the romantic believes that the women of the border will be

more beautiful and complacent than those at home; the unhappy man imagines least a different hell; the suicidal traveler expects the death he never finds. The atmosphere of the border—it is like starting over again; there is something about it like a good confession: poised for a few happy moments between sin and sin."

Recently, while I was once again ruminating over Greene, I realized that my own view has shifted. What I once sought solely on the Mexican side of the border, I have somehow come to find on the U.S. side as well. Or, more to the point, I have stopped seeking what only one side can offer me, and find this desert sticking together all around me, no matter what side I am on. Although my home has been just six miles away from the international divide that attempts to cut this desert in half, I am no citizen of the borderlands. Nope. I think I know what Douglas Kent Hall meant when he claimed that the borderland "has a national characteristic of its own, as though it were a narrow fledgling nation two thousand miles in length." Still, I can only pledge allegiance to a certain bunch of creatures, and peculiar cohort of cultures, that have somehow stayed in sync with the underlying desert of Greater Sonora—that is, parts of Arizona, a sliver of Alta California, the bulk of Baja, and the state of Sonora itself. I'm not saying this desert feels caged up with political boundaries; I only reckon it will outlive them.

Let me say it in another way: that fence cannot divide those of us who live on either side. We need one another. That's why we gather on flyways, migration routes, and underground railroads. We've learned to outmaneuver governments. Oh, they can hinder us, but I doubt they'll ever halt our flow.

And when it comes to how we feel about this fence, I am not speaking for myself and a few radicals. I also speak for the paisano, or what some here call the tadai, the churea, the correcaminos—that rakish roadrunner who hops up on a strand of barbwire stretched between two republics, wags his tail, shits, and darts over to the other side. I speak for the nectar-feeding bats—the ones that in summer hang out in old mine shafts across the border during the day and squirt red all over my toolshed at night. I speak for las familias Antonio, Elias, Tanori, Vasquez, Corrella, Ronstadt, Escalante, Alvarez, Cruz, Meling, Murrieta and Valenquela. The ones of O'odham, Dutch, Cucupa, Hispanic, Dinéh, German, Opata, Lebanese and Yaqui descent. They have their cousins on both sides of the divide.

Finally, I speak for a wild gourd, with a vine that crazily twines over the razor blades, marking the top strand between here and there. I've watched that vine, how it seems to pay those blades no mind. It crawls across them, then dives to the ground, rooting itself from the nodes wherever it touches the earth.

A Misplaced Vision

I don't have visions often. I have never sought them, never will, and I remain highly suspicious of anyone who does. But let me tell you about one such apparition I had a few years ago. I was driving out to work in some Indian bean fields, grinding along the road that runs parallel to the border between Tucson and the Tohono O'odham Reservation to the west. That's where it happened.

It lumped into one single image all that I had been imagining about "the other side" until that time.

I woke up early that morning when the stars were still brilliant. The remaining cool of the night made me shiver as I entered my truck and began to drive out to Papaguería—that's the old name for the country of the Tohono O'odham, both their reservation and the surrounding turf they were swindled out of. A cup of hot café combate steamed up from my lap, enough to fog up the windshield. I finally had to crack open a window to let the temperature inside square off with that outside, so I could see where I was going. All the while, night moved through twilight and then on to dawn.

When the sun began to brighten the day, I had made it out as far as La Avra Plains. Its low-angled beams suddenly warmed the air out on the plains, but the heavier pockets of cool air were still tucked down, out of reach in the arroyo beds below. As I swallowed the last dregs in my cup and glanced toward the Altar Valley in the southwest, sun spilled into that heavy air mass. A number of buttes and mesas loomed up before me. There, on the desert grassland rim between the Atascosas and Baboquivaris, mirror images of Sonoran landforms tilted up upon one another. They created hourglasses out of pyramidal buttes, and anvils out of flat-topped mesas. I dallied on the roadside, dumbfounded, as they wavered in front of my eyes, as if a wind were shaking them. There they were, quaking in the heavy air, which was as unstable as quicksand. Then they toppled and, just like that, fell back below the horizon forty or fifty miles away in Mexico. Gone. Gone from view in a split second.

It dawned on me: I had been seeing most everything on the other side in a wildly distorted way. Each giant cactus, each hacienda, each mountaintop shrine on the Mexican side of the desert had become exaggerated. Each culturally charged image had become a mirage by the simple act of looking across a political boundary.

Braiding Rural Lives Back Together

As this specter vanished from my sight, I moved the truck back onto the asphalt and hightailed it to the reservation. I sweated through that day with old men who wanted to fix up their fields, which had been left in disarray. These Indian farmers knew what they were doing, or wanted to do, but it was still no easy feat. We figured out that the dirt in their fields had been turning poor, starved of what Sonorans call agua puerca, "hog water," so called because it carries suspended vegetable and animal manure. Some cattlemen down by the border had built water impoundments upstream, forgetting that the old guys down here needed the floods to run into their fields. Without floods to bring the hog water with its enriching detritus into their fields, their beans and melons and maize had begun to wither and wane.

We tried to make up for this loss the hard way, hauling truckload after truckload of manure and mesquite litter into their fields. We'd go to a nearby corral, or a "cattle lounge" beneath a big mesquite tree, and shovel the dark rich stuff into the truck. Then, when we tried to find a tractor or a team to plow under the manure, our luck ran out. The John Deeres out there had seen better days, and there was not a spare parts store for another hundred miles. And no one with draft horses had the proper tack for hitching a team in front of a moldboard plow.

"Where did you get tack for your teams before?" I asked one of those old Indian men, taking my sombrero off and wiping the sweat on my brow.

He ruminated for a moment, then answered me: "We used to have our own hihilio. What do you call them, herreros or blacksmiths? Some of them were tack makers and horse doctors too. Some were so good at fixing up horses that we let them fix us up too when we got cut up or sore. A few became O'odham mamakai, our medicine men. Now they're all gone, so whenever we break our plowshares or lose our tack, we have to go over there"— he nodded southward —"to Jujkam Ha-Jewed [Mexican's earth]. If we don't cross to the other side to get what we need, we can't farm."

Their farming tradition had unraveled when the intrusion of the border cut their homeland in two. First there was the Gadsden Purchase in 1853, which gave some of them U.S. citizenship, but which began to wean them from practices thoroughly Mexican. Then, in the 1930s, the governments decided to put up a fence along their imaginary line. The fence had enough gates in it and got washed out frequently enough that at first it didn't stop the trading of cattle, horses, squashes, queso asadero and other goods.

The hoof-and-mouth disease quarantine finally nailed the lid on the coffin. Fearing that the intermixing of livestock from both sides of the border would further endanger the American cattle industry, U.S. officials forbade the Arizona O'odham from riding down to the ocean on their salt pilgrimage, to Magdalena on the pilgrimage for their Saint Francis or to Stoa Doag to gather cactus fruit for summer ceremonies. Then they rounded up 500 horses and cows, shooting, burning and burying them near the village of Komelik. Several hundred more were massacred on the other side at Pozo Verde.

"That was all we had to our names—like your savings. Except we *knew* those animals. The smell was so bad, it spoiled the air for miles around. One old man cried, 'Why don't they go ahead and shoot us too?'"

In villages where eight teams of horses and mules had worked together to keep the fields plowed and cultivated, suddenly there were none. The farming families who couldn't stand to see their fields fallow drifted off to work in the irrigated cotton fields that southern whites had begun around Eloy and Picacho. Back home as the 1950s drought hit, the dry ditches filled up with debris, the check dams atrophied and tumbleweeds overran formerly productive fields.

On the Mexican side, there remained enough horses, blacksmiths, muleskinners and tack makers, but not enough O'odham who had the seeds and knew the prayers to sow the fields, to keep the rains coming and the ditches clean. Young men in Sonora heard that they could get real cash for doing the same work that, up to that time, had only offered a winter's supply of food. They, too, wanted what was on the other side, as badly as I had wanted to live the adventures, dance with the guapas and sing the words to old corrido ballads when I discovered Sonora in my twenties. They left home to find work in Arizona lettuce fields the same time I left home for Sonora, to find the ancient seeds, the hand-forged plowshares, draft horses and stories.

While most greenhorns felt this way about the other side, the older men felt that to be whole again, their pueblos needed to repair the fabric ultimately essential to both sides, to stitch it together once more. It was not simply their tack or their seeds that had fallen into disuse. The broken, unraveled cords of their lives needed to be braided together again. Somehow, I got it into my head that I could help with that braiding.

My cousins—mis primos—that's why I'm still here.

Camera of Dirt

CHARLES BOWDEN

Aperture Magazine #159, Spring 2000

He rises, his lean body unfolds from the chair in the hubbub of the market, and then he moves with feline grace, camera in hand. The table is short, dark teenagers from Oaxaca, country people who have come up more than a 1,000 miles to the border because they have heard rumors of work. The boys wear watches, the girls new clothes. He leans into them, his voice soft, face smiling. They have been here six months, they have a shack they share, they have jobs, and today they have Sunday off and can eat in the public market and enjoy the throb of the city. The camera comes up, he slowly bends toward the targets, the film whirls and Julián Cardona feeds. He has been at this for almost 20 years. No one asked him to do this work. That does not matter, he is about his business and his business is this border city of bruises, death, dirt and love.

Talking about dirt, dust in the air chewing the city, dirt choking the lungs on a windy day, streets of dirt, yards of dirt, a city of dirt and mud and dust, talking about Juárez, two million people huddling in shacks on the flanks of the dunes to the south and west, talking about dirt and dust and mud and Juárez, the city Julián Cardona loves.

"This street," he says, "this street is where I walked with my girl."

The calle is dust, rock and ruts. Here, he wants it known, here when he was a boy, a teenager, he walked with his girl, down this dirt street, and see? She lived over there; and down there and up the hill, that's where he lived, back then, when he was young and in love in the city of dirt. Smoke from cooking fires floods the air, night is falling, the wind blows, he is in love, he is back there, walking with his girl. The turf is K-13, the most vicious of the hundreds of gangs in the city of dirt. No matter. Love. Here, then, and now.

El Paso lights up in the dusk, not even a mile away. He hates it there, it is too cold, he explains. With a ninth-grade education, he managed to learn English. "Do you know this essay," he asks, "by Gore Vidal?" The dust coats the tongue, the smoke sweetens the air, sewage comes off the privies.

He was two, he thinks, when he declared his life for beauty. Ten when he gave up on eternity. About 20 when he was working in a factory here and he stumbled into photography, bought magazines, got a camera, taught himself everything. After that came a time working for blood-and-guts working-class tabloids, finally the move up to the daily paper, and now at 39, the life of beauty. Beauty is everywhere, even in a pebble he spied at age two. Eternity is incomprehensible, there is only now. The photograph, the thing curators call the image, is now, this moment of beauty that exists for a second. Until devoured by the camera and made into comprehensible eternity. That's it, it is that simple.

The girl he used to walk with, she married someone else. Julián Cardona lives alone and says with a laugh that the camera is his wife. And the beauty is here, in this sprawling slum of a city packed with workers in cardboard shacks, racked by drug killings, ruled by endless corruption, ignored by the rest of the planet. Beauty is here in the city of dirt and dust and mud and love and Julián Cardona is here to prove it and taste it and capture it and admire it and love it in turn.

Talking about dirt.

He is a brown man in a brown city. Juárez lacks water and is first and last dust. Grass, trees, flowers, they are for somewhere else. The city is a holding pen for cheap labor sucked north from the hopeless interior of Mexico. Hundreds of factories, mainly owned by Americans, assemble goods for the U.S. market safe within the tariff wall of NAFTA. The wages are $25 to $50 bucks a week. No one can live on them. No one. Turnover runs from 11 percent to 25 percent a week in the plants. And there are plants—General Motors has 30 alone in Juárez. Cheap labor, impossible living conditions, the bottomless U.S. market, violence, and dirt. There is nothing more to say about it, except to tell lies.

"I have witnessed a lot of deaths," he offers, "and when you are a photographer you have a chance to die so many times. You see a kid of 11 playing an accordion in the street—what will he become? What if he is you? The woman is dying. What if she is your sister? Photography is a mirror of yourself."

Julián lives in a cement building of two rooms he threw up himself. The patio, a cement slab waiting for some next phase with no due date, looks down on the other little houses and shacks huddling on the bare hillside. Julián Cardona opens a bottle of red wine from Zacatecas. He is a quiet man, a pair of eyes that takes things in and feels no need to speak of what he sees. In his monk's room are a few books of photography with plates he studies and a simple cot. The other room is a kitchen.

Out here is red wine, night and talk.

He offers, "I think a photograph uncovers what is hidden and then what is hidden comes before the public eye. You must confront yourself in this mirror of reality. And the photo must seek beauty in even the worst things, it must capture the primitive things that move a human being—loneliness, hope and love. Dreams."

In the mercado público, he eats menudo amid the din of Sunday shoppers. A band of old men plays country songs. His eye drifts, the girl two tables away has fine cheekbones and the face of a child. He moves, talks, sits with her. The camera comes up and feeds. She is a teenager working in an American factory and her face shines with experiments in cosmetics. He never stops. Her name, phone number. He will visit and take yet more images. The photo will nail her in his vision of eternity.

He never knew his father, and his mother left him to the care of her parents. His grandfather was a farmer who formed an ejido, a collective, after the revolution. He tried to teach Julián the earth and its animals. When Julián was in his early 20s, he faltered after working for five years in a maquiladora and with two friends decided to go back to that ejido his grandfather had founded. The peasants agreed to let him join and have ground out of respect for his grandfather. It all came to nothing. His friends fell away from the scheme, Julián fell in love with a beautiful and rich woman. So it ends this way: he gives his patch of ground to another peasant and asks that, if possible, someday the ejido build a library or clinic and name it after his grandfather because, he says, "He was like millions of farmers and animals. No one will ever know they existed and who they were."

The beautiful rich woman marries someone else. Julián lives on the streets of Juárez for months. He does not explain this period except to make the point that he had it easy since he had money for food. Then he returns to the camera, the beauty. He takes that first shot: two men dressed as clowns standing one atop the other's shoulders in traffic and begging for change. The man on top juggles. The camera clicks. It is twilight, forever.

He spends day after day haunting the central city, the market, the whores, the cathedral, the plaza. He is the thin, silent man, the one almost unnoticed. See him, right over there, in those shadows, that man holding a camera. These spells come and go but now he is in the midst of one. He will capture that eternity, that beauty amid the stench and dust and dirt and broken glass and painted lips on the young girls soliciting in the doorways. And finally, as always, he is broken, worn out and so he does what he must do. He goes to his aunt's house and leaves his camera with her. The house is teeming with cousins and their wives and their children. Everyone sleeps in shifts, everyone works in the maquiladoras. This is the safe house for Julián. So he leaves the camera for two weeks.

Now he can rest.

He creeps into the maquiladoras, a zone of work barred to the press except for company controlled publicity shots. Julián has learned to shoot secretly in low light and so a flow of photographs begins, men and women looking blankly at the camera with eyes chastened by a five-and-a-half day week. They are a nation of Mexicans from the interior suddenly meeting the culture of the machine and being broken to the habits of presses, drills and assembly lines. Julián at night leans over the tiny light table in his room and stares at the slides of the place he escaped, the dull grind he fled for the ejido, and then the streets and finally the marriage to his camera. No one wants these images. The press of Juárez is in thrall to the economic might of the maquiladoras. The press of the United States is oblivious to the carnage just below the surface of the pat phrase, Free Trade. No matter. Julián is on his mission, and he takes his wife, the camera, with him into the mills. And finds the beauty of dead end lives.

Tijuana Wonderland

Luis Alberto Urrea

from *Nobody's Son,* 1998

When I was a boy, Tijuana was a place of magic and wonder, a place of dusty gardens laden with fruit, of pretty women, dogs, food, music. Everywhere you looked, there were secrets and astonishments. And everyone was laughing.

The crime writer Ovid Demaris had an early success with a lurid book about Tijuana called Poso del Mundo. The Hole of the World. *That pretty much sums up all our feelings about "the Calcutta of the border." Along with several other writers, I have made a certain career lately of exploring the demonic face of Tijuana. But what I never told you about the place is that it was also Wonderland—my favorite town on earth.*

We Have Always Lived Near the Castle

My grandfather was a visionary who came north to Tijuana before I was born. His hope was to establish a commune. The members thought to bake health bread to support themselves. Along with this commune, my grandfather intended to pursue his explorations into Rosicrucianism and occult science, as well as launch a career as a poet. Nobody is quite clear about why he chose Tijuana, but then, why does anyone choose Tijuana? In the old days, when Tía Juana's whorehouse lay on the low bank of that meandering nameless river, everybody knew why. But Grandpa had the border-urge-for-no-reason, even down in Sinaloa. It's an itch we have gotten to know all too well; the rash seems to be an epidemic sweeping Latin America.

Grandfather wrote his poems on a giant scroll, rolling the pages onto the ever-thickening tube of verse. In an unexpected development, he died, and his children burned all his poems. No one seems to know why these poems had to go, but go they did, leaving one stubborn line that resonated in my own father's mind for decades: "Give me two wings and watch me fly."

I always suspected this line came from the day my grandfather realized that gravity did not exist. It happened on the train ride with my father, then a young boy, from Sinaloa into the interior. They were waiting for the train to pull out. My grandfather pointed out a fly hovering in the middle of the car. When the train began to move, the fly remained exactly in place. The train sped up; the fly stayed hovering over the exact spot on the floor. "Why does he not zoom backwards and hit the back wall?" my grandfather asked. "There is no gravity," he answered himself.

This lesson stayed with my father, and he passed it on to me.

The family house seemed to grow out of a hillside in Colonia Independencia. It's still there, if you know where to look, though my cousin Hugo might shoot you if you show up unannounced. Hugo has his pistols loaded with buckshot instead of slugs. One time a neighborhood drunk kept disturbing Hugo's beloved throat-eating herd of Dobermans. Hugo came out of the house and ran down the street shooting at the guy until the guy's pants were soaked in piss as he ran and begged for his life. This is the kind of joke Hugo appreciates. If you stop by, be polite.

My grandfather built the house, energized by the lack of gravity. However, some other mysterious force slowed down the construction, and the house remained unfinished. It was a two-story, but the slope of the hill made the front door actually open on the second floor; the first floor was half subterranean and hidden. Hey, no problem: the house next door had a home-built balcony that pitched and yawed most gently. The walkers upon it had the aspect of sailors on a small boat. Later, the entire house hunched its shoulders and leaned out of plumb. It was vaguely trapezoidal and somehow jolly for its angle.

Our house had a living room and a bedroom and a dining room and a kitchen on the top (first) floor. There was also to be a second bedroom, but that mysterious power stopped my grandfather from actually putting it up, so the dining room opened onto a wonderful open room that overlooked the canyons and bustling streets of Tijuana. There, drooping clotheslines waved the Urrea flag: giant old lady underpants.

I spent much time out there, shooting toy guns, watching eclipses, inspecting the arcana of panties, fooling with the ubiquitous Tijuana geraniums and spying through windows with Hugo's telescope. Underpants in action!

Also on this sort-of room/more-or-less roof were dogs who delighted in hanging their heads over the edge and engaging passing dogs, cats and humans in a crazed, ear-flopping, vertical volley of insults and slobber.

Next door, Ernesto James had an outhouse that would kill a warthog at twenty paces. Pigeons, perversely delighting in the stench clouds, lived in its rafters. Hugo showed no mercy for birds that smelled like cosmic turds, so he'd plink them out of the air with a BB gun he got somewhere. Ernesto James, not to be outdone, got drunk some nights and chased the moon around his yard. We could hear him shouting, "Son of a bitch! *Luna cabrona!*" and then he'd shoot at it. He had a revolver that made a dull pop like a firecracker, and we'd stay inside lest a stray moon-shot drill us through the tops of our heads. As far as I know, he never did hit the moon.

Elsewhere in the house's history: the biggest ants north of the equator have been trying steadily since 1955 to undermine the house and send it into the arroyo. They tunnel and excavate, but some stubbornness in the foundation won't let the house collapse yet. Besides, the ants think that gravity will help, but we know better.

We watched gringo TV and Mexican TV. My heroes were Johnny Downs ("Howdy-howdy-howdy!") and Bob Dale. But I also had Juan Luis Curiel—general-purpose host to every available show "espectacular" on channel twelve, and the Four Seasons of Tijuana—Los Moonglow. In terms of TV, I was doubly rich.

Downstairs, there were a couple of bedrooms, a toilet and the demon. But we'll get back to the demon later.

Nobody in the barrio knew what to make of the castle. Oh sure, this fellow had come along and bought a small pinnacle above the foot of Rampa Independencia (the spectacularly unpaved road that tried to destroy every car making its way to the Colonia). That was suspicious enough—who would want a hill to himself? This proved outright that something was seriously wrong. At the very least, he probably thought he was better than everybody else, and nothing could make a Mexican madder.

Work began on the mystery man's dream home. People took it in stride.

But then this man on the hill revealed his intentions. He turned his cement-block house into a castle. A castle! Old folks gawked. Battlements, little archery slots along the roof line. Nobody could see if there was a drawbridge and moat or not. His towers threw their shadows upon the small gaggle of houses and beauty shops across the Rampa. These shops, by the way, were built with their front doors exactly five-and-a-half feet away from the open mouth of a storm drain that carried rain floods away from the castle. Presumably, these storm surges would come through the front door, maybe pause for a perm and a quick cuticle job, before tearing on down the hill and flooding the Cine Reforma.

Rumors flew. He was a general, a retired general, a colonel. The president. The former president. A warlock. A Mafia kingpin. A white slaver. He was kind, rich, evil, mad, a Russian or a gringo. Then, as if sensing the consternation in the neighborhood and savoring it, the bastard painted the whole thing bright yellow!

It loomed up there, visible from a mile away. Nobody knew exactly what was afoot, but the yellow paint could mean only one thing: the colonel was laughing at us. As far as I know, nobody ever went up there and asked him what was the deal.

One sunny day, beneath this suspicious yellow insult, in a deep pit, I first discovered death.

Viva la Muerte

Hugo was nuts for "The Outer Limits." He was also the newest karateka in the family, mastering blood-freezing karate moves in his underground kingdom—our downstairs second floor. He pounded his fists and fingertips into buckets full of gravel. "Fingers of steel," he'd warn me, going slant-eyed and holding up the deadly knife blade of his hand. "I could pull your heart out!"

The one "Outer Limits" that got under his skin was the one where David "Illya Kuryakin" McCallum got in a time machine and turned into a man from the future. His head expanded into a brain-bubble, almost exactly like the Jiffy-Pop foil container did. This future man obsessed Hugo, and he drew the bubblehead all over the walls downstairs.

I was down there checking out his drawings with his sister, my cousin Margo. Margo weighed about seven pounds—all eyelashes and eyes. She was the only girl in the world who would hold my hand. Plus she taught me feminine secrets like Dippity-Do. She smelled like soap, bubble gum and Vicks VapoRub.

There was a small craze in Tijuana in those days. Kids were taking the little rectangular batteries out of transistor radios and licking the terminals. Yow! It wasn't exactly a shock—it was kind of like a lick of Satan's salsa.

Anyone who has spent much time in Mexico knows that appalling things regularly go into our mouths. Take, for instance, those sickening little greasy shrimps you find in filthy plastic bags. Or how about blood pudding? (We call it relleno, not to be confused with chile relleno. I once made this unfortunate error and was served a steaming platter of what looked like black whipped cream full of onion chunks. A king-sized fried blood clot. I had dark orange teeth for the rest of the day.) And, of course, we have saladitos, brine-soaked prunes. Yum! Eat three of them, and you need immediate triage; an IV drip is strongly recommended.

"Let's lick the battery," Hugo suggested, opening the radio.

"No," said Margo. "Luis will do it."

"Will not!" I said, quite reasonably.

"Will too," Hugo explained, jamming the battery into my mouth.

Zzing!

I got a free perm.

After my electrocution, we went up to the street. James Brown came on. We called him "Chayss Brrong." It was as close as we could get. Also popular on the Rampa were Los Hermanos Righteous. Margo knew the dances: she could squirm like an earthworm. Hugo and I managed half-hearted shuffles in the dirt.

Suddenly Margo said, "Wanna see the bear?"

"What bear?" Hugo wanted to know.

"There's a bear down the street."

"Ha!" he scoffed.

"Come on and I'll show you."

We started off straightaway, hiking down the Rampa. On our right, the bluff at the end of which stood the castle. On our left, the slope that terminated in the backyards of a bunch of little houses below. We balanced on the crumbling edge, sending dirt clods tumbling into the yards, squinting and waving the dust away when a suicidal driver rattled and clanged over the rocks in the street. I remember whole fleets of ugly '49 Chevies, Chevies all over the hill, all of them with sun visors over their windshields.

"There," said Margo, pointing down imperiously.

Twelve feet down, looking up at us, was, as promised, a bear.

"Chingado," Hugo noted.

The bear asked, "Floob?"

It was chained to a tree stump. It was raggedy and dusty and its coat hung loose on its bones. We couldn't figure out what it was doing there. It raised its paw and waved, rattled its chain.

"Told you," Margo said.

It looked like wooden furniture under a black rug. But it also looked like a bear. I hid behind Margo.

It shook its head, got up, shuffled around, sat back down.

It was wondering what we thought we were doing in its barrio, no doubt.

It said, "Fnarff."

Hugo took control of the situation.

"Big deal," he said. "You can stand around and stare at the bear all day. But *I'm* going down the storm drain."

The storm drain!

It was absolutely, unquestionably, one hundred percent verboten. But he was already sauntering farther down the hill. Margo and I looked at each other and followed.

The bear was saying: "Moob? Mooble-fooble!"

We stood at the edge of the pit, the unseen yellow castle of evil high above us.

The drain went straight down. It was perfectly square, made of rather beautiful stone-work sunk in webs of cement. The bottom was, oh, a mile away. It had a floor of pale sand. Tijuana's usual rubble filled the corners: dry weeds, paper, bottles, rags.

"How do we get down?" I asked.

"Like this," said Hugo. He grabbed me and swung me over the edge and let me drop. I hit the bottom on my rump with a small yelp and looked up. He was gawking down at me, head upside down just like the second-story dogs back at the house. In fact, I thought he was barking, but he was laughing. Margo, beside him, stared down. I could see up her skirt.

"Ayiii!" *sensei* Hugo-san bellowed as he flew down upon me.

Margo carefully hung her toe over the edge like she was stepping into water, then scrabbled down the wall like a cat.

Before us, the black maw of the tunnel, angling down under the Rampa. In the distance, at least another 20 or 30 miles away, a small square nugget of light glowed.

"All right, cowards," Hugo said. "Let's go."

We forged ahead. I hung onto Margo's skirt. Margo hung onto Hugo's shirt. Hugo said stuff like: "Beware…of the…*giant…hungry…tarantulas!*" Margo and I had just suffered through *Rodan,* and there were these giant slugs in a flooded tunnel that ate Japanese soldiers and we just didn't think it was that funny. "Bats," Hugo said, *"that eat…out…your…eyeballs."*

We smelled it first.

This awful stench came at us with delicate fingers, sort of tickled at our noses in the dark.

"Who farted?" Hugo wanted to know.

But the stink got worse: it was the worst thing I'd ever smelled.

"I'm gonna barf!" I said.

"Not on me," said Margo, snatching her skirt away.

"Hey!" I said, waving my hands around trying to find her hem.

"Be quiet," said Hugo.

Then we heard it—this slurpy wet sound. I knew it! It was those Japanese tunnel worms!

"Better look," said Hugo.

He dug in his pockets. He always had contraband in his pockets: bullets, cigarettes, knives, tops. He pulled out some matches and lit one.

We gasped.

There, lying on its side and smiling broadly at us was the corpse of a pig. Its forelegs were crossed casually. Its whole body was packed full of maggots. We watched its sides ripple and undulate as the maggots ate frantically.

"Mmm-mm, bacon!" Hugo enthused.

"Gyah!" Margo said.

"Mamá!" I cried.

Hugo's match went out. He lit another.

"Death," he said, suddenly 50 years old. "It's just death. Fuck it. It's got nothing to do with us. Let's go buy some ice cream."

And he led us out.

Chronicle of a Death Forestalled

Of course, death is as familiar to a Mexican as life: it is a constant companion. I'd already learned where life comes from. An older boy had taken me into a field and shown me little gauzy spider egg sacs in the tall grass.

"Know what that is?" he said.

"No."

"That's unborn babies!"

"It is?"

"Yeah. When your mom wants a baby, she comes out here and picks one of these and puts it up her thing. Then it grows into a baby inside her thing."

"Wow!"

I was afraid to walk in that grass—what if I squished a couple of future camaradas?

Now I knew what death looked like, too. Nobody could tell me where death came from, only what it was. However, we all knew what—or who—came from death.

I remember my uncle Carlos Hubbard telling me once, "Every alley in Mexico has its own ghost."

Forget the Haunted House—if you want ghosts, we got 'em here. Tijuana is the Haunted City.

We had no proof that the bear on the Rampa was a real bear and not a ghost. We discussed going down and touching it in a limited caucus, but the motion was voted down in a landslide: Margo and Luis voting no, and the karate delegate voting yes. And who knew what wraiths floated through the halls of the castle?

My Aunt Irma, Ladies' Bowling Champeen of Mexico, claimed that Grandpa's ghost could be summoned from the land of the dead. "He's my father," she told me. "He still has his responsibilities."

"Why do you call him, Tía?" I asked.

"For bowling, of course!"

Apparently, Grandpa swooped into whatever bowling alley Aunt Irma was dominating, and he laid his spirit hands upon her Brunswick ball and guided it to strikes. He was especially effective at cleaning up a troubling 7-10 split. He apparently made several appearances across the border at the Bowler. I'm not sure if winning a tournament by means of ghosts is cheating or not.

The Urreas thought those ghosts were a riot.

A big party event at the Rampa was levitating tables. The adults would gather around card tables and lay their hands on them and up they'd go. Rising off the ground, everybody hooting. Also, rapping was great dead-guy fun. (Not "Baby Got Back"—knocking on things.) They'd light up their ever-present Pall Malls and talk to whatever lonesome dead guy was floating around, and he'd knock on the table.

I got rather worried about the dead for a while. What if some dead woman floated into the bathroom while I was pooing? Did dead little girls watch me take baths? What if Grandpa caught me *touching my weenie*?

Personally, I found these dead folks intrusive.

I had good reason, too. Family legend has it that a ghost used to visit me in my crib. The weird thing is that I remember him.

My father used to say that he'd carry me downstairs and put me in my crib, then stand at the door and watch me. He said I used to stare up at the ceiling and laugh, reach out to somebody, watch something fly all over the room. Okay, Dad. Fine.

I do have a memory of what was in the room, though. It was a black wisp of smoke in the shape of a man. He wore a trench coat and hat. He came up from under the door, wafting out of the crack at the bottom.

Either that, or I'm remembering a Bela Lugosi movie that was on *Science Fiction Theater*.

Grandpa Urrea is not the only meddlesome ghost in the family. According to Rampa tales, he himself was intervened upon by the dead.

Things had gone badly for the visionary commune he'd planned. Apparently, baking bread was not the ticket, but they couldn't find out what the ticket was. The commune went bust. Furthermore, his dabblings in arcane Rosicrucian secrets got him into serious trouble with the Catholic Church. My father always insisted that he was excommunicated, though he was probably boasting.

Grandpa's whole world was falling in around him, and one night he paced and paced, unable to sleep. He had a pistol, some say, and he was planning to shoot himself. He walked in the garden, around and around, smoking, trying to get up the nerve to pull the trigger.

The kids were watching. They heard a woman's voice softly talking to him. They couldn't see her in the dark. He stopped at one point to light a fresh cigarette, and in the match flare, they saw a beautiful woman with long hair held up by a crimson comb.

After a time, he calmed down and came inside.

Not another word was said until many years later, after he'd died. Due to some development down in the homeland (the details are never in sharp focus in these tales), several of the brothers were called on to supervise the moving of Grandpa Urrea's mother's grave. Our great-grandmother. She had died many years before the garden incident. And—you can see this coming, can't you?—when the casket was exhumed, it fell open, and there was a skull with a crimson comb stuck in its remaining hair! The old-timers insisted that she had returned from the dead to make her son live.

I was so aware of ghosts at this point that anything macabre seemed possible. My grandmother burned incense compulsively. When I found the little gray cones of ash, poised perfectly on bookshelves and countertops, I was terrified. I thought they were the ashes of burned-up bodies. One time I touched one and it collapsed. I hightailed it out to the yard and hid behind the pomegranate tree.

Stairway to Heaven

This part sounds like a bad joke: "There were two dogs, stuck together in the street." However, there were these two dogs, stuck together in the street. I kept watching them through the window. They were facing in opposite directions. If they'd been facing the right way, I might have gotten it. But I was having a little trouble catching the drift.

We all thought concretely. My father was having some trouble with English. "I don't get it," he'd say. "I go to the bathroom, right? And I'm supposed to *take a piss.*" He'd think a minute. "But I'm not *taking* a piss. I'm *leaving* a piss!"

This really disturbed him. He spent years trying to get to the bottom of the mystery. "Am I taking the piss *to* the toilet?"

Sometimes we'd sit around and work on it. "If I'm taking a crap, where am I taking it?"

So, concretely speaking, the dogs were a puzzle.

I called my aunt.

I said, "Tía, somebody tied these dogs together!"

She came out from the kitchen for a look.

"Idiot!" she said.

She had a funny way of dealing with us kids. Hugo, Margo and I were often known as "idiots" for whatever breach of reason we'd managed. Once, when I was sleeping on the couch, I was startled to hear her in the other room farting. Whoa! I'd never heard a woman fart. *Brroom!* my aunt exulted. *Frrapp!*

I almost gagged on my pillow, I was laughing so hard. Suddenly, her door banged open in the dark and she said: "You idiot! Haven't you ever heard a God-damned fart before?"

Brraptt!

Needless to say, she wasn't impressed.

"You think you're so innocent," she said. She went back into the kitchen in a huff. Apparently, I had made an appallingly offensive scene without having any idea of what I was doing.

The dogs, looking somewhat abashed by now, scooted around, backward and forward.

"Stop watching that," said my aunt. She handed me some change. "Go out and buy me a kilo of tortillas. Make yourself useful."

I took the money and headed out the door.

The Colonia was lively as ever. Aside from the push-me-pull-you dogs, scruffy gangs of kids were playing marbles in the dirt. The ice cream man pushed his little wooden wagon selling paletas. Another man pushing the exact same wagon was selling steaming hot ears of corn. Their magic skill really involved my brain: how did one keep his treats icy while the other kept his hot? Huge water trucks rumbled through with bad boys hanging onto the backs. Old ladies swept tides of dust off sidewalks. The mailman marched sharply from yard to yard blowing his whistle. Brilliant kites rattled in the phone lines like slaughtered pterodactyls. The hill was jumpin'.

The tortillería was the world's jolliest sweat lodge. The heat was always high from the massive sheet of iron kept hot by eternally burning propane burners. Six or eight women worked in there all day, sweating and yelling over the sound of a radio. You could smell the holy maíz heating and sending out its incense all over the street. You could smell it from two blocks away. And the sound of their palms on the corn dough was audible from at least one block distant. *Pit-pat, pit-pat, pit-pat.*

That sound lies within the heart of everyone who relied on fresh corn tortillas every day, a sound now replaced by heartless machinery that presses out tortilla analogues on conveyer belts. That's why Old Town San Diego keeps tortilla makers in restaurant windows. Something sacred is going on and it gets in the blood.

I would stand at the counter and peer up at them. Those women, with all their mysteries and their laughter. *Pit-pat, pit-pat.* Everybody was poor, but who knew? Their arms—the richest most enjoyable brown—jiggled as they worked. Their hair, deep black, wound into immense braids, lay pinned to their necks or held back by cloth. *Pit-pat.*

They ground the corn in big stone metates, both the corn and the stone handed down through generations from the Aztecs, still bearing Aztec names. Their hands repeated the motions of millions of hands and hundreds of years. Their hands, grinding and patting and laying the corn patties upon the hot metal, were a time machine. You could fly back to Tenochtitlán on their palms any day of the week.

They fed all us gawking kids. You could hang out at the tortillería and eat a pound of soft hot tortillas. They'd give them to us plain—good enough! Or they'd roll a few drops of lemon juice in one, or a pinch of salt, or both. I ate a couple of these mini-tacos while I waited.

They pulled pure white wrapping paper off a huge roll—just like my Grandpa's poetry roll—and tore off a foot or so and wrapped the tortillas snugly. The paper tucks were snug as diapers.

I headed home with the bundle hot and pulsing comfortably against my gut.

I stopped in the botica, the pharmacy/candy store/juju center/soda shop/icon seller/ toy store, for a candy. My aunt knew I was going to steal some of her change. I was addicted to these rubbery, square banana-flavored Mexican candies. They tasted exactly like my mom's nail polish smelled. This was too marvelous, and I explored its ramifications every chance I got.

I was coming out, busy pulling the fillings out of my teeth, when Hugo caught up with me.

"Come on," he said.

"Where to?" I asked.

"Got to show you something."

"Tortillas," I said.

"They can wait," he said.

I followed him around the corner and up to the top end of the Rampa. I'd never been up there before. There was no reason to walk up there, and the car was too exhausted by the time it got to the house to go any farther. All it could manage was to turn around and fling itself back downhill.

We slipped between two houses. Down the hill. Into a small canyon.

"Where are we going?"

"I found something," he said.

We climbed up the narrowing arroyo. We stopped. He pointed.

There was a stairway. A big cement stairway. It flared a little at the bottom. It had railings. It went up about 30 steps. Then it ended. It went nowhere.

We stood on the bottom step and looked up it.

"Strange, huh?" he said.

"Yeah," I said. "And guess what? Somebody tied these two dogs together in the street."

Got the Devil in My Closet

Let me tell you about the demon before I go. You probably won't believe it. Gringos have a strangely difficult time with the bizarre details of the daily life of Latinos. People scoff at personal testimonials of wonders, but they love to read them in novels from Colombia. To us, however, magic realism is basically reality.

I'll admit, I have some trouble myself. A woman I knew in Tijuana inspected the rash on her husband's back and said:

"You're hungry for chicharrones!"

"No, I'm not," he said.

"Yes, you are," she insisted. "You have a craving for them."

"But I don't," he said.

"You do, but you just don't know it," she said. "That's why you got this rash—it looks like chicharrones."

He couldn't see it all that well, so he had to take her word for it.

What she did was, she boiled a bunch of chicharrones until they were soft, then she plastered the boiling slop onto his back. That the rash disappeared was taken to be a miraculous cure, though none of us suggested she had simply burned about three layers of skin off his back.

I can see where that's too magical. Chicharrón lust is silly. And the dreaded agua de coco is silly, too. It's a love potion made from menses and slipped into an unsuspecting man's coffee. When my relatives point out who put it in whose coffee to make him such a hapless love slave, I can laugh it off with the best of them. And when an extended family member's mother was caught in the middle of a black-magic incantation by her son, *and she had a pig's head instead of a human head,* I can, sort of, you know, ignore it.

Still, I'm not sure what to make of my Aunt Irma's bottle of holy water.

She told my father she'd been sensing the evil eye on him. Somebody had been shooting him the wicked mojo from a passing car, or some such nonsense. So, she had gone out to a shop and bought an evil-eye protector. It was a bottle of holy water tied up in a red velvet sack. She opened the sack and showed us the water: yes, we agree, it was definitely a little bottle full of water. My father was to keep the bottle in his glove compartment, and it would soak up any evil eye fired his way.

My father, by the way, was not above crank ideas. For example, he wore a bracelet of magnets that supposedly sucked out all his ills through his wrists. Illness, arthritis and impotence were all apparently cured by these miraculous magnets. Still, the holy water was too much. "Bullshit," he said when we got in the car. He threw it in the glove compartment and forgot about it.

Months later, of course, I opened the glove compartment looking for something else and found the pouch.

"Look, Dad!" I said.

We laughed.

I opened it.

The little bottle was full of black sludge. It looked just like old motor oil.

You figure it out!

In the downstairs second story, there was a small room. It was partially underground—its one grimy window looked out at ground level. Its roof was angled, and its floor was at least two feet above the level of the main rooms' floors. It was a dark anomaly in the northeast corner of the house. I could never figure out what my grandfather had in mind when he built it.

It was always rumored to have an evil presence. One of the items of evidence the family offered was that everyone who stayed downstairs ended up with some sort of respiratory illness. I, for example, got TB. The fact that a family of tubercular schoolgirls lived directly behind my bedroom didn't enter into the family myth.

The demon-in-the-backroom event didn't happen until after I was long gone, had come to the United States and the realm of reason. I was not there to witness any of it, so the whole story is secondhand. I took it on faith; you may not be able to.

Irma, the bowler aunt, and her sister, the farting aunt, teamed up to exorcise the foul being from the little room. They went to the Independencia church and filched some holy water, and they somehow procured some church incense—perhaps from my grandmother's extensive booty. They went downstairs together, flinging droplets all over the place and blowing holy smoke in all the corners. They supposedly entered the room and demanded that the being leave. Then, they say with straight faces, they were physically picked up and thrown out.

All around them, the banana trees in the yard bore fruit; the neighbor's trapezoidal house refused to fall; Margo developed a marvelous skill for talking to birds—she could make them land on her fingers. Ernesto James ran out of bullets. Tijuana's Christmas decorations got fancier year by year, then grew old and faded and tattered. Margo moved away. Her mother moved away. The second first-story dogs grew old and died. In the street, a new generation of dogs got tied together to launch yet another generation of dogs. Hugo got married and had lovely daughters. My grandmother went dotty, once making the following announcement about me: "This man has a pee-pee this big!" Then, she died. Dope-fiend cholos crept into the darker corners and whispered curses at passersby. The tortilla shop's women were replaced by a machine. The botica stopped selling those chemical banana candies. The yellow castle faded to off-white, and there hasn't been a bear in sight for 30 years. And it never rains.

The saddest part is that they finally paved the Rampa. They made it easy to go there, and people who have not earned the hill traverse it blindly. Day and night, all manner of cars and trucks rush up and back, none of the drivers aware that they have come somewhere. They have crossed over into another, wilder, more beautiful land. A land that is now as invisible as its ghosts.

Everything is Going
to be Different

*In the little town of Santa Ana de Guadalupe, Jalisco,
the street vendors sell "a pocket-size Migrants Prayer
Book which opens with a bon voyage message from
the local bishop and includes prayers for migrants to recite
on their journey to the United States. Among them is the
prayer for Crossing Without Documents. 'I feel I am a citizen
of the world,' it says, 'and of a church without borders.'"*
—New York Times, August 14, 2002

The Shadow of the Polleros

Francisco Vásquez Mendoza

translated by Rus Bradburd
Diario Público, October 21, 2001

Editor's note: *Like all underworld subcultures, the world of polleros and pollos (see our dictionary on page 57) has created its own rich vocabulary, so each of the subdivisions of labor within the pollero gang usually has its own slang designators. For the sake of comfortable reading, we've decided to use some of the Spanish terminology, but to keep it at a minimum. We will use words like polleros, pollos and migra because they are rapidly becoming part of the border vocabulary on the U.S. side. U.S. readers should remember that Vásquez Mendoza writes from a Mexican perspective: to him "the northern border" is the U.S./Mexico border.*

Calle Coahuila is the capital of the Pollero Republic. The street runs alongside the high fence that marks the border. It's so close that at night it receives a little glow from the Border Patrol's powerful searchlights.

It's also the main street of the zona roja (red-light district) of Tijuana, commonly known as "La Cagüila."[1] Here the women range from wide-bodies to five-star beauties. There are bars, table dances, motels and food stands. The noisy chatter and the jukeboxes mix with the dealings between the polleros and the guys hustling the pollos. Throughout the district there are dealers, users, and junkies on crutches whose feet are swollen with gangrene from repeated heroin injections. On the corner of Coahuila and Constitución, the law is broken every third step.

La Cagüila is a republic where the government is the underworld and its citizens are those looking for the hope of a better life in exile.

Gathering and Selling

Taxi drivers are the main contact for anything illegal. It's unfair to say all cabbies are rustling up pollos, but whoever arrives at the main bus stop or the airport in Tijuana doesn't have to do anything. The recruiters will appear and greet new arrivals with the following: "Do you want to cross over?" If the answer is yes, the recruiters will speak rapidly, looking everywhere but into their eyes. The recruiter is usually a man over the age of 30, from another state in the republic, who has lived in this border city long enough to call it home: "This is where my homeys live, vato."

1 Cagüila is slang for "Calle Coahuila."

The recruiter rounds up two, three or five pollos and stashes them in a hotel in the red-light district. Then he sells them to a gang for 100 bucks a head.

The hotels in La Cagüila are set up to dispense with the visitors quickly: beds aren't for sleeping and baths aren't for bathing. If the undocumenteds don't use them, it's because they aren't there for reasons of business or pleasure. A typical organization that traffics in undocumenteds, one handling an average of 30 pollos a day, uses these hotels. The bigger gangs have their own safe-house where they gather their merchandise. The houses are known as clavos, or stash houses: there aren't beds in these rooms either because they'd get in the way, but maybe some easy chairs and rugs so people can make themselves as comfortable as they can. In the busy season—January, February and March—they manage to cram 30 people in a room. The door can only be opened with a key so the pollos cannot roam around the rest of the house. The place looks like a city jail. In the kitchen there is a small table and a refrigerator for soft drinks and beer, and in the bathroom soiled toilet paper is scattered outside the wastebasket.

The pollero and the pollos will have only one discussion. During the negotiation, they agree on the price and method of crossing the border. For the rest of the way, the pollero takes control, demanding respect although not necessarily following the rules of etiquette.

At 31 years of age, "Pelos"—a nickname meaning whiskers—is an experienced pollero. He's been a recruiter, lookout, trail guide, driver, courier and stash house boss. These days he deals only in pollos, guiding the undocumenteds to the border for his gang in the zona roja. Guys like him don't take risks, especially not him—he has had a record with the migra for the last 20 years.

Abuses

Pelos, well, he knows and recognizes the excesses of his line of work: "They shout at them [the undocumenteds] and some guys in this business rape the women. And they lie to them. They tell them they're going to walk for three hours and it turns out to be three days. This job has to be done sober." The ones who run the most risk are the trail guides who cross the border and the ones who drive carloads of pollos from San Diego to Los Angeles. While they're on the job, adrenaline makes the polleros' time fly by. They can get hooked on crack and heroin, the border's most popular drugs, and they suffer from stomach problems, the disease of the coyotes.

"You've got to be straight to do this job," Pelos repeats. Guys who need a fix will abandon an undocumented without remorse in the middle of the river or resting on a hill. Or they will turn into kamikaze drivers who ignore the migra's orders to halt. These are cases that become like car chases from a movie scene that wind up on reality TV like *Ocurrió así* (It Happened Like This) and *Primer Impacto* (Sudden Impact). They take risks hoping that if pursuit becomes too dangerous, the migra will let them go.

The trail guides tend to be younger than 20; this is their first job for the organization, and they are still following orders without talking back. They get paid $150 for each pollo that they manage to deliver. In two or three years, the Border Patrol will have their records on file—fingerprints, mug-shots with front and side profiles, record of arrests and short stays in U.S. jails—sufficient reason to change to a less dangerous job or to a profession where the money is easier. But the idea of a nine-to-five job and a pay-check has not lured anybody away yet.

"Wetbacks" by El Fisgón, a Mexico City political cartoonist whose artwork reflects the anger felt by Mexican intellectuals over the historical relationship between the United States and Mexico.

The drivers who make the pickups charge $150 to $250 per pollo. After outwitting the Border Patrol, the trail guides use their cell phones to meet at a predetermined place on a highway. There, the pollos are delivered to the driver, who transports the undocumenteds from the border to L.A., where he deposits them in another stash house. The drivers, whose ages range from 20 to 30, save three or four months of wages in order to take one or two months off back home.

The drivers have a taste for clothes and music. Their closets are filled with boots and cowboy hats made by Wrangler or Stetson—the always changing fashion says that this season's hats should be a little squared off in front. Nevertheless, when they are going to make a pickup there is one cardinal rule—the dirtier the better. During an arrest, the first step is to blend in with the pollos, to look sad and stare down at the floor.

"Only Cocaine"

"I only snort the 'blow.' I never buy it," Pelos claims. He describes himself as a recreational user. But five days later, a man called Flaco contradicted him while waiting to reel in a fish on a Long Beach pier. Flaco has lost a lot of money betting on fighting gamecocks and now he's intent on becoming a fisherman. "You can easily go crazy. You turn into a flashy big-shot," he adds.

In the busy seasons, these gangs manage to transport up to 150 pollos across the border. There are different methods of crossing the border, some riskier than others. The degree of difficulty is determined by the amount of cash in your pocket. If you have more than $2,000, they'll look for a more comfortable way for you—past the checkpoint booth, for example. But if you have only $1,000, they'll send you off on a three-day walk through the desert or mountains.

Crossing the border is not like you've reached your goal. There is another obstacle of equal or greater danger. The Border Patrol in California keeps three permanent checkpoints: the one at San Clemente on Interstate 5, one at Temecula on Interstate 15, and one on Interstate 8. Other checkpoints exist on the secondary highways, in the deserts and the mountains.

This is the challenge that confronts the drivers. That's why the gang, as a business expense, requires a fleet of autos, purchased or rented. It's not the same going through a checkpoint in a Grand Voyager as in a beat up van, in a brand new Toyota as in an old Sentra. On the interstate it is impossible to check all the cars, so the border patrol profiles only the most suspicious ones. To complete the masquerade, if the Bronco is crammed with pollos and they can't hide them under the seats or in equally ingenious hiding places, the gang makes the whitest guy or the best looking woman ride shotgun. "Imagine," Flaco says, "if I put a wide-eyed young girl from a village in Oaxaca in the front seat who is scared to death."

The Customized Vans

These vans have customized shocks that won't sink, a sure giveaway that the Border Patrol looks for. If their path is through the desert they put out the brake-lights so they can travel in constant darkness. They use these and other strategies daily to trick a Border Patrol equipped with helicopters field-tested in Vietnam, powerful infra-red glasses used in Iraq and heat sensors controlled from a computerized INS office. Mexican ingenuity knows no limits. "Out of every five trips, they average stopping us once," Flaco says.

To reduce their arrests, the gang with the most material and human resources will send a couple of people to study the movements of the Border Patrol. They'll investigate checkpoint agents, secondary highways, sparse stretches of road and every option in order to give the Border Patrol the slip. They know California like the back of their hands. They might note the hour an agent takes a break for a cold drink. They'll alert others by cell-phone that now is the perfect time to go for it, to put the pedal to the metal.

In a black neighborhood near downtown L.A., a certain house always has the door locked. Latinos are usually chatting on the street or playing cards in the front yard. Some gangs have their own stash houses, or someone sets up and rents them to different gangs at a rate of $50 per pollo. This is the last step in the job, and it also has its risks.

There are some pollos who become piedras, or stone. A stone is an undocumented already in the U.S. who can't pay up. Perhaps they didn't bring enough money, or their relatives disown them or they're simply playing dumb. For dead weight like this, there is no solution—the polleros lock them for a few days in the stash house and later dump them on the border.

Woman Crossing Border, Río Grande, El Paso, Texas

Flaco has already been a recruiter, trail guide and driver. Last June, he was stopped with a full load, and they dragged him into court. "The gringo judge told me, 'We're going to deny you entrance to the United States for five years.' And just to be an ass, I told him, 'Make it fifteen.' And the bastard took me up on it." That's why Flaco doesn't go near the border anymore. Now, for $30 to $70 apiece, he parcels out the undocumenteds that come to the safe-house. Then they are delivered to street corners and shopping centers. Or they're put on the bus, Amtrak or plane, depending on how far they are headed.

But the stones are not the worst of it. There are acquaintances who will steal the pollos by force. So Flaco carries a baseball bat; other delivery guys carry guns.

A delivery guy shouldn't work alone. Other gangs make it their business to attack the stash houses. They take advantage of the ones who have done the work and then take the spoils: the $1,200 to $3,000 that the undocumented has cost. "Two weeks ago some bastards showed up in four vans, surrounded the house and robbed us." That stash house was closed, another was opened and today each of the thugs who guard it is armed.

Despite the risks, the stash house is a basic hurdle that the pollo has to get over. It is the consulate of Cagüila Street. The undocumenteds who manage to make it up north leave behind the Republic of the Polleros forever.

Enjoying the Easy Money

Long nights, expensive women and clothes, high-stakes gambling, many kinds of drugs and risks—many risks—flavor the life of the pollero.

Flaco puts down a $50 bill at the admission booth, picks up two tickets and gets in line. It's Friday night. A norteño band called Polo Urías y su Máquina Norteña is playing inside.

The Potrero is a dance hall in East L.A. It's a hotspot, like El Lidos and The Arena. The parking lot is full of late-model pickup trucks. Any make or model—you name it and it's here.

On the dance floor, wild dancers secrete rancid fumes that saturate the air. Live music is blasting out songs of the merengue and the norteña, which is the newest fad that California Mexicans are dancing—cheek-to-cheek, facing forward, the woman wrapping her left hand around the man's neck as if she were afraid of falling, chests pressed together but waists wide apart.

Flaco enters the dancehall. At first glance he is lost among many men with the same look who appear to be clones. But don't be mistaken, brother, there's a pecking order here as well. He's a boss, he likes the best. And if the best is expensive…even better. His stingray boots ran him $600. He spent $150 on his Versace pants, the same on his shirt. His Stetson hat cost him $1,500. More than $2,400 for the whole get-up. He and his pollero pals are ready to paint the town.

The polleros were once pollos. Salaried in the United States with steady work. They recall the jobs with a grimace—plenty of work, not much fun. They abandoned those jobs. "We like easy money," they admit freely, without side-stepping. Side-stepping is for dancers, or giving the slip to the migra. But it's not all about the money. There are other motivations of equal or greater importance: the lure of danger, addiction to the adrenaline rush, the thrill of adventure. Although it may sound cynical, it's also about the joy of serving others. "When you deliver a pollo to his relatives, they truly thank you. It feels good."

Curly and the Midget

El Rizos, or Curly, was born 35 years ago in a small town in western Mexico. He and his right-hand man, the 31-year-old Pelos, know the Tijuana, Tecate and Mexicali border regions better than almost anyone—the deserts, the mountains, the canals. Eight years as polleros (they prefer to call each other vaquetones, which means "bums" or "street toughs") give weight to their words. The boss of a rival gang, Fresco, recalls, "At one time they were the ones who got the most immigrants across the Baja California border."

El Enano, the Midget, does justice to his nickname. The little town that he calls home is close to where the monarch butterflies arrive each winter. Nowadays he recalls them only when he sees the Luis Fernando Tena soccer team called the Monarchs. When Enano is working, he wears jeans, a short-sleeved sportshirt and tennis shoes. When he goes to raise hell or to his mistress' house, he changes into crocodile-skin cowboy boots. One Tuesday near the end of September, he was paid for several jobs: $1,000 in $20s and $50s, in broad daylight in the Cagüila. Then he disappeared. The last person to see him was a hooker.

"Goddamn Enano, he screwed me and then he yelled at me for charging too much." That happened Tuesday night, but now it's Friday and he hasn't shown up. His friends are seriously considering looking for him at the hospital or the morgue.

"That's why there's so many lazy bastards around here," Pelos explains. "You get paid $90 a week for a regular job, but a pollero can pull that in with just a day's work." He's sitting behind the wheel of his inconspicuous compact from the gang's fleet. The car is equipped with good shocks and engine, and cruises easily at 70 mph on the stretch between Tecate and Mexicali. "Enano showed up," Pelos says with a certain mean-spirited glee. "He said he was kidnapped." Pelos bursts out laughing.

All the polleros have a vice. The most common are cockfights, cards and horse races. And women. Rizos hangs his hat in three places: he has a woman in L.A., another in Tijuana and still another in Mexicali. Pelos has two women, one in her final month of pregnancy.

But the sport of choice is cockfighting. "In the beginning you go and bet," Rizos says. "After a while you buy roosters and put your money into them. There's nothing like raising them, training them, tying on the razors and turning them loose to fight." The roosters square off in cockpits at the local fairs, but they mostly fight at unsanctioned clandestine events. The cockfighters know and recognize each other on the street: "I have roosters, and so do you"—and a fight's put together on the spot. These days they hold the Mexicali Fair without a cockfighting ring. "It's like—no cockfighting, no fair."

Rizos and Pelos share a two-story house in a middle-class neighborhood in Tijuana. The house is only partially furnished, signaling that it changes residents continuously—every six months to a year, depending on how hot things get. In extreme cases, some of their employees betray them by informing on them.

They rarely use the house phone and hardly ever hand out the number. Instead, they work with cellphones, which they constantly change. When they buy and register a new cellphone, they use different names. This is one of the peculiarities of the subculture: the polleros don't have real names, they have nicknames.

For security reasons, the majority of the pollero bosses live on the Mexican side of the border. They've had so many run-ins with the migra—including short stays in jail—they've learned to make themselves resemble the shoppers and tourists who enter the United States legally. Besides, the U.S. government has increased the penalties considerably, and they aren't as interested in the lower-level polleros—they want the bosses. That's why the bosses continue to live on the Mexican side: they can deal with the Mexican police departments. Rizos says, "There are some asshole cops who will hit on you for a bribe even if they don't catch you with a pollo. If they catch you with somebody, the cost goes way up." The polleros keep money handy just for this occasion. Rizos, Pelos or Flaco have never seen the inside of a Mexican jail.

The pollo business is in crisis. Rizos' gang has fallen on hard times. There were better years when they were rolling in the bucks. They used to bring performers from TV's Star Channel to the cockfights in their hometowns. They paid for the fireworks at holiday festivals. They made—and lost—thousands of dollars on their roosters. Easy come, easy go. It's all right with Pelos; nobody recovers what's been lost: "If I die, there's no problem," he says, while driving through the zona roja of the Coagüila. "I've done what I wanted to do and had a great time. I have no regrets." Last night he enjoyed a good time with Cynthia, a short cutie from the state of Guerrero who is new to the border.

JULIÁN CARDONA

A broad expanse of desert in southern Arizona has been the nation's busiest region for illegal border crossings for the past five years, with more than 333,000 arrests by the Border Patrol in the fiscal year ending September 30, 2002. With 261 miles of border, the area has become even more active since the September 11 terrorist attacks, which brought increased enforcement of restrictions on crossings in California and Texas. The harsh conditions of Arizona's deserts led to the deaths of at least 134 migrants, primarily from dehydration and exposure, up from 11 in 1998. The number is more than double that of the second-most-perilous district in eastern California, where 63 people died in the last fiscal year.

Rizos, however, is a little worried because he has several debts. He didn't take good care of his finances, a common problem among the polleros. The Chamber of Commerce has even reprimanded him. But he attributes his troubles to a spiritual problem: he is certain that some of the many women in his life have put a curse on him. That's why Rizos is anxiously awaiting the return of his spiritual advisor, a white witch. She's been gone on vacation for the last several months to her home in a small town in the state of Michoacán. When she returns, Rizos confides, the cleansing power of her ceremonies will fix everything. Then—then, his rooster will rule and his pollos will be plentiful.

EVERYTHING IS GOING TO BE DIFFERENT

POLLEROS—A DICTIONARY OF SLANG

Words like taloneros, clavos, piedras and vaquetones are jargon in the clandestine and illegal world of the gangs who smuggle undocumented persons into the United States. Below is a list of some of these slang words, most of which appeared in the Vasquez Mendoza text, others we thought may be interesting to language buffs. Nearly all deal with various job descriptions within the smuggling organization, so instead of arranging the words alphabetically, we list the terms in chronological sequence, following the immigrants as they move north.

Pollo and **pollero**: Pollo means chicken; here it identifies immigrants who are crossing into the United States illegally. Pollero, or chicken farmer, applies to anybody who makes his living smuggling undocumented persons, the pollos, into the U.S.

Mojado and **coyote**: Synonyms for pollo and pollero. Mojado as a noun is a person who is wet, and in this context, an illegal migrant who has gotten wet by crossing the Rio Grande. The English word "wetback" predates mojado and has long been used in the U.S. to stereotype and denigrate all Mexicans living in the U.S. Mojado is one of those words that has various shades of meaning. Mexican-Americans may use it to badmouth Mexican immigrants, but Mexican immigrants may use it with a touch of pride. Coyote, of course, is the sneaky dog, the trickster, that thrives in the American Southwest and northern Mexico. But along the border a coyote is also a pollero, a smuggler of human beings.

Enganchador: Comes from the verb enganchar meaning to hook, to connect or, in military circles, to recruit. Thus, the enganchador is a recruiter of undocumented immigrants wanting to go north.

Talonero: Talón means heel, like the heel of a foot, or the Achilles heel. It can mean a "street walker," like a street hustler, or, if feminine (talonera) can refer to a prostitute. In pollero slang, the talonero is the person who recruits the immigrants, so we translated it, like enganchador, as a recruiter. A talonero working independently will sell the pollos he recruits to a gang of polleros.

Clavo: Means spike or nail. A clavo is a stash house on either side of the line where the smuggler (pollero) stores the immigrants who have paid him to move them to the next location.

Encargado: The person in charge of a stash house (clavo) on either side of the line. He or she is responsible for feeding the illegal immigrants, seeing they are locked up and unable to escape, and also making sure they are not stolen by other gangs.

Encaminador: Responsible for buying the pollos from the recruiters (taloneros) and escorting them to the stash house (clavo) or to the guía who will take them across the border (línea).

Línea: This cognate means line and refers to the U.S./Mexico border. East of El Paso, where the Río Grande is the border between the two countries, people refer to the border as el río, the river. People on both sides of the border speak of the neighboring country as el otro lado, the other side.

Migra: A Spanish word, rooted in the verb migrar (to migrate). La migra means immigration police and along the border refers specifically to the U.S. Border Patrol.

Guía and chofer: El guía, or guide, is the person responsible for guiding the immigrants north through the desert. The walk may be only a short distance, but with heightened surveillance on the U.S. side, the walk has become a trek requiring days and is extremely dangerous. The guía's job is to deliver the immigrants to the chofer, or chauffeur, the person responsible for driving the pollos north after they have successfully crossed the border. These two jobs, guía and chofer, are the most dangerous occupations in the pollero chain and are usually assigned to the younger and wilder members of a pollero gang. When a guía or chofer gets older and has been arrested a few times, he may graduate to another of the pollero occupations.

Piedra: Piedra means stone, but here is translated "dead weight." A piedra is an undocumented already in the U.S. who is in debt to the pollero gang who brought him or her north. Perhaps the piedra didn't bring enough money, or relatives refuse to help, or he or she may simply be playing dumb. For dead weight like this there is no solution—the polleros may lock up piedras for a few days in the clavo and later discard them on the border.

Repartidor: The repartidor is responsible for the last task in the pollero chain—parceling out the immigrants to their various destinations, making sure they get on the busses, planes and trains to their particular destinations in the U.S.

Vaquetón: A street-tough, a guy who gets by on the streets by his wits and toughness. In the Vasquez Mendoza text, El Pelos and El Rizos like to refer to themselves as vaquetones instead of polleros, the latter being more labor specific. Both of these vaquetones, who were in their 30s when this was written, have been in the pollero business a long time and have worked in most of the jobs described above.

Driving While Mexican* vs. the 4th Amendment

Amendment IV to the Constitution of the United States of America
THE RIGHT OF THE PEOPLE TO BE SECURE IN THEIR PERSONS, HOUSES, PAPERS,
AND EFFECTS, AGAINST UNREASONABLE SEARCHES AND SEIZURES, SHALL NOT BE VIOLATED,
AND NO WARRANTS SHALL ISSUE, BUT UPON PROBABLE CAUSE, SUPPORTED BY OATH
OR AFFIRMATION, AND PARTICULARLY DESCRIBING THE PLACE TO BE SEARCHED,
AND THE PERSONS OR THINGS TO BE SEIZED.

THE UNITED STATES OF AMERICA
v. EUGENIO ZAPATA-IBARRA, AUGUST 10, 2000

Judge Jacques L. Weiner, appointed to the U.S. Court of Appeals 5th Circuit by President
George H. Bush, argued that the legal system has given law enforcement free reign in search
and seizure of automobiles and people near the border in his dissenting opinion to *The
United States of America v. Eugenio Zapata-Ibarra.*

He states:

> I am embarrassed that the federal courts have forced the dedicated, at-risk officers
> of these agencies to engage in the charade of "articulating facts" just so that we can
> point to something as the underpinnings of our retrospective findings of "reason-
> able suspicion" when we uphold vehicle stops that otherwise offend the Fourth
> Amendment. It is we, not law enforcement, who have constructed the straw man of
> articulatable facts and we who then accept as justifiable suspicion virtually anything
> and everything thus articulated:
>
> The vehicle was suspiciously dirty and muddy, or the vehicle was suspiciously
> squeaky-clean; the driver was suspiciously dirty, shabbily dressed and unkempt, or
> the driver was too clean; the vehicle was suspiciously traveling fast, or was traveling
> suspiciously slow (or even was traveling suspiciously at precisely the legal speed
> limit); the [old car, new car, big car, station wagon, camper, oilfield service truck,
> SUV, van] is the kind of vehicle typically used for smuggling aliens or drugs; the

---

* "DWM" is a slang term used by some Border Patrol agents to describe their rationale for stopping and
searching Latino drivers near the Mexican border.

driver would not make eye contact with the agent, or the driver made eye contact too readily; the driver appeared nervous (or the driver even appeared too cool, calm, and collected); the time of day [early morning, mid-morning, late afternoon, early evening, late evening, middle of the night] is when "they" tend to smuggle contraband or aliens; the vehicle was riding suspiciously low (overloaded), or suspiciously high (equipped with heavy duty shocks and springs); the passengers were slumped suspiciously in their seats, presumably to avoid detection, or the passengers were sitting suspiciously ramrod-erect; the vehicle suspiciously slowed when being overtaken by the patrol car traveling at a high rate of speed with its high-beam lights on, or the vehicle suspiciously maintained its same speed and direction despite being overtaken by a patrol car traveling at a high speed with its high-beam lights on; and on and on ad nauseam.

Judge Weiner concluded his dissent with the following statement:

In summary, I take but slight issue with my colleagues of the panel majority or with the agent who stopped Zapata-Ibarra. Rather, the bone I pick is with the judiciary as a whole for the part we have played and continue to play in rolling back the Fourth Amendment to points many miles this side of our border with Mexico.

Shame on us. At least the war that prompted the Supreme Court to condone the internment of Japanese Americans was a full-fledged, Congressionally-declared, "shooting" war. These are the reasons why I respectfully dissent.

Ña'a ta'ka ani'mai: What Will Be in My Heart

Isaías Ignacio Vázquez Pimentel

translated by Paul Fallon

from *Lo que estará en mi corazón*, 1994

TRANSLATOR'S NOTE: *These vignettes relate border-crossing experiences that Isaías Ignacio Vázquez Pimentel reported in a 1992 interview to Luis Humberto Crosthwaite, later published as part of the book,* Lo que estará en mi corazón (Ña'a ta'ka ani'mai). *A Mixtecan from the southern state of Oaxaca, Sr. Vázquez learned Spanish as a second language. I have tried to maintain the oral rhythm of the stories and convey the inconsistencies of a non-native speaker that the author himself kept in the book. The text is broken into three sections: Sr. Vázquez' anecdotes of his father's time in the U.S.; his own first and second border crossings; and his capture by the migra after his second trip across. Though the accounts here focus on crossing the border, they form a part of Sr. Vázquez' larger narrative as one of thousands of indigenous people who left their southern homelands to find jobs in the north of Mexico or in the United States. Sr. Vázquez also tells of his growing political awareness and his participation in movements working for indigenous communities' and tenants' rights in the San Quintín Valley near Tijuana.*

Part I: 1957

The bracero: My Dad

Once my dad went to the United States when the hiring was going on in 1957. I was nine years old. My father went to Imperial Valley. He came back lighter-skinned. He began to tell me that the United States were pretty and all, but the work was a pain in the ass. He went to pick cotton, asparagus, to pick lettuce. Your back hurts, and then the breeze gets your pants wet. The dollars are nice, but it's a big pain in the ass, that's what he'd say to me.

"I am not going back. If we don't go fast one minute, they just about fire us from the job. They're just so hard ass."

When my dad and them got to Mexicali, on the border in Mexico, they took all of their clothes. They made them bend down, and they looked at everything that men have, and they squeezed where they pee to see if they were not sick. They looked to see if no pus came out. And with many of them pus came out. They didn't enter to the United States. It was sad. There they were in Mexicali, asking for charity, holding out their straw hats.

They hired the workers in Yucuñuti. There was a man named Emiliano Rodríguez. He had a friend in Tezoatlán who hired people for the gavachos. He got a group together in

Yucuñuti to hand them over to the guy from Tezoatlán. The workers left on a train. They had to pay their own way. They gave 150 pesos to the contractor. As soon as they arrived at the line, the border, every single one of them was frisked, all over. People from Oaxaca, Guerrero, Michoacán, Zacatecas, Durango, Nayarit, lots of people in Mexicali. Then they'd wash them with a liquid. All of the men were white white, they fumigate 'em. The ones that bring dry tortilla, bring red tortilla, bring white tortilla, bring yellow tortilla, they throw all that away. And there's my dad looking at his totopos,[1] all thrown away. Ever'thing they bring, clothes and all, was fumigated. They make my dad get naked, they took him to a room and there's a doctor there. Completely stripped they go, bare naked all of them. There're some men that are really big, they're not ashamed or embarrassed, there they go with their big ol' things. The immigration people grabs'em and if pus came out, back they go. Then they make them bend over and they look to see how their ass was. There're some poor guys that have rashes, so much sitting in the train, and these guys don't get to come across because they're scraped up. And by now my dad was happy because he did get to go and the others from Yucuñuti felt sad because they returned. They had to help each other out for the trip back to Oaxaca.

It gladdened my father's heart when he found out he was going to go on. He put his clothes on, but they kept his tortillas. He went on to Calexico, in the United States, and continued to the Imperial Valley. There he got work picking cotton.

"They have a cook," my dad would tell me, "a man-cook that would give them their food, he'd give them their plates. Early, already at three in the morning a little bell is ringing so the workers get up for breakfast. And who wants to eat breakfast at that hour?" But they have to eat their milk with rice or their beans 'n' eggs. My dad used to say that it didn't taste very good because corn was mixed with beans, or butter with beans and it's not very tasty. The time comes to begin work. And at noon the man-cook returns, bringing chicken, meat, fruit. Then they gave the workers their *breiks* at nine in the morning.

"What's a *breik*?" I asked my dad.

"They give you 15 minutes so you can rest and grab an apple or some other fruit, to rest a while."

They were braceros. They are not illegals. The migra doesn't look for them. They didn't call them "pollos" like they call us. There were thousands of them, there were so many. Daily, day after day, the line full of people.

"What's the line?" I'd say.

"The line is where the division is, where the immigration of the gavachos is, where Mexico ends and the United States begins."

My dad sent us many, many letters. When he left home, 20 days later the first one had already arrived. When he got there, he wrote my mom telling her what had happened, that he had met good people. Many compadres didn't get across, the letter said. My mom would take the letter to a compadre so he could read it to her, and there I'd go with her, grabbing

1 Totopos are dried or fried tortillas.

on to her dress. My dad would write in Spanish. My mom was sad because she didn't want my dad to go, but soon as she received the first letter she was glad, she got a little happier.

"Your dad has already arrived, son, soon now we'll have a little money."

My mom went to church daily with her flowers for the saint, Saint Sebastian. Her, praying Mixtec. Me, just looking around. An hour, an hour a half sometimes. When my grandma would do something to her, my mom would cry in church, praying and crying. She's asking God not to let anything bad happen to my dad. Many men go and come back dead, they die. My mom saw this with the rest of the people and it scared her.

"Why'd you let him go? 'Tis really far, it's another nation," they'd tell my mother. Then she'd tell me about it.

"What's all this about another nation?" I'd ask her.

"It's not Mexico, son, it's another nation—the United States."

"Who knows what that is?" I'd say.

And lots really did come back dead. One man, Don Juan Montes, fell from a truck, he got hit and there he stayed, dead. He didn't even come back, they buried him over there. Another one died, but the other braceros brought him back themselves. Others died of hunger, cars hit other ones. And there are a lot of robbers that snatch their money away and kill them. They rob the poor bracero and sometimes the bracero goes crazy for his money, he wants to defend himself, and they kill him.

After five months his contract ended and my dad came back lighter-skinned, with his suitcase and his red boots. He brought my mom a dress and cloth so she could have other dresses sewn, and he gave her the money he made.

He got back home all of a sudden; we knew he was gonna come because he sent a letter but we didn't know when he'd get home. I was asleep; it was already late at night; before, we didn't even use a clock—we didn't even know what a clock was—but it was already the wee hours of the morning. He arrived and began to talk with my mom. I got up running, really happy to see my dad.

We didn't greet each other with a hug. With a hug, no. My dad just arrived and I said: "You're back, dad?"

"I'm back, my son," and he gripped my little hand.

"A ni sa'o, jee? —You came back, son?" my mom asked him.

"Yes, I came back, daughter."

And later he went to see the littlest ones: Guadalupe and Rodrigo. He brought us sweets, cookies to enjoy. My mom got up and made him dinner; we talked 'til dawn.

My dad wanted to return to the United States but now my mom wouldn't let him.

Part II: 1973

I was going crazy

Tijuana was the very border of Mexico. It was really ugly; the only place I liked was the center of the city. We arrived at the station about six or seven in the afternoon and in the letter it said for us to get to the Hotel Económico that was next to the station on the left hand side. We went out and my brother looked around and we found the hotel easy. We went over quickly to talk on the phone. We called and a man told us that Raúl Soriano wasn't there, that he went out at four in the afternoon, so if you want, you can speak with him at six or seven in the morning, whatever you want. That man was his friend. He told us:

"Don't move from that hotel and tomorrow Raúl will tell you who's the person who's going to bring you."

We looked at the beds and the beds were nice in that hotel. It was a fancy hotel. We bathed and my brother was rubbing his hands together, he was so happy to go over to the other side, to the United States.

"You like it, brother?"

"Yeah, now we're going to get to know the dollars."

It was the year 1973.

We began to count the money; I brung 150 pesos, which was a lot of money, and my brother another 450 pesos. We went to buy a six-pack of Tecate in cans and we stuck them in a paper bag because we were embarrassed to enter the hotel with the beers. We opened the cans and we began to drink very happy. Since we were young, with the third can, I started to enjoy myself and I grabbed another one. I felt half drunk and we still wanted to drink more, but Rodrigo told me that we should wait for the telephone call tomorrow morning. And so, better we get under the covers and go to sleep.

Before four in the morning, my brother was already awake. We began to talk:

"I hope we can get across."

"Yeah, brother."

"Soon as we get across, we'll get work and send a letter to our family, so our wives and our parents will be happy," my brother said. And he hugged me and tickled me out of joy. He was going crazy, but from being happy; he had never seen Tijuana or Culiacán. Just talking and talking. *I wonder how our children are?* I was thinking about my wife because I left her only a little money. It wasn't going to be enough. We were talking about a lot of things and we didn't see what time it was, and since we didn't have a clock, my brother went down about three times to talk to the man downstairs. The first time he went down and asked they told him it's a little past four. A while later he went down again to ask if it was six. "No, it's only a little past five." It was about ten to six when we went down together. I grabbed the telephone and the hotel owner himself dialed the number. My compadre was already waiting.

"Compadre, I'm here now, in Tijuana," I tell him.

"And, how did you do it, compadre?"

"Well, with the exact same address you gave me."

"Ooooof, well, it's already been a long time since I sent it to you."

"Well, yeah—it's because I was in Culiacán and now I'm here with my brother Rodrigo and I need your help."

"Okay, don't worry, compadre, don't fret, I'll help you out. I have money for you but I'm going to do what I can to get a little more for your brother."

My brother got a pen from the hotel and began to take notes.

"Go out of the Hotel Económico and go to the left hand side and you go straight up for about four or five blocks on your left hand side until Guerrero Street. Look for the store Ensenada and you go in that store and talk to Mrs. Regina. Tell her that Raúl Soriano sent you. She already knows because I talked to her on the phone."

"Thanks a lot, compadre. And when do you think we are gonna cross?"

"Well, I don't know, we'll see when they bring you over. But I trust this person a lot."

"That's awright, compadre, thanks a lot. That's what we'll do."

"Good enough then. And don't go out walking around because it's really dangerous walking around in Tijuana—there's a lot of violence."

That's what he told me. And we hung up. My brother even danced, he was so happy.

The contact

Asking and asking until Guerrero Street: one, two, three, four blocks. We started to look for the numbers. We walked a little and there was the store. We went in and asked.

"Good morning, ma'am."

"Good morning, young men."

And the woman didn't want to talk. There was a girl there who told us that no Regina lived there.

"Ask over around the corner," they told us.

When we went out, there was the woman waiting for us. It was Mrs. Regina but she didn't want to talk to us about it inside the store. We went over and sat down at a table and the woman asked us questions about if we wanted to cross over to the other side.

The woman didn't bring over the pollos, she just got them together; she'd sell us over into the hands of the coyotes, and they'd pay twenty-five dollars to the woman, leaving one hundred fifty for the coyote. She made us some really big steaks, huge plates for me and my brother. In Oaxaca, we'd eat meat but just little pieces. I had never eaten a piece so big. The woman treated us very well. They gave us milk, juice and a banana.

"La banda del carro rojo" / The Red Car Gang

At about three in the afternoon, the coyote arrived. He had a big 'ol moustache, and he gets to talking with Mrs. Regina.

"Don't worry, I'll come for you at five."

My brother was wringing his hands. At five another person came and it scared us because it wasn't the same guy. I didn't know they worked together. They're the same people, the woman told us. They told us to buy a bus ticket to Tecate. There in the bus station there were more people, all of them with their dufflebags. We bought a ticket. There were 16 of us in all. We got off before we got to Tecate. My brother said, "Move it." We were going right alongside the coyote.

"Real careful, boys," the coyote said. "Don't spread out because there's snakes."

When he said snakes I got more scared. My brother, too. And we're going and we're going. We got off the bus at about nine at night. We walked six or seven hours on the Mexican side. We got to a little town and we crouched down, we got ourselves scrunched down beneath some bushes. We stayed like that about an hour. We stayed just crouched down; we weren't supposed to make noise but there were a lot of dry branches. And the coyote standing, he was standing up. It seemed like some cars came close and flashed their lights on us, but the cars're far away. We arrived at another place and we got into a big car, a paneled wagon. We got in lying down, some on our backs, some on our stomachs, piled up like logs. One would come in and lie on top of the others. I was on top of one man, my head next to somebody else's stomach and my brother next to my knee and someone else came and got on top of me, well, like firewood. And the coyotes began to fight amongst themselves:

"What are you doing? Do something."

"I'm taking care of these guys. You're drinking coffee."

"If we're screwed, it's because of you."

The coyotes brought their beer and the smell of the beer reached us and they put on a cassette of Los Tigres del Norte, "La banda del carro rojo." I hadn't heard them in Oaxaca. I'm just listening. You could hear the coyotes opening their beer cans. I'm hearing it, and they're just happy as can be; you could hear that they were throwing the beers down. They were drinking and their "Banda del carro rojo" just playing. How pretty, I thought to myself. I was pleased with the music. My body ached, but what could I do? What I wanted to do was to get over to the other side.

"Contrabando y traición" / Contraband and betrayal

We crossed over through the range near Tecate, easy, there's no wire, there's nothing, and we arrive at Tecatito. In that little pueblo, it's already the other side; it's already the United States. We arrived at San Clemente and they returned because it wasn't possible to cross now. They argued, saying go back, leave them right there and get them out, and be careful with them, said the biggest coyote, the boss coyote. And we went right back. They took us to the edge of a gorge.

"Get out and get yourselves up there."

It was getting to be light out already. Really cold, all of us in the ravine. You could see lights but in the distance. We made a fire, we thought about a lot of things.

"It's rough, this crossing."

The others said: "These sons of bitches might just leave us here." And us without money.

It was clear morning by six o'clock, but it was a really deep ravine and we couldn't see the sun 'til noon, and then it began to warm up a little. At one in the afternoon, the coyote came with gallons of milk, with bags of bread. Before I didn't drink milk. Yeah, I drank it—cow's milk; my mom would boil it, and she'd sprinkle a cornmeal inside. That milk was tasty. But this milk was not boiled, in a gallon jug, and since we couldn't stand going hungry we had to drink that milk. It was cold and frozen, and then the bread was white bread, Bimbo bread. I don't like Bimbo bread. I didn't eat Bimbo, but since hunger is a bad, bad thing, I had to eat two pieces and my brother did, too. But no sooner did my poor brother drink the milk, then he began to bring the food right back up. The milk bothered us; we weren't used to it. They brought food, then they left again. They came back again about ten at night. It was dark. They came in the car.

"Let's go, all of Morales' people."

That was the name of the coyote, guy named Marco Morales. All the people from different coyotes were concentrated there together. There were some sixty of us. We stood up and got into the car and we left the ravine. They stopped in a marketa, they bought beer, they began to drink and they put on some music, "Contrabando y traición." Los Tigres del Norte again. I liked them a lot. That's when I learned these lines:

> They crossed o´er at San Clemente
> Immigration stopped them
> Asked them for their documents
> And asked them, "Where are you from?"

The coyote

We arrived in Los Angeles. He told us it was Los Angeles. Some big buildings in that place. We got out at the coyote's house. There he had his carpets, everything fancy where the pollos rested. There was food, but since I was shy, since I was a little embarrassed, I waited for them to give me something to eat, but no, there every man was for himself. The ones who know better stand up first and grab their disposable plate and there they all go, and we're at the end of the line and there was nothin' but little wings left for us because we didn't know any better. We were still hungry. A really huge pot of mole. And then chicken and bread. How great it would be if there were some tortillas.

The house was pretty. It was like the color blue inside. They were some stacked-up houses. We went up some steps. There was another house below. Now the bread and the milk had more or less settled in my stomach. My brother's stomach still hurt, but not so much then. We finished eating, everybody with their plate in the trash. The coyote goes and right in the middle of all of us, he says:

"Let's see, guy, what's your address, where're you going?"

"I'm going to Los Angeles," one said.

"Okay, first the ones for Los Angeles. Your address, your telephone number."

The coyote pulls his telephone over in the middle and talks. He gets tired of his chair and crosses his legs in the floor, on the rug. Everyone has their address and telephone number. He began to separate all those for Los Angeles, all those for San Fernando, up to the last ones for Santa Ana. We were shut in. I would have really liked to get out, I would have really liked some fresh air but I couldn't. We got in the car, they're taking us and the coyotes don't find the address. They get out to call by telephone and the phone did not answer.

"Well, let's go back, I don't know what happened, seems that we hit a bad streak with you two. You should pay more."

"I don't know about that," my brother said. He was the more direct one. "We don't know what the deal is. You turn us over and arrange it with our family."

We went back to the coyote's house about three in the morning. We laid down and the coyote locked us in so we couldn't leave. The sun came up and he got himself up about nine in the morning. We were awake since six. The coyote went to take a shower. He was a while combing his hair. He looked in the mirror, and then he stretched out on the bed for a while. "Man, I'm really tired," he says. The coyote Marco Morales, with so much money, he wasn't even worried about us any more.

"Spent a lot of gas with you. Tell your friends to see if they can come up with some more money because we're driving around a lot."

"Yessir, alright," we told him.

What else were we going to tell him?

Back in the United States again

I told my wife that I wasn't going but I had to go. I returned because a friend encouraged me. It was my cousin Raymundo Sanmorán and my brother Rodrigo.

Suriana was sad. She was hurt because she didn't want me to go.

"Don't be sad because this time everything's going to be good for me. Raymundo says that San Bernardino is really good with lots of oranges."

"Yes, but I don't want you to go."

"Don't be sad. I'm just going for two months, 's all."

She didn't say anything else, but she was hurt, she was sad.

It was a lot more than two months. I went with Raymundo and Rodrigo and Pablo Vázquez and a nephew of his. Raymundo took us to El Chupe, a pollo crossing from Mexicali. He took us over through the Tecate mountains. We walked five days. My wife made totopos. I brought forty huge tortilla totopos with salt. In Tecate, I broke them into little pieces. That Chupe guy knew Lolo Montes, a man from Michoacán, a foreman for oranges. We were going to the shelter of the orange tree. We crossed near Tecate. There aren't any migra or anything. We walked at night, with Chupe in front. He'd go on smoking cigarettes. We entered the United States. The only danger was the snakes.

We walked all night to Highway 80 when dawn came up on us. We climbed up to the top of a hill. We slept there. We went down when it got late. We walked all night. There were a lot of torch pines, and gavachos' orchards, lots of orange trees, lots of lemon trees.

Through the Tecate mountains, it was desert, nothing but desert, nothing but rocks, thorns, bushes; after the highway, it was nothing but orchards, nothing but gavacho gardens, apples, grapefruits. We'd walk real quiet all night without resting, nothing but desert. We all brought totopos. We stepped on snow. My brother Rodrigo drank the snow because he was really thirsty and it got him sick. We tried to get to a highway. The sun came up on us. We had to wait out the day. We went to sleep in some ditches.

The only thing we ate were totopos—Chupe brought canned beans—the whole day until we went down into the Valle del Borrego. There you could see cattle, corrals of bulls, calves. We scared the horses. There were eight or nine of us. I couldn't stand it; I wasn't wearing a jacket. In the Valle del Borrego, it began to rain, too much rain. We were going through the corrals. I had a swollen foot. I was already limping; I needed a stick to walk with. My brother helped me with the totopos. I began to get cold; my whole body was soaked. I found a wet jacket and I covered myself—I was walking way behind.

We walked the whole day. We got to a river, we rolled up our pants. The arroyos were big because of the rain. My huarache sandals came apart on me. Chupe wore big boots. He wasn't a bit tired. We got to the little pueblo Nanza. They looked for a car and I stayed in a little house; I slept all curled up. Later I couldn't stand up; my feet, my legs went to sleep on me. When the car arrived, I couldn't stand up. I wanted to stand up but I couldn't. Chupe was getting mad because the migra was going to get us, because it was getting to be light out. He took us to Jemes Mountains. We got up on a hill again because it was dawn again. Soon as the sun went down, Chupe went down to a marketa and went to get food. We ate and we began to go down little by little. We went into some olive trees. My feet couldn't stand it any more.

Part III
The migra comes down on us
There you took whatever job you could get. Sometimes there was work, sometimes there wasn't. We were working at thinning the cotton plants. My uncle Pablo Vázquez was there, too. It was 'bout nine in the morning. The migra comes down on us. It was the cops. The migra came. We saw 'em. There were about 30 men in each row. The cops stopped, the migrant agent stopped, and there I go; I throw down the hoe and I tell him, "Uncle, here comes the migra." And the people go, some here and others there and then I up and go just like that, and my boots were just sinking in the loose dirt and I go straight, then I go left and there a migra was coming, a pocho[2] with a big moustache, just flying, running, he left the paddy wagon. I didn't want him to grab me because it was payday. It was my little pay and I wanted to see my bit of money; it was Saturday, we were all ready to leave. I went left and here comes the pocho. I wanted to get to the freeway but as I'm goin' I see there was a migra

2 "Pocho" is a perjorative term, much like "traitor" or "Uncle Tom," used by Mexicans to denigrate Mexican-Americans or fellow Mexicans who have become too Americanized.

pick-up and I took off going the other way. And then the migrant agent tells me, "Hold up, hold up, stupid pendejo," the pocho said in Spanish, foam coming out of his mouth like a pig. I would look back and run faster and a fat guy from Michoacán comes running, too. He was coming behind me.

And they grabbed my uncle and they grabbed his nephew, and I'm running, and as I'm going, I break to the left. I'm just going 'round in circles, and the migrant agent hangs on to the neck of the guy from Michoacán and the two of them fall down. I saw them rolling around together, and I saw a canal floodgate. I wanted to get into the water to escape. Just when I was about to get close, the wagon comes and then a migra grabs me. He grabbed me by the jacket; he stretches out his hand and he grabs me. The one who was driving sticks his hand out of the window and I just go down on my ass, and I fall down. Well, I'm moving forward and really quick another one gets out of the truck to grab me and when I tried to get up, he gives me a whack on the neck with the butt of his pistol, and then he gives me another one on my head and another one on my head and hard and heavy, really ugly, and another one on the cheek. And oh, how my uncle Pablo's heart hurt to see how they hit me, and I felt my skin split open, the other migras just watching and they cross my hands together and they put handcuffs on me. And then once I'm cuffed, another one on my head, about eight shots, and they hit me in the ribs and in the legs with the billy club. They're all pochos. They say they're Texans; they're Mexicans, they're really cruel. And they put me up into the wagon. "Stupid pendejo," they call me. "Get in." They were tired, drenched in sweat, and I'm all balled up little and they're beating me. No blood came out, nothing but lumps came up.

They beat others, too.

There were 30 of us and of the 30, one escaped because he kept hoeing while the rest of us ran. The migra came and they chased after the ones that ran and he knew what to do. While the others ran, he just kept hoeing. Then, while the migra go after the others, he gets away through the canal floodgates. That guy, he knew what to do.

They took us to the big coop, to the office in Fresno, in the United States. They frisked us. How much money did we have with us? I didn't have any money. The ones that had $100, they took it from them, to pay for the trip. From some they took $40, $30, $20. They did this in the big coop in Fresno, and they passed us over to another set of bars, like a prison.

We were there the whole day until the bus left, the bus to Mexicali, the whole day, until eight at night, and the migrant agent didn't give us anything to eat. Everybody was hungry.

"We're hungry, migra," everybody said.

And a big fat migra just sat there looking at us, just eating his potato chips.

Chronology:
Changes in Immigration and Naturalization Law

Adapted from and provided courtesy of the National Immigration Forum Website 2001.

1790—Naturalization is authorized for "free white persons" who have resided in the United States for at least two years and swear loyalty to the U.S. Constitution. The racial requirement remained on the federal books until 1952, although naturalization was opened to certain Asian nationalities in the 1940s.

1798—The Alien and Sedition Acts authorize the President to deport any foreigner deemed to be dangerous and make it a crime to speak, write, or publish anything "of a false, scandalous and malicious nature" about the President or Congress. An amended Naturalization Act imposes a 14-year residency requirement for prospective citizens; in 1802, Congress reduced the waiting period to five years, a provision that remains in effect today.

1882—The Chinese Exclusion Act suspends immigration by Chinese laborers for ten years; the measure was extended and tightened in 1892 and a permanent ban enacted in 1902. This marks the first time the United States restricted immigration on the basis of race or national origin.

1891—To the list of undesirables ineligible for immigration, Congress adds polygamists, "persons suffering from a loathsome or a dangerous contagious disease" and those convicted of "a misdemeanor involving moral turpitude."

1906—The first language requirement is adopted for naturalization: the ability to speak and understand English.

1907-1908—Under a so-called "gentlemen's agreement," the United States promises not to ban Japanese immigration in exchange for Japan's pledge not to issue passports to Japanese laborers for travel to the continental United States (although they remain welcome to become agricultural workers in Hawaii). By a separate executive order, President Theodore Roosevelt prohibits secondary migration by Japanese from Hawaii to the mainland.

1917—Over President Wilson's veto, Congress enacts a literacy requirement for all new immigrants: ability to read 40 words in some language. Most significant in limiting the flow of newcomers, it designates Asia as a "barred zone" (excepting Japan and the Philippines) from which immigration will be prohibited.

1921—A new form of immigration restriction is born: the national-origins quota system. Admissions from each European country will be limited to three percent of each foreign-born nationality in the 1910 census. The effect is to favor Northern Europeans at the expense of Southern and Eastern Europeans. Immigration from Western Hemisphere nations remains unrestricted; most Asians continue to face exclusion.

1924—Restrictionists' decisive stroke, the Johnson-Reed Act, embodies the principle of pre-serving America's "racial" composition. Immigration quotas will be based on the ethnic makeup of the U.S. population as a whole in 1920. The new national-origins quota system is even more discriminatory than the 1921 version. "America must be kept American," says President Coolidge as he signs the bill into law. Another provision bans all immigration by persons "ineligible to citizenship"—primarily affecting the Japanese.

1943—To appease a wartime ally, a token quota (105) is created for Chinese immigration. Yet unlike white immigrants, whose quotas depend on country of residence, all persons of "Chinese race" will be counted under the Chinese quota regardless of where they reside.

1950—The Internal Security Act, enacted over President Truman's veto, bars admission to any foreigner who might engage in activities "which would be prejudicial to the public in-terest, or would endanger the welfare or safety of the United States." It excludes immigra-tion and permits deportation of non-citizens who belong to the U.S. Communist Party or whose future activities might be "subversive to the national security."

1952—The McCarran-Walter Act retains the national-origins quota system and "internal se-curity" restrictions, despite Truman's opposition. For the first time, however, Congress sets aside minimum annual quotas for all countries, opening the door to numerous nationalities previously kept out on racial grounds. Naturalization now requires ability to read and write, as well as speak and understand, English.

1965—The United States finally eliminates racial criteria from its immigration laws. Each country, regardless of ethnicity, will receive an annual quota of 20,000, under a ceiling of 170,000. Up to 120,000 may emigrate from Western Hemisphere nations, which are still not subject to country quotas (an exception Congress would eliminate in 1976).

1986—The Immigration Reform and Control Act gives amnesty to approximately three mil-lion undocumented residents. For the first time, the law punishes employers who hire per-sons who are here illegally. The aim of employer sanctions is to make it difficult for the un-documented to find employment. The law has a side effect: employment discrimination against those who look or sound "foreign."

1990—The Immigration Act of 1990 raises the limit for legal immigration to 700,000 people a year.

1996—A persistent recession in the U.S. in the early 90s, among other reasons, leads to calls for new restrictions on immigration. The Illegal Immigration Reform and Immigrant Respon-sibility Act is passed, toughening border enforcement, closing opportunities for undocu-mented immigrants to adjust their status and making it more difficult to gain asylum. The law greatly expands the grounds for deporting even long-resident immigrants. It strips im-migrants of many due process rights and their access to the courts. New income require-ments are established for sponsors of legal immigrants. In the Personal Responsibility and Work Opportunity Act, Congress makes citizenship a condition of eligibility for public ben-efits for most immigrants.

Everything is Going to be Different

1997—A new Congress mitigates some of the overly harsh restrictions passed by the previous Congress. In the Balanced Budget Agreement with the President, some public benefits are restored for elderly and disabled immigrants who had been receiving them prior to the 1996 changes. With the Nicaraguan Adjustment and Central American Relief Act, Congress restores an opportunity for certain war refugees living in legal limbo to become permanent residents.

1998—Congress continues to mitigate some of the nativist provisions passed by Congress in 1996 by partially restoring access to public benefits for additional groups of legal immigrants. The Haitian Refugee Immigration Fairness Act resolves the legal limbo status of certain Haitian refugees, and allows them to become permanent U.S. residents. Responding to the pleas of powerful employer groups, Congress passes the American Competitiveness and Workforce Improvement Act, which significantly raises the number of skilled temporary foreign workers U.S. employers are allowed to bring to the U.S.

2000—Congress continues to move incrementally in a pro-immigrant direction, passing the compromise Legal Immigration Family Equity Act, which creates a narrow window for immigrants with family or employer sponsors to adjust to legal status in the U.S., resolves the legal limbo of certain immigrants denied legalization in the mid-1980's, and provides temporary visas for certain family-sponsored immigrants waiting for their green cards. For the second time in three years, Congress significantly raises the ceiling for skilled temporary workers. The Child Citizenship Act grants automatic U.S. citizenship to foreign-born adopted children. The Victims of Trafficking and Violence Protection Act provides visas for trafficking and crime victims. Congress modifies the Naturalization law to allow severely disabled immigrants to become citizens even if they cannot understand the Oath of Allegiance.

The Border Patrol State

Leslie Marmon Silko

The Nation, October 17, 1994

I used to travel the highways of New Mexico and Arizona with a wonderful sensation of absolute freedom as I cruised down the open road and across the vast desert plateaus. On the Laguna Pueblo reservation, where I was raised, the people were patriotic despite the way the U.S. government had treated Native Americans. As proud citizens, we grew up believing the freedom to travel was our inalienable right, a right that some Native Americans had been denied in the early twentieth century. Our cousin, old Bill Pratt, used to ride his horse 300 miles overland from Laguna, New Mexico, to Prescott, Arizona, every summer to work as a fire lookout.

In school in the 1950s, we were taught that our right to travel from state to state without special papers or threat of detainment was a right that citizens under communist and totalitarian governments did not possess. That wide open highway told us we were U.S. citizens; we were free...

Not so long ago, my companion Gus and I were driving south from Albuquerque, returning to Tucson after a book promotion for the paperback edition of my novel *Almanac of the Dead.* I had settled back and gone to sleep while Gus drove, but I was awakened when I felt the car slowing to a stop. It was nearly midnight on New Mexico State Road 26, a dark, lonely stretch of two-lane highway between Hatch and Deming. When I sat up, I saw the headlights and emergency flashers of six vehicles—Border Patrol cars and a van were blocking both lanes of the highway. Gus stopped the car and rolled down the window to ask what was wrong. But the closest Border Patrolman and his companion did not reply; instead, the first agent ordered us to "step out of the car." Gus asked why, but his question seemed to set them off. Two more Border Patrol agents immediately approached our car, and one of them snapped, "Are you looking for trouble?" as if he would relish it.

I will never forget that night beside the highway. There was an awful feeling of menace and violence straining to break loose. It was clear that the uniformed men would be only too happy to drag us out of the car if we did not speedily comply with their request (asking a question is tantamount to resistance, it seems). So we stepped out of the car and they motioned for us to stand on the shoulder of the road. The night was very dark, and no other traffic had come down the road since we had been stopped. All I could think about was a book I had read—*Nunca Más*—the official report of a human rights commission that

EVERYTHING IS GOING TO BE DIFFERENT

investigated and certified more than 12,000 "disappearances" during Argentina's "dirty war" in the late 1970s.

The weird anger of the Border Patrolmen made me think about descriptions in the report of Argentine police and military officers who became addicted to interrogation, torture and the murder that followed. When the military and police ran out of political suspects to torture and kill, they resorted to the random abduction of citizens off the streets. I thought how easy it would be for the Border Patrol to shoot us and leave our bodies and car beside the highway, like so many bodies found in these parts and ascribed to "drug runners."

Two other Border Patrolmen stood by the white van. The one who had asked if we were looking for trouble ordered his partner to "get the dog," and from the back of the van another patrolman brought a small female German shepherd on a leash. The dog apparently did not heel well enough to suit him, and the handler jerked the leash. They opened the doors of our car and pulled the dog's head into it, but I saw immediately from the expression in her eyes that the dog hated them, and that she would not serve them. When she showed no interest in the inside of the car, they brought her around back to the trunk, near where we were standing. They half-dragged her up into the trunk, but still she did not indicate any stowed-away human being or illegal drugs.

The mood got uglier; the officers seemed outraged that the dog could not find any contraband, and they dragged her over to us and commanded her to sniff our legs and feet. To my relief, the strange violence the Border Patrol agents had focused on us now seemed shifted to the dog. I no longer felt so strongly that we would be murdered. We exchanged looks—the dog and I. She was afraid of what they might do, just as I was. The dog's handler jerked the leash sharply as she sniffed us, as if to make her perform better, but the dog refused to accuse us—she had an innate dignity that did not permit her to serve the murderous impulses of those men. I can't forget the expression in the dog's eyes; it was as if she were embarrassed to be associated with them. I had a small amount of medicinal marijuana in my purse that night, but she refused to expose me. I am not partial to dogs, but I will always remember that small German shepherd.

Unfortunately, what happened to me is an everyday occurrence here now. Since the 1980s, on top of greatly expanding border checkpoints, the Immigration and Naturalization Service (INS) and the Border Patrol have implemented policies that interfere with the rights of U.S. citizens to travel freely within our borders. INS agents now patrol all interstate highways and roads that lead to or from the U.S./Mexico border in Texas, New Mexico, Arizona and California. Now, when you drive east from Tucson on Interstate 10 toward El Paso, you encounter an INS check station outside Las Cruces, New Mexico. When you drive north from Las Cruces up Interstate 25, two miles north of the town of Truth or Consequences, the highway is blocked with orange emergency barriers, and all traffic is diverted into a two-lane Border Patrol checkpoint—ninety-five miles north of the U.S./Mexico border.[1]

1 These checkpoints have been moved. [Editor's note.]

I was detained once at Truth or Consequences, despite my and my companion's Arizona driver's licenses. Two men, both Chicanos, were detained at the same time, despite the fact that they too presented IDs and spoke English without the thick Texas accents of the Border Patrol agents. While we were stopped, we watched as other vehicles—whose occupants were white—were waved through the checkpoint. White people traveling with brown people, however, can expect to be stopped on suspicion they work with the sanctuary movement, which shelters refugees. White people who appear to be clergy, those who wear ethnic clothing or jewelry and women with very long hair or very short hair (they could be nuns) are also frequently detained; white men with beards or men with long hair are likely to be detained, too, because Border Patrol agents have "profiles" of "those sorts" of white people who may help political refugees. (Most of the political refugees from Guatemala and El Salvador are Native American or mestizo because the indigenous people of the Americas have continued to resist efforts by invaders to displace them from their ancestral lands.) Alleged increases in illegal immigration by people of Asian ancestry mean that the Border Patrol now routinely detains anyone who appears to be Asian or part Asian, as well.

Once your car is diverted from the Interstate Highway into the checkpoint area, you are under the control of the Border Patrol, which in practical terms exercises a power that no highway patrol or city patrolman possesses. They are willing to detain anyone, for no apparent reason. Other law-enforcement officers need a shred of probable cause in order to detain someone. On the books, so does the Border Patrol, but on the road, it's another matter. They'll order you to stop your car and step out; then they'll ask you to open the trunk. If you ask why or request a search warrant, you'll be told that they'll have to have a dog sniff the car before they can request a search warrant, and the dog might not get there for two or three hours. The search warrant might require an hour or two past that. They make it clear that if you force them to obtain a search warrant for the car, they will make you submit to a strip search as well.

Traveling in the open, though, the sense of violation can be even worse. Never mind high-profile cases like that of former Border Patrol agent Michael Elmer, acquitted of murder by claiming self-defense, despite admitting that as an officer he shot an "illegal" immigrant in the back and then hid the body, which remained undiscovered until another Border Patrolman reported the event. (Elmer was convicted of reckless endangerment in a separate incident, for shooting at least ten rounds from his M-16 too close to a group of immigrants as they were crossing illegally into Nogales in March 1992.) Or that in El Paso, a high school football coach driving a vanload of players in full uniform was pulled over on the freeway and a Border Patrol agent put a cocked revolver to his head. (The football coach was Mexican-American, as were most of the players in his van; the incident eventually caused a federal judge to issue a restraining order against the Border Patrol.) We've a mountain of personal experiences like that which never make the newspapers. A history professor at UCLA told me she had been traveling by train from Los Angeles to Albuquerque twice a month doing research. On each of her trips, she had noticed that the Border Patrol

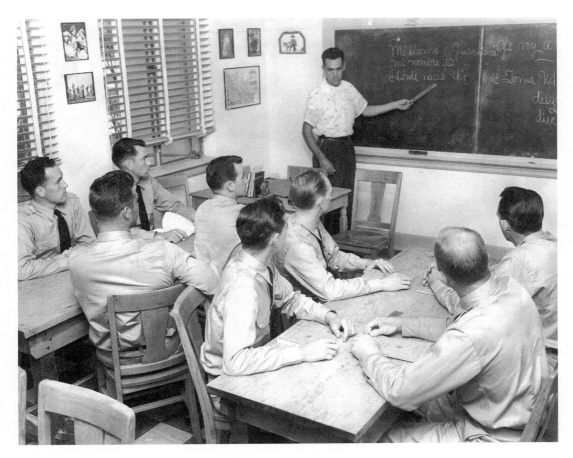

INS agents taking Spanish lessons in the 1950s. Today, according to Tim Dunn, author of The Militarization of the Border, *the Border Patrol is the most Latino (mostly Mexican-American) agency in the U.S. Government. Oddly, turnover hovers around 15% every year, a very high average for a federal agency.*

agents were at the station in Albuquerque scrutinizing the passengers. Since she is six feet tall and of Irish and German ancestry, she was not particularly concerned. Then one day when she stepped off the train in Albuquerque, two Border Patrolmen accosted her, wanting to know what she was doing, and why she was traveling between Los Angeles and Albuquerque twice a month. She presented identification and an explanation deemed "suitable" by the agents, and was allowed to go about her business.

Just the other day, I mentioned to a friend that I was writing this article and he told me about his 73-year-old father who is half-Chinese and who had set out alone by car from Tucson to Albuquerque the week before. His father had become confused by road construction and missed a turnoff from Interstate 10 to Interstate 25; when he turned around and circled back, he missed the turnoff a second time. But when he looped back for yet another try, Border Patrol agents stopped him and forced him to open his trunk. After they satisfied themselves that he was not smuggling Chinese immigrants, they sent him on his way. He was so rattled by the event that he had to be driven home by his daughter.

This is the police state that has developed in the southwestern United States since the 1980s. No person, no citizen, is free to travel without the scrutiny of the Border Patrol. In the city of South Tucson, where 80 percent of the respondents were Chicano or Mexicano, a joint research project by the University of Wisconsin and the University of Arizona recently concluded that one out of every five people there had been detained, mistreated verbally or nonverbally, or questioned by INS agents in the past two years.

LEE BYRD

Sign at a Border Checkpoint. All individuals traveling in the Border regions, whether they've been in Mexico or not, must travel through such secondary checkpoints, approximately 50 to 100 miles north of the Mexican border, in order to fully "enter" the U.S. Usually a simple declaration of U.S. citizenship allows you to pass. These checkpoints do not exist below the U.S./Canada Border.

Manifest Destiny may lack its old grandeur of theft and blood—"lock the door" is what it means now, with racism a trump card to be played again and again, shamelessly, by both major political parties. "Immigration," like "street crime" and "welfare fraud," is a political euphemism that refers to people of color. Politicians and media people talk about "illegal aliens" to dehumanize and demonize undocumented immigrants, who are for the most part people of color. Even in the days of Spanish and Mexican rule, no attempts were made to interfere with the flow of people and goods from south to north and north to south. It is the U.S. government that has continually attempted to sever contact between the tribal people north of the border and those to the south.[2]

2 The Treaty of Guadalupe Hidalgo, signed in 1848, recognizes the right of Tohono O'odham people to move freely across the U.S./Mexico border without documents. A treaty with Canada guarantees similar rights to those of the Iroquois nation in traversing the U.S./Canada border.

Everything is Going to be Different

Now that the "Iron Curtain" is gone, it is ironic that the U.S. government and its Border Patrol are constructing a steel wall ten feet high to span sections of the border with Mexico. While politicians and multinational corporations extol the virtues of NAFTA and "free trade" (in goods, not flesh), the ominous curtain is already up in a six-mile section at the border crossing at Mexicali; two miles are being erected but are not yet finished at Naco; and at Nogales, 60 miles south of Tucson, the steel wall has been rubber-stamped and awaits construction likely to begin in March[1995]. Like the pathetic multimillion-dollar "antidrug" border surveillance balloons that were continuously being deflated by high winds and made only a couple of meager interceptions before they blew away, the fence along the border is a theatrical prop, a bit of pork for contractors. Border entrepreneurs have already used blowtorches to cut passageways through the fence to collect "tolls," and are doing a brisk business. Back in Washington, the INS announces a $300-million-dollar computer contract to modernize its record-keeping and Congress passes a crime bill that shunts $255 million to the

EL FISGÓN

Mexican immigrant Serafín Olvera died on February 24, 2002, from injuries he received at the hands of INS agents almost a year earlier. INS agents beat Olvera after taking him into custody during a March 24, 2001, raid on a home in Bryan, Texas, northwest of Houston; one agent broke Olvera's spine with his knee. Olvera was paralyzed from the neck down and remained hospitalized for nearly a year before doctors declared him brain dead and his family had him removed from life support. Olvera's five children were born in the U.S.; he worked as a roofer before the beating incident. Immigrants who witnessed Olvera's beating were deported before they could be interviewed; however, with the help of the Mexican consulate in Houston, eyewitnesses were identified and a civil lawsuit was filed in federal court.

INS for 1995, $181 million earmarked for border control, which is to include 700 new partners for the men who stopped Gus and me in our travels, and the history professor, and my friend's father and as many as they could from South Tucson.

It is no use; borders haven't worked, and they won't work, not now, as the indigenous people of the Americas reassert their kinship and solidarity with one another. A mass migration is already under way; its roots are not simply economic. The Uto-Aztecan languages are spoken as far north as Taos Pueblo near the Colorado border, all the way south to Mexico City. Before the arrival of the Europeans, the indigenous communities throughout this region not only conducted commerce; the people shared cosmologies and oral narratives about the Maize Mothers, the Twin Brothers and the Grandmother, Spider Woman, as well as Quetzalcoatl the benevolent snake. The great human migration within the Americas cannot be stopped; human beings are natural forces of the Earth, just as rivers and winds are natural forces.

Deep down, the issue is simple: the so-called "Indian Wars" from the days of Sitting Bull and Red Cloud have never really ended in the Americas. The Indian people of southern Mexico, of Guatemala and those left in El Salvador, too, are still fighting for their lives and for their land against the "cavalry" patrols sent out by the governments of those lands. The Americas are Indian country, and the "Indian problem" is not about to go away.

According to the late Dr. Dale Hathaway in his book *Allies Across the Border* (South End Press, 2000), the walls and fences that the U.S. government constructed between Mexican and U.S. urban areas have had little effect and have been the cause of increased deaths. He quotes statistics provided by the Centro de Apoyo al Migrante in Tijuana that document the deaths of migrants crossing into the U.S. The data show that before 1994, when the Tijuana wall was constructed, deaths were about 21 per year. In 1998, after the walls, deaths soared to 145. The number of crossings was not diminished.

One evening at sundown, we were stopped in traffic at a railroad crossing in downtown Tucson while a freight train passed us, slowly gaining speed as it headed north to Phoenix. In the twilight, I saw the most amazing sight: dozens of human beings, mostly young men, were riding the train. They were everywhere—on flat cars, in wide-open boxcars, perched on top of boxcars, hanging off ladders on tank cars and between boxcars. I couldn't count fast enough, but I saw 50 or 60 people headed north. They were dark young men, Indian and mestizo. They were smiling and a few of them waved at us in our cars. I was reminded of the ancient story of Aztlán, told by the Aztecs but known in other Uto-Aztecan communities as well. Aztlán is the beautiful land to the north, the origin place of the Aztec people. I don't remember how or why the people left Aztlán to journey farther south, but the old story says that one day, they will return.

Everything is Going to be Different

People Migrate

PHOTO ESSAY / JULIÁN CARDONA

IMMIGRATION FACTS *from the AFL-CIO, and the National Network for Immigrant and Refugee Rights "Bridge" Curriculum*

In 1999, 26.4 million foreign-born people resided in the United States, representing 10.4% of the population. The present percentage of immigrants in the United States is lower than in other periods. From 1870-1920, predominantly European immigrants made up 15% of the U.S. population.
US Census Bureau, 2000, and Poverty and Race, March/April 1995

Of the over 125 million people in the world who live outside of their countries of origin as immigrants or temporary migrants, less than 2% of these migrants come to the United States.
Migration World, 2000 and INS Annual Report, 1999

The number of documented immigrants admitted in 1998 totaled 660,000,
the lowest level since 1988. 54% of these were female.

The majority of immigrants come to the U.S. legally.
About eight of 11 legal immigrants come to join close family members.

About 60% of all undocumented immigrants enter the country legally
and then overstay their visas.
Michael Fix & Jeffrey Passel, "Immigration and Immigrants: Setting the Record Straight," 1994

Immigrants provide more to the nation's economy and government services than
they use, adding about $10 billion each year to the U.S. economy and paying
at least $133 billion in taxes, according to a 1998 study, *A Fiscal Portrait of the
Newest Americans*, by the National Immigration Forum and the Cato Institute.
The typical immigrant and his or her descendants pay an estimated $80,000 more
in taxes than they will receive in local, state and federal benefits over their lifetime.

EVERYTHING IS GOING TO BE DIFFERENT

The total net benefit (taxes paid over benefits received) to the
Social Security system in today's dollars from continuing current levels
of immigration is nearly $500 billion for the 1998-2002 period.
Citizens, legal permanent residents and undocumented workers alike enjoy the
same workplace rights under such key labor laws as the National Labor Relations Act,
the Railway Labor Act, Occupational Safety and Health Act, Americans with Disabilities Act,
Title VII of the Civil Rights Act of 1964 and the Fair Labor Standards Act. Such laws
include the requirement of minimum wage and overtime, providing a workplace free
of discrimination based on race, gender, religion and ethnicity, and the right to
form and join unions, no matter what your immigration status is.

Only four out of ten undocumented migrants cross the Southern border,
but 85% of all border enforcement personnel is located on that border.
Michael Fix and Jeffrey Passel, "Immigration and Immigrants: Setting the Record Straight," 1994

The INS budget for its activities on the U.S.-Mexico border was increased by $59.2 million in 1999. Its budget for enforcement along the Southern border funds both the employment of over 9,000 INS agents, as well as surveillance and enforcement technology adopted from the military. Over 1,450 migrants have died along the border as INS strategies have pushed immigrants to cross in some of the most remote and dangerous areas of the United States. In 1993, less than 4,500 agents policed the U.S.-Mexico border. Today, approximately 9,000 agents are stationed on the border.
INS, 1999, and Operation Gatekeeper, 2000

"The illegal immigrant is the bravest among us.
The most modern among us: the prophet.
The peasant knows the reality of our world decades before
the California suburbanite will ever get the point."
—Richard Rodriguez

EVERYTHING IS GOING TO BE DIFFERENT

All Jokes Will Be Taken Seriously

David Romo

Texas Observer, **April 26, 2002**

Rules for crossing border checkpoints for those of us who fit profiles:
1. Keep your answers short, simple and unambiguous.
2. Make eye contact but not too much. It might be interpreted as defiance or contempt.
3. All jokes will be taken seriously.

Israel

When I turned 20, I lived in Israel for two-and-a-half years. Whenever I share this fact with Jewish friends from New York they inevitably want to know why a non-Jew, a Chicano from the Texas-Mexico border, would end up living in Israel for a couple of years. To learn Hebrew, I tell them. What for? they insist. I'm not sure, I tell them. Some insist some more. I learned Hebrew so that I could read the Bible in its original tongue and so that I could pick up Israeli women. My Jewish friends are never sure if I'm joking or not.

The Israeli woman who checked my bags at the Ben Gurion airport security checkpoint wasn't sure what a dark-skinned, Palestinian-looking guy like me who carried an American passport had been doing in Israel either. Her skin was like sabbath challah bread, light and sweet, the Jewish version of Mexican pan dulce, the kind you dip in milk. It was 5:30 in the morning, I had gotten to the airport three hours before my El Al plane took off back to Rome and I was in a half-daze, not fully awake and especially susceptible to female beauty.

What was the purpose of your visit to Israel? she asked me.

I answered her in Hebrew. I came to visit a girlfriend of mine. I mean, she used to be my girlfriend.

She leafed through my American passport and stopped at my East German entrance visa stamp.

Did you meet or talk to any Palestinians during your visit?

Sure.

Name them.

Well, there's Lucia Sarsar, her mother, her father, her brother.

What was your relationship to her? she asked.

We used to be very close, I said with a smile. I noticed her silver-plated *chai* earrings, the Hebrew word for life. I imagined she was real tough, a *sabra*, an Israeli prickly pear. She probably knew how to handle an Uzi machine gun, but her earrings made her look soft and delicate.

Is this the girlfriend you came to visit? she asked me.

No, that was Michal. . .Cohen. She lives in the Jewish side. Lucia lives in the Arab side.

You were involved with both of them?

Yeah. I cleared my throat.

At the same time?

Yeah. I nodded slowly various times. My face was flushed. I blush easily during interrogations. I get flustered. But that was 10 years ago, I added, hoping that would somehow justify me.

Are you Jewish?

No, I'm Chicano. I was still clearing my throat.

You're from Chicago?

No. Chicano. I was born on the U.S. side, but my parents are from the Mexican side.

So what were you doing in Israel? My interrogator seemed genuinely confused. She switched from Hebrew to English.

I was going to feed her the line about women, the Bible and the original tongue but I held back. I did not want to push my luck.

I...well...I'm not really...I guess I just...

Finally I muttered something about being enrolled at the Hebrew University of Jerusalem while I worked as an interpreter and courier for a fundamentalist Christian television crew.

I was already in trouble. My story wasn't making any sense to her. Will you please come with me? she ordered me politely. Bring your suitcases. She took me to a different section of the airport, a makeshift room, separated from the rest of the airport with black curtains. It looked almost like the backstage of a theater. She asked me to please open my suitcase.

In Hebrew, please is *bevakasha*. I was infatuated with the way she said it. *Bevakasha*. I decided then and there that she would be the inspiration for the rest of my life, at least for the rest of the day. When King Solomon praised his beloved in the Song of Songs, he compared her neck to the Tower of David and her breasts to twin gazelles. Duke Ellington had an even better line—"Darling, you sure know how to make a nice dress look mighty fine."

But I was hypnotized by my beloved's earrings and couldn't come up with anything more eloquent than *Betach* in response to her request. *Betach* is Hebrew for sure, of course, seguro. It shares the same root with *bitachon*, which means security. I tried to say it with as much self-composure as possible to assure her that I was safe, I was no terrorist, I wasn't carrying any bombs.

She searched my suitcase thoroughly. Passed her hand through every possible hidden compartment and a metal detector through my clothes.

What is this? she asked leafing through a notebook.

My writings, I said.

She leafed through them. Then she started reading them carefully, page by page. I was flattered.

U.S./Mexico border

The customs officials ordered Joe Díaz to take down his pants. They were looking for drugs up his anus, which I guess makes sense to them. But sometimes it's hard to tell the difference between an investigation and a seduction.

How many assholes a month do customs officials worldwide get to check? I wonder if they keep any official statistics.

Joe Díaz was in the car with me. It was my fault that they were looking up his rectum. I've crossed the Santa Fe Bridge from Juárez to El Paso a few thousand times at least, but almost every time I hit the checkpoint I turn deep Indian red. Interrogations always make me feel guilty.

What are you bringing back from Mexico? Usually nothing illegal, but my mind races through the hundreds of possibilities. Maybe Angie left some pot in the ashtray. I've been told that even if someone who just smoked pot touches your car, it gets the search dogs all riled up.

Or maybe, let me think, I forgot I'm carrying some forbidden fruits in the trunk: guayabas, sugar cane, lemons, mangoes, hierba buena or anything else that has the potential of propagating on our side of the border.

I'm paranoid, I know, but maybe the border checkpoint computer revealed that Joe Díaz and I belonged to P.E.R.L.A, an internationally subversive organization with its headquarters at U.T. El Paso. Perla means pearl in Spanish. It was also the name of a beautiful woman we knew. But P.E.R.L.A stood for Political Expediency Revisited in Latin America. Don't ask me what that meant.

There were always at least five of us in the group. We protested everything. We would march around in circles at the University's Union plaza. Willivaldo waved around his banners facetiously. Inez walked around with a placard without words, only with his drawings of the planet Saturn. I'm still not sure what he meant by that. Andres, a recent immigrant from Argentina, and his girlfriend of Anglo-Polish descent marched around wearing tight cycling shorts. During a demonstration protesting the contras in Nicaragua, we marched around in circles chanting that ancient sixties slogan "Peace Now," but with our international accents, people in the audience thought we were saying "Piss Now."

One summer P.E.R.L.A followed the joint INS and police patrols that walked around downtown El Paso checking the IDs of anyone who looked too Mexican. A couple of civil rights lawyers hired us to document civil rights violations by city police who were illegally doing the job of the INS. Everyone walking downtown El Paso is Mexican, but only the INS is trained to recognize the difference between Mexicans with and Mexicans without papers. I once read a border patrolman's memoir in which he claimed that when he tracked Mexicans through the desert, he could tell the difference between the feces of an undocumented

Mexican and a legal citizen. The shit of a poor Mexican has a distinct smell and texture due to the inferior nutritional content of the illegal alien's diet.

The customs agent who noticed my discomfort asked us to drive over to a secondary stall. Dogs came and sniffed inside my car. We were led to a small room, the size of a fitting room at a men's clothing store. I waited in a wooden bench outside while they checked Joe Díaz's private orifice.

You can go now, they told us.

Guatemala-Mexico border

Once the same uncle who invited me to Israel invited me to Guatemala on a church choir missionary tour. We drove in a caravan of private cars and crossed the Guatemalan border from Mexico after dark. The soldiers stopped us and fumigated our cars. They flirted with the young women in the choir. There were fireflies in the jungle and the night was peaceful. Suddenly, we heard muffled screams from a wooden shack next to the custom's house. I didn't know anything about Guatemala then. Like the soldiers, I also had been flirting with the choir girls. One girl had been sitting next to me in the car and when she took off her sandals, I fell in love with her, her bare feet and her painted toe nails. I didn't know anything about Guatemalan right-wing death squads, the kaibiles, who received "anti-terrorist" training from the Israelis. I didn't know their methods included ripping open the stomachs of pregnant Mayan Indian women with a knife. I didn't know back then that you're supposed to fight terror with terror even if it means killing tens of thousands of communistic-minded indios for the sake of peace. I had no clue why a man was screaming inside the shack at the border. I figured he must be a criminal or a contrabandista.

I was just glad I was crossing the border into the Guatemalan night, sitting next to a girl with beautiful sexy feet.

I had never seen so many fireflies. Anywhere.

Israel

Michal was part Sephardic. Her mother was born in Iraq; her father's family had lived in Jerusalem for generations. I dated her for a year. Her sister was dating an Arab, which was quite dangerous in the '80s, but not quite as dangerous as it would be now after the many *Intifadas* and many martyrs. Back then, the odds that a couple could survive a transgressive sexual relationship between an Israeli Jew and a Palestinian Arab weren't too bad.

In the early '80s, there was some level of accommodation between Jews and Arabs. Sure, the language in the Israeli press was often one of extreme disdain for the Palestinian *jukim* (cockroaches) and *schwarze chai* (black animals). Hebrew, the holy language, can sometimes also be a godawful language. *Ani soneh otam, kuulam*, I once overheard an Israeli soldier sitting next to me on a bus say. I hate them, the whole bunch of them, he hissed, oozing globs of acid from his tongue.

But things weren't so bad, despite the bombings, the Arab homes razed by bulldozers and the occasional *Katyusha* rockets launched from the Lebanese Border. On most days, Israelis or Arabs could still walk into each other's neighborhoods without getting stabbed, stoned, shot, arrested or tortured.

The truth is that I liked and respected both sides. Both Israelis and Palestinians were for the most part coarse, direct, honest and intense as hell. Both their cultures were wells dug deep into the desert. Both cultures reminded me of my own.

Michal was Israel to me. She had skin dark like the mud of Qumran and reddish-brown hair with wild curls, wild as everything around her. Her bosom was large and maternal. When I entered her, I entered the land of milk and honey. She had been a paratrooper in the army. Her dream was to visit Mexico and I was the closest thing to Mexico. Although she laughed at me often, she never once asked me what the hell a Mexican-American was doing in her country.

I never told her about the time I tried to hide behind a tree stump after hearing machine gun fire near me. I was hiking along a forest near Jerusalem when I saw a small hot-air balloon over my head. I heard shots. I'd heard gunshots before but these were different. These shots were meant to kill. Gunshots that are aimed to eliminate a human being have a different sound; they travel on an entirely different wavelength than non-lethal gunshots, especially if you're not sure who those shots are aimed at. I awkwardly crouched behind a tree stump, which was only tall enough to cover my knees. I heard three more shots, which I thought were coming from behind me, and I instinctively jumped to the other side of the stump. A couple of Israeli fighter jets flew toward the hot-air balloon which, instead of hosting a terrorist attack, turned out to be a runaway balloon set afloat by the local boy scouts.

I was afraid if I told Michal what happened that day she would have laughed at me. Michal was beautiful and tough as hell. She once asked me if she could beat me with a leather belt while we were making love. I said no. Michal turned out to be too much for me. I had to leave her and her country behind.

U.S./Mexico Border

If you were a Mexican maid like my great-aunt Adela, crossing into El Paso from Juárez in 1915, you would be required to take a bath on the American side. You put your clothes in a huge dryer machine. Sometimes they would use kerosene to disinfect you. "Me sentí muy avergonzada. I was embarrassed that they thought I was dirty," my great-aunt told us. "I once had to put my shoes in the dryer and they melted."

School districts kept records of how many baths they administered to the Mexican children during the first part of the twentieth century. One senator called the Americanization of the dark-skins "the bleaching process." Germ theory was catching fire in America then. Dirt was more than physical, it was social. Real Americans were afraid of being contaminated by us. Those Americans didn't see themselves as backward and racist at all. Quite the opposite. They saw themselves as progressive and very scientific.

They still do.

The first time my father crossed illegally into the U.S. through the Tijuana border, an INS agent caught him and handcuffed him to a telephone pole while the agent chased after another illegal. Before handcuffing my father to the pole, the migra, who was pissed off at my father for running, threw my father's sack lunch at his face. There was a bottle inside the sack that broke and gashed my father's forehead. "The wound wasn't too serious," my father tells me. That was in 1953. My father was 14 years old.

Today my father is a wealthy man. Last year he took a pilgrimage of sorts, which led him to the spot where he was handcuffed to a pole. There's a fancy restaurant near that spot where he and my mother sat down to eat the most expensive meal they could order. That was all the revenge he needed. My father, who is Pentecostal and a believer in the theology of forgiveness, is not a bitter man.

My mother is also Pentecostal, yet she's bitter as hell. In a very Pentecostal way. Pentecostalism is a very emotional and intense religion. When my father is being "blessed by the Holy Spirit," his whole body shakes as if he were being struck by lightning. Pentecostals are often at each other's throats. That's why they're one of the fastest growing denominations in the world. They get into spiritual fights, separate from each other, then rent new buildings, start their own churches and replicate endlessly like amoebas.

My mother is one of those fighters. Cursing is sinful—that's why whenever she's pissed off at one of her brothers or sisters in Christ, she simply tells them "God bless you" in the most acerbic tone of voice she can muster. God bless you is her way of saying Fuck you.

I think I take after my mother's side. My father won't say anything bad about this country so I'll say it for him.

God bless you, America. God bless you.

Israel

My airport interrogator kept after me for more than two hours. My notebook was scrawled with poems, observations, newspaper clippings, free associations, to-do lists, phone numbers. I'd never seen anyone fit into a uniform quite the way she did. I wondered how long it would take me to unzip it. She jotted down the phone numbers and asked who they belonged to.

To Michal, my former girlfriend who now has a husband and two children; to Yehuda Rapiguano, an archeologist from Phoenix who teaches at the Hebrew University; to Andrew Burrows, a Biblical scholar from Yale who recently bought a house in Jerusalem. She queried me some more about them, about friends in Israel and friends at home, about the countries I had visited, about my experiences crossing borders. She even asked me about some of the music CDs I was carrying. With a different interrogator, I would have probably been irritated as hell. Not with her.

She pointed out a poem I had copied from a Hebrew anthology by Yehuda Amichai. Do you understand this poem? she asked me.

Sure. It's a poem about being able to love in the midst of war, I said.

Do you plan to come back to Israel? she asked.

I shrugged. I don't think so. Not for a long time at least.

At the end of the interrogation, she asked me to step into a different room where a male security agent would pat me down.

Taaseh ma she atah hoshev, she told him. Do whatever your gut tells you.

My gut doesn't tell me anything, he answered. He let me go.

She helped me pack my bags and rushed me through passport control, since I was about to miss my flight.

She apologized for holding me up so long.

I didn't mind, I told her and complimented her earrings.

She touched her earrings, revealing the palm of her hand to me and asked me again if I had plans to return to Israel.

Again I told her I didn't think so.

She seemed disappointed but I wasn't sure.

To this day I'm not sure what was just an interrogation and what was more than that. When you're crossing borders it's hard to be sure.

Ramón Castillo

"What I did was to come here illegally, and this is against the law of the United States. But it is not against the law of my family. Nor is it against my law. Even if they're American, they can't tell me, 'You can't work to support your family—no.' This is the right that I have to make sure my family is OK. And no one can take that away from me. It's the right I have earned. It's mine. It's my responsibility."

Ramón Castillo made this statement during an interview with Heather Courtney for her documentary, *Los Trabajadores*, which was filmed in Austin, Texas. Ramón worked for PEMEX, Mexico's national oil company, for 11 years before he and 22,000 other PEMEX workers were laid off after the peso devaluation that followed the beginning of Carlos Salinas' presidency in 1994. The estimated number of Mexicans who lost their jobs during that time was over a million. In February 1999, Ramón traveled to Austin from his home in Cardenas, Tabasco in search of work. He lived and worked in the United States before returning to Tabasco for a Christmas visit with his family. In February 2000, shortly after he began the return trip to Austin, he was hospitalized with pancreatitis and passed away before he could complete his journey. He is survived by his wife Virginia and two daughters, Jade and Gema.

¿Quién Está
Manejando la Plaza?

*Mexico, generally, has offered only two routes of
real economic progress to its poor and uneducated
rural folk. One is emigration to the United States. The other,
more recent, is growing and smuggling drugs.*
—Sam Quinones

La Plaza

Terrence Poppa

from *Drug Lord: A True Story. The Life & Death of a Mexican Kingpin, 1998*

EDITORS' NOTE: *In the early part of his book* Druglord, *which is a case study of Pablo Acosta's reign as the druglord of the Ojinaga "plaza," Terrence Poppa details the evolution of drug smuggling along the Texas/Chihuahua section of the U.S./Mexico Border. Poppa discusses the inception and the gradual ascendancy of Ojinaga—a dusty little town on the other side of the Río Grande from the equally small and dusty town of Presidio—as a primary hub for the passage of a large percentage of drugs flowing into the United States. The book follows the passing of the plaza from Manual Carrasco to Shorty Lopez to Pablo Acosta. An element of the Mexican army—traveling by helicopter across U.S. soil and supported by the U.S. government —attacked and killed Acosta in Santa Elena, a tiny community within walking distance of a camping area and store in Big Bend National Park. Fuentes Carrillo, the infamous "Lord of the Skies," then assumed management of the plaza and moved its headquarters to Juárez, Chihuahua. Fuentes Carrillo allegedly died on an operating table in Mexico City undergoing plastic surgery. As of this writing, no one person has yet been identified as manejando la plaza. The editors chose this early section of the book* Druglord *because it defines a "plaza" as a business franchise that is subservient to authority entrenched within the Mexican government. This concept of a centralized power controlling operations is essential to understanding the trade in illegal drugs in Mexico.*

"¿Quién está manejando la plaza?"

In Mexico this question is generally understood to mean "Who's in charge?" or "Who's running the show?"

In its most literal sense, the word "plaza" refers to a place of gathering—a town square, a marketplace, a bullring. Thus "la plaza de armas" is the parade ground, "la plaza de toros" is the bullring and so forth. Colloquially, however, la plaza refers to a police authority and a police commander's jurisdiction. And so the question "Who's in charge here?" would bring the answer, "Comandante So-and-So."

To the Mexican drug underworld, however, a question about who is in charge has another meaning, a very precise and well-understood meaning. When someone in the drug trafficking world asks who has the plaza, the question is interpreted to mean, "Who has the concession to run the narcotics racket?"

For decades, Mexican informants tried to explain the idea to their law enforcement contacts in the United States. When somebody had the plaza, it meant that he was paying an authority or authorities with sufficient power to ensure that he would not be bothered by state or federal police or by the military. The protection money went up the ladder, with percentages shaved off at each level up the chain of command until reaching the Grand Protector or the Grand Protectors in the scheme.

To stay in the good graces of his patrons in power, the plaza holder had a dual obligation: to generate money for his protectors and to lend his intelligence-gathering abilities by fingering the independent operators—those narcotics traffickers and drug growers who tried to avoid paying the necessary tribute. The independents were the ones who got busted by the Mexican Federal Judicial Police, the Mexican equivalent of the FBI, or by the army, providing Mexico with statistics to show it was involved in authentic drug enforcement. That most of the seized narcotics were then recycled—sold to favored trafficking groups or outrightly smuggled by police groups—was irrelevant. The seizures were in fact made and there were headlines and photos to prove it.

Usually, the authorities would protect their man from rivals; other times they would not, preferring a variety of natural selection to determine who should run the plaza. If the authorities arrested or killed the plaza holder, it was usually because he had stopped making payments, or because his name had started to appear in the press too frequently and the trafficker had become a liability. Sometimes international pressure became so strong that the government was forced to take action against a specific individual—regardless of how much money he was generating for the system.

It was a system that enabled the Mexican political and police structures to keep a lid on drugs and profit handsomely from it at the same time.

When Pablo Acosta fled New Mexico for Ojinaga, Chihuahua, in late 1976, the Ojinaga underworld was in a state of flux.

Manuel Carrasco, Pablo's source of marijuana and heroin and the drug trafficker who had converted Ojinaga into an important hub for narcotics, was on the run. The Ojinaga plaza was up for grabs.

These changes came as a result of a relatively insignificant accidental shooting that later flared up into a full-scale gun battle, bringing Carrasco's career to an end, at least in Ojinaga. The shooting took place one evening in March 1976, in the town's outlying zona de tolerancia, the red light district, eight months before Pablo Acosta fled to Mexico. Carrasco and several drug associates had been getting drunk and shooting their pistols in the air in revelry with several bar girls. One of the rounds ricocheted, hitting one of the girls in the foot.

According to informed accounts given of this pivotal incident, Carrasco was in the bar in the company of Heraclio Rodriguez Avilez, nephew of a powerful drug kingpin in Parral some 150 miles south of Ojinaga and one of Carrasco's chief suppliers. Heraclio had flown into town in a light airplane earlier that week with three gunmen to discuss money that

Carrasco owed the Parral drug boss. Heraclio was a trusted member of the Parral clan who evidently knew how to take care of situations. Only two weeks earlier, he and his men had disarmed the entire municipal police force of Parral to show who was truly in charge of the agricultural community. They marched the city cops at gunpoint to a hill outside town where the traffickers tied them up and left them.

Heraclio's visit to Ojinaga, it is believed, was tied to a financial crisis Carrasco was experiencing due to a string of serious losses—major drug shipments that had been fronted to him by the Parral drug lord but that had been seized in the United States. During the previous nine months, 30 pounds of Carrasco's heroin and a ton of his marijuana had been confiscated in drug busts in California, Illinois and Texas. An airplane he had borrowed from the Avilezes had crashed. In all, the dope busts represented multimillion-dollar losses for Carrasco. The Ojinaga drug don still had to pay for these loads, and that was the purpose of Heraclio's visit. How—and when—was he going to make good on those debts? Carrasco had apparently satisfied the nephew of his source, for they were having a grand time partying together in the zona until the bullet hit the girl.

The drunken group drove the wounded girl to the home of Dr. Artemio Gallegos, a retired military surgeon who ran a private practice out of his book-lined home near the town square, not far from the police station and the army garrison. While Carrasco, Heraclio and his men sat in the waiting room, the doctor set about fixing up the wounded woman. Just as he finished cleansing the wound, however, a carload of municipal policemen led by the chief of police pulled up in front to investigate.

Heraclio had been sober when he marched the Parral municipal police force out of town at gunpoint. But when the Ojinaga police chief accompanied by other municipal cops walked into the waiting room, a drunken Heraclio pointed his semiautomatic pistol at the police chief and began to squeeze the trigger. The police chief had only time enough to grab Heraclio by the arm and shove him; Heraclio pushed the policeman backward to free his gun hand. Then everyone started shooting. Drunken dopers and terrified cops ran in confusion from book-lined room to book-lined room or out into the street, shooting back and forth. The doctor, the nurse and the wounded bargirl ducked behind the examination table just as one of the pistoleros fired a machine gun at them.

The incident would have had a Keystone Cops quality to it if no one had been hurt. But during this gun battle, Heraclio was shot through the heart and died instantly. One of the policemen was shot in the arm. Manuel Carrasco was hit in the lower back. The gunfire ended when someone in the street shouted that soldiers were coming. The remaining gunmen fled.

The troops arrived moments later, but Heraclio's men were able to escape the dragnet. Manuel Carrasco was taken to a hospital in Chihuahua City. The wound was not serious and he was soon released.

In the meantime, rumors began circulating that the gunfight was the result of a power struggle for control of the Ojinaga plaza. Someone had wanted Manuel Carrasco out of the way, a logical assumption due to Ojinaga's growing importance as a transit point for narcotics.

State police in New Mexico, however, later picked up a scenario that American narcotics officers thought was more likely: Manuel Carrasco took advantage of the unexpected confusion to shoot Heraclio to clear the drug debt. Manuel could then claim that he had already paid off the big debt he owed in Parral and did not know what Heraclio or his men had done with the money.

But then Manuel got shot too.

According to accounts later picked up by the New Mexico State Police, the older Avilez, then in his seventies, called the hospital in Chihuahua City where Manuel was getting patched up and asked him what happened to Heraclio. Manuel reportedly said in a saddened voice, "There's been a problem, Señor Avilez. Heraclio has been killed."

After Manuel gave an edited account of the shooting, the older Avilez asked, "And what about the money?"

"I don't know; I gave it to him earlier that day. I don't know what he did with it."

But Heraclio's pistoleros had a different story to tell. They had eluded the army and made it back to Parral about five days later. One of them, a pilot named Huitaro, supposedly said, "That's bullshit. I *saw* Manuel shoot Heraclio." None of the survivors could remember any money being handed over to Heraclio.

Old man Avilez not only put a price on Manuel Carrasco's head, he also put out a contract for every one of the municipal cops in Ojinaga. They were *all* to be killed.

Rumors flashed around town that two airplanes full of Avilez men armed with machetes and machine guns were on the way with orders to butcher the policemen. To the last man, the Ojinaga police force fled to the United States. Some of them went to towns in New Mexico, others to communities in Oklahoma where they had relatives. U.S. Immigration and Customs authorities in Presidio proved very understanding. They obtained special permits for the police chief and the deputy police chief and their families. And they looked the other way as the remainder of the Ojinaga police force came to the United States, bringing their families with them.

Manuel Carrasco disappeared too, and his vanishing act left the Ojinaga underworld in disarray. Treacherous himself, he suspected everyone else of sinister intent and did not say a word of his whereabouts even to his closest associates. He simply abandoned a lucrative plaza. It was as if the proprietor of a multimillion-dollar firm walked out the door one day without saying goodbye to any of his employees and never came back.

Rumors later circulated that "higher-ups" had decided to promote Carrasco to a bigger, more challenging plaza in the state of Sinoloa. Other stories circulated that he was able to buy his way into the military and was now the general of an army unit in the state of Durango. Other rumors had him hiding out from old man Avilez' vengeance in the port city of Veracruz.

For a short time one of Manuel Carrasco's cousins was thought to be running the plaza, but he was soon arrested in the United States.

The Ojinaga plaza fell by default to Shorty Lopez, Pablo Acosta's pal from Fort Leavenworth. Like Pablo, Shorty had distributed heroin and marijuana in West Texas for Manuel Carrasco. But while Pablo was content to base his operation in Odessa and later in Eunice, Shorty preferred to work out of Ojinaga. He had married a woman from the town and gradually started spending more time there than in the United States. He would run drug loads to American clients, then head back to Mexico with suitcases full of money.

Shorty's star in the Carrasco organization began to rise the night Texas Department of Public Safety officers chased him through the mountains on Highway 67 between Marfa and Presidio. He was returning to Ojinaga late one night with money for a marijuana load he had smuggled to Fort Stockton across the dirt ranch roads of the Big Bend. With the money in a satchel, he took the two-lane highway to Presidio for the easy return trip. But ten miles from the border, a police car pulled up behind him, red lights flashing. Shorty didn't know if he was being pulled over for speeding or if someone had informed on him. As soon as he saw lights, he gunned his souped-up pickup and tried to outrun the law. It *would* have been awfully hard explaining how an ex-con came by the tens of thousands of dollars in that leather bag. And Ojinaga was only ten miles away. All he had to do was make a mad dash for the border. The high-speed chase ended at a sharp bend near Presidio. Shorty lost control, skidding off the highway. His truck rolled down the slope. The policemen thought they were going to find a mangled body at the bottom of the ravine. All they found was a wrecked pickup truck, broken mesquite bushes, crushed cactuses, flattened greasewood and a few traces of blood heading off into the desert.

Shorty broke his leg as he was thrown from the truck. His face and chest were cut and bleeding. The way he later told the story, he managed to elude the police and drag himself to the Río Grande just west of Ojinaga. He swam across with the satchel firmly gripped in his mouth, then hobbled up to an adobe shack near the river's edge. He banged on the door to wake up the elderly widower who lived there alone. "Listen, old man," Shorty said, gritting his teeth in pain. "I'll make it worth your while. Go find Manuel Carrasco and tell him to come and get me. I'm hurt, and I'm hurt bad."

The accident left him with a permanent limp, but his resourcefulness and daring earned him Manuel Carrasco's esteem—and a promotion: Manuel put him in charge of a big desert ranch southeast of Ojinaga where Carrasco raised cattle and goats. The animals were a front; the ranch's real purpose lay in a long dirt runway and the bulk cargo that arrived constantly from distant parts as well as in the underground warehouses where the merchandise was kept from prying eyes.

As his importance to Manuel grew, Shorty began dealing directly with more of the drug lord's buyers, and with his drug suppliers in the mountains of Chihuahua, Oaxaca and Sinaloa. Shorty soon came to see the drug business in its broad outlines rather than just in its parts. Eventually he was handling the movement of drugs all along the border from Pilares, a village 100 miles upstream from Ojinaga, to Boquillas, 150 miles downstream near the Chihuahua-Coahuila state line—the stretch of the Río Grande that roughly defined

Manuel Carrasco's Ojinaga plaza. But it was always Manuel Carrasco who dealt with the authorities, jealously guarding his official contacts.

That changed after Manuel disappeared.

When Carrasco could not be located for the plaza money, his protectors began investigating who was left in charge. Manuel Carrasco reputedly had been paying a $100,000 on the tenth of every month. The unpaid balance began climbing as the months went by. Several months after Manuel vanished, Shorty started getting official visits from Chihuahua City. Manuel was not making his payments and was falling behind, Shorty was informed. *Someone* named Shorty Lopez had better come up with the money.

Shorty protested the amount. He had been privy to much of Manuel's dealings, sure, but not *all* of his dealings. A hundred thousand dollars a month was predicated upon the total volume of Manuel's drug movement. For Shorty, just starting to pick up the pieces of an organization abandoned by its chief, the sum would be ruinous. Ultimately, Shorty struck a deal and was left in peace to work the plaza.

Former underworld associates of Shorty Lopez said that Shorty at first made the payments in Manuel's name, but as the months went by he began to consider the plaza his own. After all, he was the one generating the money for the plaza payments now, not Manuel. Manuel had left him in an ambiguous situation and had not tried to contact him, not the other way around.

Adding to his self-importance, Shorty quickly got big in his own right. He soon had all the trappings of a drug lord—his own ranch equipped with a runway, a warehouse for marijuana storage and his own pilots and runners. The focal point of the smuggling operations shifted away from Manuel's property to his own.

"So what am I supposed to do?" Shorty once asked an American friend. "If Manuel's not here to pay the plaza fee and they make me pay instead, that means I have the plaza and not Manuel. I don't owe him nothing."

By the time Pablo Acosta reached Ojinaga—the day after his close call with the police outside of Eunice[1]—Shorty had been making the plaza payments for five or six months. Their meeting in Ojinaga was like a slaphappy reunion of boyhood chums.

Shorty handed Pablo a machine gun and a semiautomatic pistol and put him to work. At first Pablo worked as Shorty's chauffeur and bodyguard and escorted his friend and boss here and there in the dusty border town or to Shorty's desert ranch east of San Carlos, La Hacienda Oriental. It was barely 40 miles from Ojinaga, but it took six hours to get there along a bumpy and frequently washed-out dirt road.

Pablo, meanwhile, worked his own drug deals, supplying the American networks he had left behind from his Mexican sanctuary. When the indictment against him for the

---

1 From 1974-1976, Pablo Acosta, an American citizen, owned a roofing company in Eunice, New Mexico. The company was a front for his drug distribution business. In November, he narrowly escaped a DEA sting operation and fled to Mexico.

heroin deal in Eunice was handed down in January 1977, Pablo knew there was no going back. He hired his own runners to take loads for him and had his brothers and others collect. Occasionally, he drove to the narrow international bridge, half a mile from his brick house on Calle Sexta, and watched the activity at the port of entry on the American side.

He was untouchable in Mexico so long as he remained under Shorty's wing. Shorty guaranteed his protection in exchange for a percentage of each deal Pablo cut. If Manuel Carrasco had still been in charge of the plaza, Pablo would have paid Carrasco instead. There *were* laws to be obeyed, but they were not the ones written down in the code books.

As he became settled, Pablo opened a small clothing boutique on Avenida Trasviña y Retes for his wife Olivia. They called it *Karen's* after their daughter. He also opened a hole-in-the-wall restaurant in downtown Ojinaga in one

Pablo Acosta, druglord of the Ojinaga plaza. Acosta operated the Plaza from 1982 until his violent death on April 24, 1987.

of the adobe buildings near the town square. The restaurant specialized in cabrito, roast baby goat, and was a favorite rendezvous in the early afternoon for local hoodlums. He also did a lot of business there with Americans who came down with stolen automobiles or other goods they wanted to exchange for drugs.

In the United States, Pablo had rarely gone around armed. In Mexico, it was a necessity. A clean, well-lubricated .45 semiautomatic was just as much an article of clothing as were cowboy boots and oval belt buckles. Pablo believed he was going to have to defend himself sooner or later, and he wanted to be prepared. He kept his pistol stuffed in his belt at the hollow of his back. He never failed to take advantage of opportunities to practice shooting.

Driving Shorty to his ranch or while with friends out in the desert, he would suddenly slam on the brakes if he saw a rabbit or a quail, leap out with his .45 already drawn and Bam! Bam! Bam! let off round after round until he had either killed the scurrying animal or run out of ammunition. He got to the point where he could hit a quail at 40 yards with his .45 semiautomatic.

He and Shorty liked to draw on each other for practice, but Pablo took the roughhousing even further. Many of the drug mafiosos gathered in the morning or afternoons to water, feed and exercise their quarter horses at stables owned by Fermin Arevalo, one of Manuel Carrasco's former associates. Like the other dopers, Pablo had acquired horses and went about his chores at the stables just like everyone else. But he had a habit of drawing on everybody, a quirk that made his victims nervous. He would appear out of nowhere, his chrome-plated semiautomatic flashing into his hands. Or he would spin around to aim at someone behind him, or draw face-to-face like an old-time gunslinger.

Some just waved him off as a trigger-happy punk. "Ah, go stick it up your ass," they would tell him.

Pablo just shrugged.

One day, he was certain, a fast draw would make the crucial difference between his life and someone else's.

Like many of the campesino-traffickers, Shorty was detached from the effects of the substances he dealt. He could sell a pound of black-tar heroin, his mind whizzing and clicking as he tallied up the profit, yet perhaps never once give any thought to the thousands of doses of chemical enslavement his profits represented. Then he could turn around and give much of the money to the poor in the Ojinaga area.

It was the tradition of a drug lord to take care of people in need, of course. For one thing, it was good for business. Give a peasant food for his malnourished children, he will become a loyal pair of eyes and ears in the sinister desert. A lot of small-time welfare added up to a big-time intelligence network.

But with Shorty, generosity was not mere pragmatism. He enjoyed helping the underfed campesinos who scrounged for a marginal living on the harsh land. Stories were told of how Shorty would fill his pickup truck with groceries in Ojinaga before making a trip to his ranch. On the way he would stop at this adobe hovel and that, distributing the food and supplies, having nothing left by the time he got to his ranch. One of the beneficiaries of Shorty's generosity was an invalid with the nickname Pegleg, a one-legged man who had a big family and lived in a village outside Ojinaga. One of Shorty's former associates recalled how Shorty drove up to Pegleg's primitive adobe one day and tooted his horn to rouse the man from the shack.

"Goddammit, you lazy old fart, I'm going to put you to work," Shorty said, slapping the astonished man on the back.

He took Pegleg around the ranches and ejidos, bought him a couple hundred hogs, a truckload of feed and started the man and his family raising pigs. With similar directness he got other people to raise goats, sheep, chickens, turkeys.

Many ranchers in the area of San Carlos, a pueblo of 2,000 people near Shorty's La Hacienda Oriental, owed their well pumps, tractors and fencing to Shorty's impulsive altruism. During his short reign as drug lord of Ojinaga, Shorty came to be known as the benefactor of San Carlos.

Shorty could afford to be generous. Business boomed the moment he took over from Manuel Carrasco. With the marijuana and opium-poppy harvest that fall of 1976, trucks streamed from the interior of Mexico to Ojinaga with a dual cargo: carrots, apples, woolen Oaxacan blankets and an endless variety of goods for Ojinaga merchants. Under some of those loads were secret cargoes for Shorty.

It was so easy to sell marijuana! A bonanza for dope sellers like Shorty was assured from the hippies and ranchers, campers and hunters, Hispanics and Anglos, Blacks and Indians, from as far away as California, Montana or North Carolina who drove up to low spots in the river looking to score some dope. They knew where to go. Once they spotted someone on the other side who could only be there for one reason, all they had to do was holler something like, "Hey, you a Messkin?"

The man on the other side of the muddy river would cup his hands to his mouth and yell back, "Yeah, gringo. Whaddya want?"

"Twenty kilos."

"I can get it for you."

"How much?"

"Come across, let's talk."

And the deal was on.

Such small-time river deals along the sparsely inhabited and poorly patrolled Big Bend could dispose of an entire truckload of marijuana in no time.

Shorty also sent trusted runners up to Fort Stockton across the dirt backroads of the desert with 1,500 pound loads stashed in campers. Light airplanes also flew directly to Shorty's ranch, loaded up and left at night, returning undetected to the United States through the mountain passes of the Big Bend with 400 or 700 or 1,000 pounds of marijuana per trip.

The money was rolling in. Shorty was making his monthly plaza payments. Everybody was happy.

Everybody except Manuel Carrasco.

Toward the end of 1976, word began spreading in Ojinaga and in the surrounding ejidos and towns that Manuel Carrasco, still in hiding from Avilez, was planning to kill Shorty. The rumors became so strong that finally Pablo and some of the other drug dealers began urging Shorty to leave town for a while.

Manuel Carrasco considered Shorty a traitor. Shorty had taken advantage of his self-imposed exile to grab what was rightfully Manuel's. It didn't matter that Manuel had not trusted Shorty enough to contact him and clarify the situation. It only mattered that Shorty now considered himself master of the plaza, that he was boasting about it and making money Manuel thought was his. Shorty was going to pay for it with his blood.

Shorty kept a pistol and an American assault rifle on the floor of his truck, but he did not walk about town armed and he did not always have a bodyguard with him.

In the early spring of 1977, Shorty accidentally ran into Manuel Carrasco in Chihuahua City. He and a couple of his men had taken some Ojinaga girls to the state capital for an outing, spending several days shopping and partying. One afternoon they turned a corner in one of the quieter downtown side streets near the state government buildings. There was Manuel Carrasco, arm-in-arm with his wife, walking toward them! It was like finding the proverbial needle in the haystack, only they had not even been looking.

Manuel Carrasco was tall in his cowboy boots, with a look of stolid dignity in his ranchero suit and hat.

"You little son of a bitch," Carrasco sneered when he recognized Shorty. "If I don't kill you right now, it's out of respect for my wife."

It didn't take much to throw the 110-pound Shorty Lopez into a bantam-rooster flutter. He marched up to Manuel, who towered over him by about ten inches. "I'll fight you any time you want," Shorty yelled. "You name the time and place."

Manuel's wife nervously tugged on her husband's arm. Shorty's men pulled him away. Without another word, Manuel and his wife brushed past the small group from Ojinaga and disappeared around a corner.

During the three-hour drive back, Shorty's men tried to reason with him. If Shorty hadn't been so goddamn cocky, he could have settled it with Manuel right then and there in Chihuahua City. All it would have taken was a few words explaining how Manuel had left him in the lurch.

"Why don't you make a deal with him? You could still work it out with him," one of the men said.

"Oh, the hell with him!" Shorty said.

Manuel Carrasco caught up with Shorty on May 1, 1977, outside the river village of Santa Elena. Shorty had a load of marijuana to ship north that day and had his runners take it across the Río Grande somewhere downstream from the tiny village. Following the smuggling operation, he returned to Santa Elena with his driver to party with the locals.

Manuel Valdez, the driver, was a young, eager campesino who worked on Shorty's ranch with two older brothers. The young Valdez occasionally chauffeured the drug lord around the desert, doubling as bodyguard.

A week earlier Manuel Carrasco had spread the word from Chihuahua City that Shorty's end was imminent—the kind of psychological terrorism Manuel seemed to relish. Shorty kept on about his business.

Shorty was convinced he could come out on top in a shoot-out with Manuel Carrasco. Manuel could choose the time and the place, but Shorty's intelligence network, the fruit of his generosity, would alert him ahead of time to the danger.

And he was right.

Late that afternoon, Shorty and Valdez left Santa Elena to drive back to the ranch in the desert highlands. They had to drive 10 miles downriver, then cut south into the mountains. The bumpy road was tough even on the sturdiest four-wheel drive. The road followed the foothills below the mammoth limestone wall of the Sierra Ponce, going in and out of broad arroyos, sometimes following the floor of dry washes for a mile before turning again onto higher ground.

Several miles from the fork, Shorty saw a pickup approaching, the driver waving frantically. They stopped next to one another in a swirl of dust. The pickup's driver had benefited from Shorty's largesse at one time. "Be careful," he said.

El Fisgón

Every year the United States requires nations that receive aid to be certified as supporting efforts to stop the flow of illegal drugs into the U.S. Mexico has long argued that drug certification is a unilateral process that demeans the Mexican government. The Drug Enforcement Administration estimates that 55% of the cocaine in the U.S. comes across the U.S./Mexico Border, and most experts agree that drug certification does not stem the flow of drugs. Richard Schwein, a retired FBI agent who served in El Paso from 1987-94, stated: "With or without certification, the drugs keep pouring across. We're never going to decertify Mexico because doing so would cause such a big stir with our next-door neighbor. The answer to the problem is for people in this country to stop using drugs, but I don't see that happening either."

—El Paso Times, 9/27/02

"They're waiting up ahead to kill you—Manuel Carrasco's gunmen."

The rancher had learned of the ambush by driving into it. A man with a mouthful of steel-capped teeth had stepped out in front of his truck and yelled "Judicial!" Other men brandishing machine guns who also passed themselves off as judiciales searched his truck. They were up by the fork, on the other side of an arroyo. The rancher did not know if Manuel Carrasco was there himself, but he had seen plenty of men.

Shorty's blood began to boil; he wasn't about to run. He was going to show them what kind of stuff he was made of. He grabbed an assault rifle from the floor. He slapped an ammunition clip into it. "You drive on. I'm getting in the back," he shouted to Manuel Valdez.

Shorty grabbed some extra clips, shoved one of the semiautomatic pistols into his belt and jumped into the back of the truck. Valdez checked his own handguns and placed them—chambered and cocked—next to him on the seat. He put the truck in gear and moved on up the bumpy road. Shorty lay flat in the bed of the pickup, ready to spring up at the right moment.

The ambush site was several miles away. The road dropped nearly 10 feet into a wide, flat-bottomed arroyo. One had to drive across the arroyo bed and climb the steep slope on the opposite side to get back onto the road. Carrasco's gunmen were waiting on both sides, on the top of the rises. As soon as they knew it was Shorty in the middle of the arroyo they were going to gun him down.

But the advance warning had allowed Shorty to prepare. When Valdez drove down into the wash, the gunmen could see only one man—and it wasn't Shorty. They let Valdez drive through and up the other side. Once the truck had bounced up to the top of the wash, the man with steel-capped teeth walked into its path and shouted, "Judicial!"

What happened next took place in the space of time it takes for about a dozen men firing simultaneously to shoot several hundred rounds of ammunition.

Shorty jumped up from the bed of the truck, firing a burst from his AR-15 at Steel-Tooth, then turning his fire on the group of men that had started to emerge from the mesquite brush the moment Steel-Tooth halted the truck. Several of those men fell. Valdez leaped from the pickup cab at the same moment, firing toward the other side of the road. The hammering of machine guns became thunderous. Bullets coming from three directions tore into the pickup. Manuel Valdez was hit and fell to the ground. Shorty jumped down from the truck and shot backward as he ran up the road.

Steel-Tooth had only been grazed by Shorty's initial spray of bullets, and had hugged the ground to keep out of the line of fire. When he saw Shorty running, he got to his knees and aimed. A .45-caliber bullet tore into Shorty's spine. He fell face forward to the ground.

The marks people later saw in the dirt showed that Shorty crawled a short distance, scratching and clawing the ground, then writhed in the scorching sand. Tire tracks showed that a heavy vehicle had driven again and again over his frail body before finally driving over his head. Shorty was probably already dead when someone stood over him, lifted a heavy machete high and then brought it down with savage force that cut off the top of his skull at the hairline.

Only the bodies of Shorty Lopez and Manuel Valdez were found later. The assailants fled with their own dead and wounded. Reports later reached San Carlos that several men had checked into clinics in towns across the state line in Coahuila. One of the men had steel-capped teeth and claimed to be a judicial.

¿Quién Está Manejando la Plaza?

Several days after the shooting, the town of San Carlos was full of the grim festivity of a rural funeral. The small stone church at one end of the town square was festooned in black. People who had come from all over for Shorty's funeral jammed the square. A priest celebrated a requiem mass in the belief that Shorty's charity absolved at least some of his sin. Then the pallbearers—mafiosos wearing Western clothes and cowboy boots—emerged from the church with the coffin on their shoulders and carried it through the thick crowd to the hearse. The hearse drove to Shorty's ranch where he was buried to the music of a norteño group that sang ballads about his exploits.

Shorty's memory lived on in the ballads—and in irregularly shaped bone fragments about the size of a quarter said to have been cut from the portion of Shorty's skull severed by the machete. Holes had been drilled through the fragments allowing thin gold chains to be inserted. The skull-fragment pendants started showing up around the necks of Ojinaga traffickers, giving grounds for rumor that Manuel Carrasco remained in charge even though he was rarely seen again in Ojinaga.

The skull fragments were emblems of loyalty—and were grim warnings against betrayal.

Corridos

Ballad of Martín "El Shorty" López

Pasaron por Providencia
ya venían de Santa Elena,
donde les habían pagado
treinta kilos de la buena,
Manuel Valdez y Martín
sufrieron terrible pena.

They had passed through Providencia
and were now coming from Santa Elena
where they had been paid
for 30 kilos of the good stuff,
Manuel Valdez and Martín
suffered a terrible punishment.

Por el camino donde iban
los estaban esperando
no faltó quien les dijera
y se fueron separando
Martín se sube a la troca,
Manuel la llevaba arreando.

On the road they were traveling
the assassins were waiting for them,
a passer-by warned Shorty and his driver,
so the two men separated:
Martín got back in the bed of the truck,
while Manuel continued driving in the cab.

Llegó el momento esperado
ya estaban los enemigos,
se formó una balacera
y cayeron tres tendidos,
después también a Martín
le pegó uno en los sentidos.

The appointed moment arrived,
the enemies leapt out of hiding,
there was a hail of bullets
and three bodies fell on the ground,
afterward Martín, too
caught a bullet through his brain.

Agarraron a Martín
y le esculcaron su ropa,
no le consiguieron nada
y le abrieron la cabeza
porque tenían que cumplir
las órdenes de la mafia.

They grabbed Martín
and searched his clothes,
they didn't find anything,
so they split open his head,
because they had to carry out
the orders from the Mafia.

Martín López se llamaba
y le apodaban "El Shorty"
era un hombre muy afamado
en la Hacienda de Orientales,
y también fue respetado
por agentes judiciales.

Martín López was his name
but they called him "Shorty,"
he was a well known man
at the Hacienda de Orientales,
and he was also respected by
the state police and federal agents.

De la mafia y del destino
nunca nadie se ha escapado,
el que anda por mal camino
debe de andar bien armado,
pero a Manuel y a Martín
la mafia los ha matad

From the Mafia nor from fate,
no one has ever escaped,
he who chooses the path of evil
had better go well armed.
But as for Manuel and Martín,
the Mafia has killed them.

From the liner notes of *The Devil's Swing:
Ballads from the Big Bend Country of the
Texas-Mexican Border / El Columpio Del Diablo:
Corridos y Tragedias de la Junta de los Rios,
2000, Arhoolie Productions Inc.*

Ballad of Pablo Acosta

De tanto cantar corridos
mi voz está muy cansada,
pero lo que ha sucedido,
es cosa muy mencionada:
ha muerto uno de los grandes,
más famosos de Ojinaga.

My voice is tired
from singing so many ballads,
but what has recently happened
is much talked about,
one of the great and most famous
men of Ojinaga has died.

Pablo Acosta fue su nombre,
de nación americana,
y puesto a jugar con lumbre,
sabiendo que se quemaba,
en las orillas del Bravo,
del estado de Chihuahua.

Pablo Acosta was his name,
and he was born a U.S. citizen,
he started playing with fire,
knowing full well that one could get burned
on the banks of the Río Bravo,
in the state of Chihuahua.

Eran quince federales
que a Santa Elena llegaron,
a orillas del Río Grande,
lugar donde aterrizaron,
venían desde Ciudad Juárez
a llevarse al alegado.

Fifteen federal policemen
arrived at Santa Elena
on the banks of the Río Grande,
the spot where their choppers landed,
they had come from Ciudad Juárez
to arrest the accused.

The gun fight started
according to the newspapers,
on April 24,
which according to the calendar
was a Friday;
it was the day that the great Czar
of traffickers lost his life.

Si alguien bien los recuerda,
y quiere mandarle flores
al hombre que hizo leyendas
y que ayudaba a los pobres,
mi cruz se encuentra clavada
en el rancho El Tecolote.

If anyone remembers him well,
and wants to send flowers to
the man who made legends,
and who helped the poor,
my cross is standing
in the ground at Rancho El Tecolote.

From the liner notes of *The Devil's Swing:
Ballads from the Big Bend Country of the
Texas-Mexican Border / El Columpio Del Diablo:
Corridos y Tragedias de la Junta de los Rios*, 2000,
Arhoolie Productions Inc.

ILLUSTRATIONS BY JOSÉ GUADALUPE POSADA

El jefe de judiciales,
de apellido Calderoni
gritaba – ¡ríndete Pablo,
con ésto son tres lecciones ! –
— ¡primero me sacan muerto
que llevarme a las prisiones ! –

The leader of the police,
by the name of Calderoni,
yelled: "Give up Pablo,
this is your last chance!"
"You'll have to kill me
before you take me to prison!"

Empezó la balacera,
según las letras del diario,
abril 24 era,
viernes marcó el calendario,
en que la vida perdiera
el gran zar del contrabando.

¿Quién Está Manejando la Plaza?

A Bankrobber on the Border

Marie "Louie" Gilot & Lou Rutigliano

El Paso Times, July 22, 2001

A Vision of Juárez

"When I was 13 there was this older kid and he was real tough, you know, with a leather jacket and hair all up like the 'Fonz'—and he gave me cigarettes and treated me like an equal. He was always talking about Juárez. I always had a vision about Juárez being very romantic," Lenny DiCarlo, the California son of an Italian immigrant, said. "I said, 'I'll rob a bank.' That was my plan. 'I'll rob a bank and go to Juárez.'"

November 17, 2000, he robbed the Bank of America in downtown Tucson, got on a Greyhound bus and arrived in El Paso at 6 a.m. the next day. He crossed the downtown Santa Fe Bridge, stopped a cab driver and pointed to the crooked maze of streets tucked in under the bridge's shadows.

"He said, 'You don't want to go there. It's Boys' Town.' Well, that's exactly where I wanted to be. I said, 'Thank you very much.'"

By the light of day, Melchor Ocampo Street, just west of Juárez Avenue, masquerades as an unremarkable extension of the tourist strip. But by 7 p.m., the street turns into an all-night drug and sex market. People there remember DiCarlo, his drug habit and his money. Pharmacist Eddy Ballesteros said DiCarlo was constantly surrounded by a horde of street urchins eagerly awaiting gifts of candy and trinkets. One of the children was the seven-year-old brother of "Fernando," a drug dealer DiCarlo befriended.

"When they took (DiCarlo) away, that boy was very upset," Ballesteros recalled.

He split his time between a room at the Bombin Hotel and the apartment shared by his new pal Fernando and his family.

"I like Wells Fargo"

On November 22, 2000, the day before Thanksgiving, DiCarlo was drug-sick and broke. He quickly decided against robbing a Juárez bank.

"I didn't have a gun," he explained. "You don't rob a bank in Juárez with a note. You'll end up killed."

He went into El Paso and settled on the Wells Fargo Bank at Bassett Center.

"I like Wells Fargo. I like their logo with the stagecoach," he said.

With a McDonald's paper bag he retrieved from a trash can, DiCarlo entered the bank. The surveillance cameras captured the image of an unshaven man hunched over the counter.

FBI agent James Rankine testified in a court document that the teller, a young woman, "realized he was attempting to rob the bank, but she could not believe it."

DiCarlo remembered it clearly.

"She's not scared at all. She told me, 'You don't have a gun.' She saw right through me. She's typing on a computer, waving to get the attention of a security guard. Finally she starts putting money in the bag. After three to four minutes, I snatch the bag. She was feisty. I liked her. I'm sure she doesn't care, but I respect her."

Outside, DiCarlo shed his top layer of clothing, put on his glasses and disappeared. He stopped for a few hours at the Gateway Hotel downtown, bought a bean burrito and a Coke. In a $24 room, he split his bank loot between his pockets and his shoes. He headed toward the bridge.

"Halfway through the bridge (on the Mexican side), I stop and exhale. I feel safe, smoke a cigarette. Looking back at El Paso, I'd see Wells Fargo, Chase (buildings). 'I'm going to get them,' I'd say."

That night in Juárez, DiCarlo, high on heroin, watched the TV news.

"I'd see myself on the news with the longer gray hair. No doubt it's me. I went to the barber shop and had it cut. Then I bought 'Just For Men' from a pharmacy on Juárez Avenue and dyed it dark. That stuff works good. That was the extent of my disguise. I went through customs like that."

Hiding in Plain Sight

The day after Thanksgiving, DiCarlo ran out of money and made good on his vow to hit the Wells Fargo branch downtown.

As he did with all his robberies, he handed the teller a note that said: "I have a gun. Do as I say and no one will get hurt. Large bills first. No dye pack. No tracking device." FBI documents say the young woman teller didn't read past the mention of the gun and surrendered the money in a panic.

About five police cars responded to the robbery. A half-dozen uniformed police officers and many plain-clothes officers, including FBI agents, were inside the building questioning employees. DiCarlo said he watched the commotion from a nearby cafe, over a hamburger.

"They expect someone to run and act suspicious. They are looking for me trying to get away," he said. By that time, the FBI had received information from an El Pasoan whom DiCarlo had briefly befriended that led them to his identity, and perhaps his location. In Juárez, too, everyone knew who he was.

"There were three bicycle cops. They would call me 'bank robber' and stick up their middle finger. 'Fuck the U.S.A.,' [they'd say]." The police officers' tolerance cost him $100 a week each, he said. "I was spending money on everybody."

Waiting for the heat of his latest robbery to die down, DiCarlo headed 60 miles west for Columbus, N.M., hoping for a bank and an easy getaway.

"Well, there's nothing in Columbus," he said, finding himself stranded and aching for drugs in the small dusty town.

He went on to nearby Deming and found a Wells Fargo Bank there, but an elderly woman recognized him and he fled.

"'I know you, you're the bank robber,' she said. I didn't know they have all the same TV stations (as El Paso)."

Desperate, he robbed two convenience stores and took off for Las Cruces, where he robbed a First Security Bank. In a room at the Imperial Sky motel, he eagerly opened the money bag. "There was $152 in one dollar bills. I had to laugh," said DiCarlo, who was used to taking in at least a couple thousand dollars.

The next day, he robbed the Mesilla Valley Bank, hid out at an Alcoholics Anonymous meeting and caught a bus back to El Paso. "I had been gone for a week. Things had cooled off."

Back in Juárez' Boys' Town, while getting high with Fernando, DiCarlo started thinking about the future.

"I wasn't going to go back to El Paso. I was going to rob banks in Nogales, Mexico, and Douglas, Arizona. Well, we got to partying. We did more drugs than we should have, spent more money than we should have. I could still have made the trip, but I wouldn't be able to pay for a hotel room or drugs. I'm thinking, 'This ain't going to work.'"

One Last Bank
On December 14, 2000, DiCarlo robbed his last bank.

At 2:45 p.m., he walked into the bank on the second floor of the Chase building at Main Street and Mesa Drive. Customers in the bank at the time said they didn't realize the bank was being robbed.

On his way back to the bridge, DiCarlo went shopping for coats for Fernando's family and stuffed them in bulky Santa Claus shopping bags. By 3:30 p.m., he was back in Juárez.

Television sets on Melchor Ocampo were periodically broadcasting the $5,000 reward for his capture and DiCarlo decided to leave Juárez the next day. At noon, he went to bid farewell to Fernando and ran into an elderly neighbor.

"Why are you still here? Leave now. There's nobody here that wouldn't take the money," the man told DiCarlo.

Inside his apartment, Fernando loaded DiCarlo full of cocaine "for old times' sake."

"At 4:45 p.m., I come out of it, and ask (Fernando's mother) where Fernando went. She said, 'I don't know, he's acting funny.' I still didn't get it."

DiCarlo said he believes Fernando turned him in for the reward money. FBI agents said an unspecified tip led them to DiCarlo, and they worked with Mexican authorities to deport him back to the United States.

Lenny DiCarlo on his way to court for his hearing.

At 5 p.m. December 15, DiCarlo pushed open the blue steel front door and was met by half a dozen Mexican state policemen. A few hours later, two Mexican police officers walked him across the bridge, back to the United States.

Near the top, as he smoked his last cigarette as a free man, DiCarlo offered them $1,000 each to let him go. "They shook their heads. They said, 'It's gone too far for that.'"

Zeta: A Borderland Newspaper

Peter Laufer

from *Mexican Media: The Oral Tradition,* July 2002

EDITOR'S NOTE: The practice of investigative journalism on the Mexico side of the border —especially if the journalist probes drug trafficking and corruption of police and government officials—is a dangerous occupation. The editors suggest the reader consult the Committee to Protect Journalists (www.cpg.org) for a complete listing of murders of journalists and attacks against them, their families and facilities. Since 1997, the CPG has reported four murders of journalists along the border.

"Free like the wind"—the *Zeta* masthead slogan

Back in 1997, J. Jesús Blancornelas—co-founder and co-director of the crusading weekly newpaper *Zeta* out of Tijuana—was the victim of a vicious assassination attempt that left him permanently injured and killed his bodyguard. As he tells the story, his car was cut off in the Tijuana traffic by gunmen who pumped over 100 rounds into it. Seeking cover as soon as the shooting started, Blancornelas managed to avoid all but four of the shots, one of which just missed his spine. He spent a month hospitalized, more time recovering at his home, and finally returned to work.

But the attack on Jesús Blancornelas was not the first attempt to silence *Zeta*. His partner, the paper's co-founder Hector Feliz Miranda, was murdered in 1988. Neither shooting slowed down the crusading reporting *Zeta* is now famous for. Instead the paper and Blancornelas became examples of a new type of Mexican journalism: investigative and courageous. He and the paper continue to win international press freedom awards.

Zeta was founded in 1980 and quickly gained a reputation for disclosing Mexican government corruption and reporting on the activities of drug traffickers. Such investigative stories were a surprise for Tijuana readers, accustomed to government corruption and drug trafficking being glossed over in most papers. Cash payoffs to publishers and their reporters—in the form of so-called government subsidies or outright bribes—long kept most Mexican papers filled with celebrity gossip, violent street crime news, and bland political coverage that was little more than the official ruling party line.

The sprawl of Tijuana—from the tourist traps downtown to the maquiladoras luring factory workers up from the interior to the squalor of its slums—makes for a vibrant news town. And *Zeta* made its pages come alive with the details inside that sprawl, providing a tribune for politicians working to overthrow the long ruling Institutional Revolutionary Party (PRI) and covering the real dope of the illegal drug scene infesting the borderlands.

Carnival of Blood—The Whacked-Out Adventures of Min and Mon

John Ross

México Bárbaro #305, April 20, 2002

Carnival, that pre-Lenten outburst of merriment and mockery that has made New Orleans and Río de Janeiro famous the world over, was not a very festive occasion in 2002 for the Arellano Felix brothers, North America's most wanted narcotraffickers, doing business as the Tijuana cartel, which is thought responsible for supplying 15% of the U.S.' 300-ton annual cocaine imports.

On Carnival Sunday, February 10, 2002 in Mazatlan, Sinaloa, traditionally Pacific Coast Mexico's most boisterous celebration, Ramón Arellano Felix ("Mon"), 37, ran into a yet-murky police ambush on the palm-tree-lined streets of that resort city. Although identification proved difficult, Ramón Arellano was officially declared defunct a month later.

Then on March 8, up in altiplano Puebla state, near San Andrés Cholula, where Carnival extends past Easter and colorful, cactus-beer-swilling contingents roam the streets for months, big brother Benjamin ("Min") Arellano was captured by an elite military team without either side getting off a shot.

The end was unusually quiet for Mexico's bloodiest drug dynasty, pursued for more than a decade on both sides of the border with scant success—both Arellanos were atop the FBI's Most Wanted list, alongside Osama bin Laden, with a $2 million USD bounty on their scalps.

Like most of Mexico's top-drawer narcos, Min and Mon were Sinaloa boys. Their uncle, Miguel Angel Felix Gallardo, the first Mexican drug baron to forge ties with the Colombian cartels, was collared in 1989 by then-president Carlos Salinas de Gortari to show then-president George Bush that Mexico meant business in the War on Drugs. The dynamic is not so different today.

With their uncle's gunslingers backing them up, the Arellano boys shot their way into Tijuana, taking the plaza (smuggling franchise) away from the Caro Payón family, another Sinaloa clan, during the shamelessly corrupt regime of Governor Xicantecatl Leyva (1984-1989).

Min was the brains and Mon brought the muscle, and their bloody footprints have been tracked through dozens of homicidal vendettas, police shootouts and brutal massacres. The killing of 19 Pai-Pai Indians, 12 of them children, at El Rodeo outside Ensenada in 1999, and the execution of 12 young men at Limoncito, Sinaloa the next year—both in dope deals that went bad—are two signature samples of the Arellanos' flair for mass murdering. San Diego FBI spokesperson William Gore pins 200 murders in southern California, Baja California and Sinaloa on the Tijuana cartel.

The Arellanos' control of the Tijuana route was repeatedly challenged down the years, most sanguinarily by the amalgamated mobs of Joaquín "El Chapo" ("The Short Guy") Guzmán and Hector "El Güero" ("The White Guy") Palma, collectively known as the Sinaloa cartel. Beginning with the November 1992 shoot-em-up at the Cristina discotheque in Puerto Vallarta—eight Arellano underlings were butchered but the brothers made it out the back door—bad blood between the two gangs has spilled like a crimson Amazon.

On May 24, 1993, six months after the blowout in Vallarta, the Arellanos went after El Chapo at the Guadalajara airport with sicarios (hit-men) imported from a San Diego street gang, the "Crazy-30s," based in the Logan Heights barrio of that California port. Six citizens were slaughtered in the crossfire, most prominently Cardinal Juan Jesus Posadas Ocampo, purportedly a victim of "mistaken identity"—despite the fact that the Cardinal bore no resemblance to El Chapo and was wearing a long black cassock and large pectoral cross when he was machine-gunned in the thorax from two feet away in the rear of his Gran Marquis town car.[1] After the killing was done, Mon and Min reportedly boarded an Aeroméxico flight for Tijuana that was being held for their tardy departure.

"In late February 2002, investigators discovered a four-by-four foot tunnel, reinforced with planks of wood, running from a ranch house in Tijuana to a house in San Diego County, 875 feet away. Railroad tracks laid along the floor transported a battery-operated cart that could pull two flatbed carts and deliver drugs from one side of the border to the next within minutes.

"The investigators believe the tunnel was constructed 10 or 12 years ago, but may have been used up to 20 years ago in a rougher form.

"Once a week, a lawyer from Tijuana would arrive at the ranch house and take the caretakers shopping. According to an article printed in the *Los Angeles Times*, the caretakers told authorities that it was odd how often the attorney took them shopping, but 'he bought groceries and clothes for them and their neighbors.' That hooked them into going with him and not asking questions.

"Elberg Johnson, who is serving a 30-year sentence for transporting 2500 pounds of cocaine, owned a pig ranch on the U.S. side of the tunnel. After he went to prison in November 2001, Belinda and Raul Alvarado bought the property and rented out the buildings. The house with the tunnel had not been rented for six months. The Alvarados have stated that they were not aware of the tunnel."

Information compiled from "Tunnel Under Border May be 20 Years Old; Secret passage was used to transport drugs to the U.S. and weapons to Mexico," by Matea Gold, *Los Angeles Times*, May 19, 2002.

---

1 The alternative version has Cardinal Posadas, a former bishop of Tijuana, being whacked for double-crossing the very devout kingpins by refusing their lavish donations to the Church once he became the powerful cardinal of Guadalajara—the neo-classic "plata o plomo" (silver or lead) proposition that narcotraficantes give to their business associates, who then have the choice of taking the money or being killed.

Apparently riddled with remorse at having Swiss-cheesed a Prince of the Church, Min and Mon showed up at the papal nuncio's Mexico City mansion in December 1993, proclaiming their innocence and carrying a mysterious package for the Pope. Nuncio Girolamo Prigione then called Los Pinos, the Mexican White House, to inform President Salinas that Mexico's two most wanted drug lords were waiting on his couch. But Salinas and his attorney general Jorge Carpizo McGregor refused to order the Arellanos' arrest—Carpizo later alibied that to do so would have violated the Vatican's diplomatic immunity—and the two were allowed to walk out of the papal embassy scot-free.

The next stop in the whacked-out adventures of Min and Mon came four months later, March 24, 1994, when Luis Donaldo Colosio Murrieta, the presidential candidate of the then-long-ruling Institutional Revolutionary Party (PRI), was assassinated on Arellano Felix turf in a Tijuana squatter colony. Just two nights before the hit, an Arellano lieutenant, Ismael "El Mayel" Higuera, had shot it out with the cops on TJ's tourist-studded Revolution Avenue and walked away from the crime scene despite many outstanding warrants and several dead men on the pavement. State, federal and private police forces were reported to be involved up to their eyeballs in the events surrounding the Colosio killing. Popular Tijuana police chief Federico Benitez, who kept secret files on the narcos' role in the hit, was himself whacked by presumed Arellano hit men.

When El Mayel was finally captured in June 2000, after neighbors complained that Higuera was shooting up his million-dollar home on the Rosarito beach, south of Tijuana, his apparent crack-up seemed emblematic of the Tijuana cartel's decline.

The Arellano combine moved hundreds of tons of Colombian cocaine into and through Mexico in small planes and secret landing strips, overland on long-haul trucks, in shipping containers and in tuna boats. The brothers' longevity—they almost seemed an institution—owed much to the quality of their protection. Not only did the Arellanos keep many top cops on the payroll, they even enlisted an army general, Alfredo Navarro, currently doing 15 years hard time, to spread their largesse around the officer corps.

And if the plata didn't work, the plomo did the talking. The Arellano hit list includes a dozen high-ranking police and army investigators plus a couple of judges. Three slain agents who collaborated with the U.S. Drug Enforcement Administration (DEA) were kidnapped near Mexicali last year, run over, tortured (their heads were flattened by a tire compressor) and tossed into a lonely ravine.

The Arellano brothers were celebrities among Tijuana's "junior" set, the scions of TJ's richest families, and several were recruited as drug runners and enforcers—"El Kitty" Pez, recently extradited to California, was a popular young killer. In late 1997, after crusading local editor Jesus Blancornelas exposed the "narco-juniors" in his weekly *Zeta*, the Arellanos ordered his execution—Blancornelas survived the assassination (his bodyguard was killed) but remains permanently disabled.

Despite their well-earned reputation for murder and mayhem, Min and Mon sought to pass themselves off as Rotary Club types—Min was masquerading as "Manuel Trevino," a

Monterrey businessman, when he was captured in Cholula. In Tijuana, the deadly duo laundered dope profits through "legitimate" businesses such as the Vida pharmacy chain and the Oasis hotel complex near Ensenada. U.S. authorities warn their citizens that they could be fined as much as a quarter-of-a-million dollars for sleeping at or shopping in either enterprise.

Another of Min and Mon's purported associates was an illustrious junior, Jorge Hank Rhon, son of the late PRI kingmaker Carlos Hank González. Jorge operates a dog track and a string of off-track betting parlors in TJ, in addition to (allegedly) being Mexico's most active trader in rare and endangered species. According to published reports (*Zeta*), Jorge Hank once secured a pair of rare red kangaroos for the narcos' private zoo on a ranch outside of Tijuana.

Despite the ubiquitous wanted posters, the Arellanos went undetected for years; when finally run to ground, they did not look radically different from their widely distributed mug shots. Despite intense U.S. pressure upon Mexican authorities to capture the kingpins, some of their years on the lam were almost certainly spent in La Jolla, California. How freely the Arellanos were able to roam both countries was illustrated by Mon's ill-starred holiday in Mazatlán, a resort that was crawling with cops at Carnival time.

Mon apparently came to Carnival gunning for Ismael "El Mayo" Zambada, the Sinaloa representative of the Chihuahua, or Juárez, cartel, once run by the late Amado Carrillo Fuentes, the so-called "Lord of the Skies," another Sinaloa boy. One story has it that Zambada, anticipating Mon's murderous mission, hired local police to get to his rival first.

What is known is that on Carnival Sunday morning, ministerial police agents stopped Ramón Arellano and an accomplice near a Gold Coast shopping mall. After showing the cops a credential issued by the Federal Judicial Police that the agency claims is apocryphal, the narcos opened fire, and Ramón and officer Arturo Arias each met with violent demises. But one problem with this scenario is that forensic studies reveal bullets in Mon's back.

Both bodies lay head to head on the sidewalk for several hours before authorities carted them off to a local funeral home, where supposed relatives of "Jorge Perez Lopez" claimed the corpse and had it cremated—thereby depriving Mexican narcs and the DEA of the DNA they needed to confirm that Ramón Arellano was no longer among the living. After Min's capture, a photo of Mon was discovered on a religious altar in the Cholula house, a find that apparently substantiates his death. Also found on the spacious premises: a small suitcase containing $4 million USD, thought to be a week's rent for the plaza of Tijuana.

No other journalist captures the surrealism of Mexican politics like John Ross from his outpost at the Hotel Isabel in Mexico City. If you would like to receive his *México Bárbaro* dispatches by email, contact *Weekly News Update on the Americas* at wnu@igc.apc.org.

Who's Running This Plaza?

The illegal drug trade has reached "staggering" proportions throughout the world and is now the most profitable underground business—and it's still growing, warns U.N. Secretary-General Kofi Annan. The illegal trade in narcotics, he points out, has a captive market of about 190 million addicts and users worldwide, and is estimated to be worth more than 400 billion dollars a year. "It is larger than the oil and gas trade, larger than the chemicals and pharmaceuticals business and twice as big as the motor vehicle industry," Annan says. The Paris-based International Police Organization (Interpol) says the drug business is second only to the world's arms trade which is estimated at more than 800 billion dollars annually.

from an International Press Service news report
"Global Drug Trade Reaches Staggering Proportions,"
by Thalif Green. Dateline: United Nations, March 2, 2002

"Drugs are a business, one of the largest on the surface of the earth, and this business exists for two reasons: the products are so very, very good and the profits are so very, very high. Nothing that creates hundreds of billions of dollars of income annually and is desired by millions of people will be stopped by any nation on this earth. A Mexican study by the nation's internal security agency CISEN (Centro de Investigación y Seguridad Nacional), which has been leaked to the press, speculates that if the drug business vanished, the U.S. economy would shrink 19 to 22 percent, the Mexican 63 percent. I stare at these numbers and have no idea if they are sound or accurate. No one can really grapple with the numbers because illegal enterprises can be glimpsed but not measured."

—Charles Bowden
Down By the River: Drugs, Money, Murder, and Family

Soldiers of Misfortune

ROBERT DRAPER

Texas Monthly, **August 1997**

On most afternoons at the edge of El Polvo—the low-water crossing that connects Redford, Texas with Mexico—a visitor who survives the mind-wilting border heat may hunker beside the Río Grande and be rewarded with a tableau as pastoral as any in Texas. The vision is preceded by an ethereal tinkling, the barest fingerprint of a sound. Then, spilling down from the northern plain, the goats come into view. There are perhaps 40 of them, accompanied by a dog of obscure pedigree. Two of the goats wear bells around their necks. Quietly gnashing at the weeds, they make their unhurried way to the water.

Behind the animals, a man and a boy materialize on horseback. Esequiel Hernandez, Sr., is a solidly built middle-aged native of Palomas, a pueblo almost visible from here. He wears a cap and a solemn but profoundly weary expression. In silence, he surveys the mangy splendor of his world. His 10-year-old son, Noel, sits atop his pony with the slack posture that suggests an easy familiarity with goat herding. In this communion, even the boy appears ancient. Meanwhile, the river glints like a shivering sheet of tinfoil. Across the water, a lone man stands beside a dusty pickup—staring vaguely at America, waiting.

Simplicity shaded with ambiguity. That is El Polvo (literally, the Dust) and the border as a whole. Its beauty is not the innocent kind. Even the boy knows. His older brother, 18-year-old Esequiel Junior, who owned this very flock of goats, was shot to death here on May 20 [1997] by U.S. Marines. Likely the inscrutable figure on the other side of the river knows about the killing, and in any case, he is no innocent, as the visitor will later see for himself. But there are crimes and there are outrages. Hernandez' death at the hands of a 22-year-old California-reared Marine named Clemente Bañuelos was at least the latter, no matter what the jury decides about the former. Newspaper readers all over America now know what tiny Redford (population: 107) always knew—that the soft-spoken, hard-working high school sophomore was as law-abiding and unthreatening as anyone drawing breath could possibly be.

Quite properly, the Texas Rangers are preoccupied with what took place the day Hernandez—carrying his grandfather's old .22 rifle to fend off a pack of wild dogs that had been ravaging his herd—allegedly fired on four low-to-the-ground shaggy figures that turned out to be heavily armed and camouflaged Marines. The investigators have already voiced their skepticism as they square the soldier's statements against the autopsy report, the shooting distance, the position of Hernandez' body, the time discrepancies, and the evidence gathered at the scene of the incident. District Attorney Albert Valadez has intimated his desire to try Corporal Bañuelos for murder, and Hernandez' parents have hired an attorney to pursue a wrongful death lawsuit against the U.S. military. While his family awaits justice, the rest of the world awaits the truth.

Senseless though the tragedy was, the greater outrage is this: Esequiel Hernandez' killing was imminently predictable. We could expect no less, really, from the quiet but growing movement to militarize an area populated with civilians. Just what was the Marines' mission at El Polvo? Was it, as we have been led to believe, an honorable episode in America's much-ballyhooed War on Drugs? The evidence plainly suggests otherwise. From inception, the Marines' mission in Redford was trivial, politically and bureaucratically freighted and doomed to fail—a blundering bullet, in effect, with Esequiel Hernandez' name on it.

From where I sat the day I observed the Hernandezes and their goats, El Polvo didn't look like a battlefield. Later, however, as I walked through the scrubby trails paralleling the river, I found abundant evidence of the Marines' presence there a month before: more than a dozen empty packages of military rations, plastic military utensils, camouflaging burlap and the duct tape used to secure it to the soldiers' uniforms.

Then, after discovering a piece of wire poking out of the dirt road at the river's edge, I dug. What I uncovered, about a foot below the surface, was a heavy plastic box, similar to a car battery, with ten-foot wires dangling from each side. "U.S. Government," read the inscription on the box, which turned out to be a sensor used to monitor movements at trafficking areas. A Redford resident I talked to had seen a U.S. Border Patrol vehicle parked at this spot late one night, about a week before Hernandez was shot. I reported this to a senior Border Patrol official. He denied the sensor was theirs and suggested that I ask the military agency that had coordinated the mission at El Polvo. I did, but the spokesperson said the sensor wasn't the military's either.

Abandoned there in the dirt, the devious instrument seemed a forlorn and impotent creature—a fitting symbol for the wayward mission it was intended to serve, and maybe for the War on Drugs as a whole. What was a U.S. government sensor doing out here in the middle of nowhere? El Polvo, just south of Redford, is one of dozens of nearby informal crossings, a relatively shallow stretch of the Río Grande that can easily be waded across by smalltime dealers. The real drug action goes on in ports of entry like Presidio-Ojinaga, 16 miles away, where notorious smugglers like Pablo Acosta Villareal and Amado Carillo Fuentes have made millions sneaking drugs into the United States. The fact is that the War on Drugs, if it is to be won by interdiction, will be won at the ports of entry and not by collaring flunkies who ford the Río Grande with bundles of pot held over their heads. But like all wars, this one must be fought on all fronts. So while U.S. Customs makes the big busts at the ports, the woefully undermanned Border Patrol must monitor the vast riverbanks, where the odd nickel-and-dimer might pop up.

This is where the story of Esequiel Hernandez' tragic demise begins: with the best intentions. In the early summer of 1996, Border Patrol assistant chief patrol agent David

Castañeda met with two informants who alerted him to a drug-backpacking operation in force at El Polvo. The news discouraged Castañeda. "In the past couple of years," he told me, "we had hurt the organizations in Ojinaga by turning the people we had caught over to the state, meaning they'd have to spend 12 to 18 months in jail before even coming to trial. Word got around in Ojinaga to the point where the operators had to go all the way down to Durango to recruit new backpackers. But the confidential sources told me they were recruiting in Ojinaga again."

Specifically, they would later learn, a Cuban-born traficante named El Cubano was signing up so-called mule trains consisting of teams of five that would haul 175 to 200 pounds of pot in backpacks across El Polvo. Each backpacker would be paid about $1,500 and get counterfeit identification papers along with a free ride into the American interior, where they could then seek honest work. El Cubano's operation was small but steady, and it took place at late-night hours, when the Border Patrol's skeleton crew was ill-equipped to react. Castañeda knew his agency needed outside help, but he also saw the operation for what it was—hardly a mission requiring immediately deployable troops. "When we need urgent assistance," he told me, "we call on the Texas National Guard." In this case, the call went out to Joint Task Force 6.

Like a grimacing cheshire cat, the military's presence along the border is both more and less than it appears. For example, Joint Task Force 6 (JTF-6), the agency that coordinates anti-drug activities for the U.S. Department of Defense (DOD), subsists on a miniscule operating budget of $25 million. As its spokesperson, Maureen Bossch, insisted to me, "There has *not* been a recent increase in the militarization of the border. We're such a small part of the overall fight against drugs." Yet from its command post in El Paso, JTF-6 deploys a U.S. military force that is allocated $808 million for use in the War on Drugs—astonishingly, more than Customs, the Border Patrol, the FBI or even the Drug Enforcement Administration.

More to the point, militarization of the border occurs not simply by funding soldiers to stand shoulder-to-shoulder with guns pointed at Mexico. Instead, a civilian zone becomes militarized when the rules of war are imposed on it. That is precisely what transpired in May of 1997, the moment four JTF-6 Marines set foot on El Polvo.

Created in 1989 by then Secretary of Defense Dick Cheney, JTF-6 also owes its existence to Joint Chiefs of Staff Chairman Colin Powell, who envisioned a key role for the military in the Bush administration's National Drug Control Strategy. When one considers the political inclinations of both Powell and Cheney, one can imagine the public-relations value they saw in this maneuver. Others in the military were less sanguine. As one Defense Department spokesperson told me, "We were ordered to get into the counterdrug policy, and believe me, we were dragged in kicking and screaming. There are a lot of hard, complicated issues to be faced when you're talking about military personnel on U.S. soil. But there was strong pressure for the military to be more involved in the drug fight. For a lot of lawmakers, this is their big political shtick."

Shrine for Esequiel Hernandez, Redford, Texas.

Beneath the rhetorical bravado, however, one finds a war that is being carried out with a near-total absence of urgency. In the dull, workday setting of vast Biggs Army Air Field, part of Fort Bliss near El Paso, some 169 soldiers and support personnel toil in JTF-6, including its commander, Brigadier General James Lovelace, who, like his predecessors, will serve 18 months before moving on to the next post. This lack of continuity exasperates other senior colleagues in the federal drug war—including one senior official at another agency who says of JTF-6: "It's basically a way station where a one-star general gets a second star, and then he moves on."

The wheezing bureaucracy that directs the military's drug warriors hardly provokes an image of a lean, mean, fighting machine. It takes months for JTF-6 translators to provide a wiretap transcript and usually a year to deploy an operational military unit. Its so-called rapid support unit renders assistance in about a month, according to spokesperson Bossch. In memos distributed to local, state and federal drug-fighting agencies, JTF-6 regularly promotes what a senior official at another agency terms "services *they* want to use, as opposed to what we need." Canine training, first-aid instruction, fence building, map reading—all useful, but are they unique or simply a way for one agency to spend another's money?

JTF-6's biggest federal client is the Border Patrol, an agency whose primary function is not narcotics interdiction, but people interdiction. When I asked a senior Border Patrol official at the Marfa sector about what use he had made of the military through JTF-6, he enthused, "They improved a shooting range out at the Marfa airport and saved us up to 70 percent of the cost. They also built a radio workshop for us much cheaper than we could've done it."

Compared with such dubious pursuits, the interdiction mission against El Cubano's backpacking operation must have resembled the invasion of Normandy in the eyes of the officials who reviewed it for merit. In truth, though, when U.S. Border Patrol assistant Marfa sector chief Rudy Rodriguez penned the proposal last June or July, he knew that the request for several LP/OPs (listening posts—observation posts) to be stationed in and around El Polvo wasn't actually going to snare El Cubano. "The backpacking situation had something to do with the request," Rodriguez told me recently, "but it wasn't just that. I knew there wasn't a pattern I could point them to by the time they got there. Mainly, we wanted to use them here as a force multiplier because of our lack of personnel."

Though Bossch of JTF-6 would later explicitly tell me, "We're not a force multiplier—they're not using us for that purpose," it seems clear that despite all the sophisticated gadgetry offered by the military, Rodriguez called upon JTF-6 for one basic reason. The Border Patrol Marfa sector—having been reminded once again that a small-time smuggling scheme could crop up anywhere within its 115,000 square-mile jurisdiction and operate with impunity—needed more bodies and didn't care where it got them.

Perhaps an objective review board would have seen through Rodriguez' request and discarded it. But there is nothing remotely objective about Operation Alliance, the bizarre outfit at Biggs Field that evaluates all agency requests for military assistance. Funded by the very federal agencies (such as the Border Patrol and Customs) that file the lion's share of the requests, Operation Alliance's 19 members happen to work for those agencies as well. Not surprisingly, then, the organization—which, apart from receiving policy guidelines from Washington, answers to no agency—dutifully passes on to JTF-6 85 to 90 percent of the requests (or about 1,500 annually), according to Operation Alliance's senior tactical coordinator, Brian Pledger.

Predictably, Operation Alliance rubberstamped the Marfa sector's request. The proposed mission, like all others, was then forwarded to one of JTF-6's four lawyers. What followed was a painstaking, time-consuming review to determine whether the project in any way violated the Reconstruction-era Posse Comitatus statute, which was enacted to ensure that the military does not get into the business of domestic law enforcement. (Though watered down somewhat in the 80s, the statute still limits domestic policing on the part of the DOD in ways that do not apply to the National Guard, the Border Patrol, Customs, the FBI and the DEA.) In signing off on the El Polvo mission, the JTF-6 lawyers would, in effect, give the lie to the fiery oratory of politicians who promised their constituents, amid the popping of flashbulbs, to wage this war the old-fashioned way.

JAMES EVANS

The Marines who killed Esequiel Hernandez wore camouflaged "ghilli" suits like this one.

Shortly after one of the attorneys okayed Rodriguez' proposal, a JTF-6 message went out to every Army and Marine base in America, soliciting volunteers for an operational mission along the Texas-Mexico border. The message billed the El Polvo mission as a real-world encounter with drug smugglers, a challenge more bracing than the usual numbing base drill. All the same, it was a military exercise. The unit that signed up for the operation would do so not to assist the War on Drugs but to satisfy one portion of the unit's "mission essential task list"—the checklist of duties any outfit must fill before becoming eligible for deployment in an actual battle. According to Bossch, the unit that was selected was simply the first that volunteered. That happened to be the 5th Battalion, 11th Marine Regiment, an artillery unit stationed at Camp Pendleton in San Diego County, California.

In October, fully four months after Castañeda had received word about the backpacking operation, the Border Patrol met with JTF-6 and Camp Pendleton officials to plan their mission. In that span of time, the backpackers had doubtless altered their route, as smugglers do. Nonetheless, Castañeda, Rodriguez and the military advisors elected to station an LP/OP unit near El Polvo, with a sensor to be buried at the crossing to signal comings and goings. Meanwhile, the 5th Battalion was transported to Biggs Field, where the troops engaged in situational military exercises, strategy sessions, and Posse Comitatus statute seminars for a few weeks. Following this, the unit returned to Camp Pendleton and intensified its mission planning, which included setting up a prototype operational center. All in all, the Marines engaged in a phenomenal flurry of activity, considering that the initial justification for the mission had long since evaporated.

Included in their standard military training was something known as the Joint Chiefs of Staff Standing Rules of Engagement. In essence, the rules of engagement dictate that when a soldier perceives an imminent threat to the lives of his fellow soldiers, he responds not as a police officer would—with a warning or intent to disarm and wound—but instead, as a warrior would on a battlefield. As Marine Colonel Thomas Kelly explained in a press conference two days after the death of Esequiel Hernandez, "If you reach the point where you fire for fear of your lives, then you usually fire to kill."

Rudy Rodriguez of the Border Patrol knew, as he put it, "In times of stress, you revert to your training." According to Rodriguez, "You'll see guns everywhere all along the border. I told them, 'In daytime, a guy with a gun is not a threat.'"

Apparently, the planners forgot to pass this information on to U.S. Marine Corporal Clemente Bañuelos.

By law, the military is required to gain permission from a landowner to conduct an exercise on private property. Unlike the other border states, Texas is composed of very little public land, and the difficulties involved in securing landowner permission therefore help explain why less than 10 percent of JTF-6's approximately 3,000 missions have taken place in Texas, according to Bossch.

The mission at El Polvo presented the worst of all possible scenarios. The military indeed received permission to encamp on acreage just down the river from the crossing. Unfortunately, the landowner resided in Kermit, 221 miles north of Redford, and seldom visited his property. The other townsfolk had no way of knowing that the Marines would be descending on El Polvo. For that matter, Presidio County Sheriff's Department didn't know either. And because there was no one to tell Redford about the Marines, no one, conversely, told the Marines about Redford. Colonel Kelly of the Camp Pendleton unit would later tell the press, "We key off of law enforcement. They have a good feel for the community. They live it, they breathe it and they're part of it. So we depend upon law enforcement's judgment as to what there is to find." This kind of communication did not occur. Kelly also said that military intelligence gatherers actually visited El Polvo three to four days before the unit was deployed there. And, of course, either JTF-6 or the Border Patrol visited the crossing and buried the sensor. Yet throughout all this preparation, the military never gathered the one bit of information that everyone in Redford knew, the one kernel of intelligence that would have saved both the mission from being aborted and, incidentally, a life—nearly every afternoon from about five to six, a young man named Esequiel Hernandez, Jr., brought his flock of goats to the riverbank.

On May 12, an advance team of Camp Pendleton officials arrived in Marfa and set up shop in a mobile home on a lot behind the sector headquarters of the Border Patrol. Two days later a C-130 airplane conveyed the remainder of the 5th Battalion to Marfa. Of the 120 or so soldiers, about 10 would remain at the command center on the Border Patrol

Established in 1989, Joint Task Force-6 is a military operation, comprised heavily of Army and Marine personnel whose official mission is to aid local law enforcement agencies in fighting the "war against drugs." Unofficially, JTF-6 is also currently one of the government's main weapons in the "war against immigrants" from Mexico and Central American nations. While JTF-6's jurisdiction now includes the entire continental U.S. and Puerto Rico, many of its operations still occur along the border region in the Southwestern states of California, Arizona, New Mexico and Texas.

JTF-6 is the largest use of military force within our domestic borders since the Civil War. Before 1980, domestic use of the military was widely regarded as unconstitutional as well as extremely dangerous. Soldiers are trained to kill, not police civilian populations. After Sept. 11th, the Bush administration announced the military would play a greater role in "homeland security." We have yet to see what exactly the administration means by a "greater role," and what part JTF-6 will play in it, but already we have seen an increase in the number of troops deployed along our borders.

The activities of JTF-6 also pose an unacceptable threat to the many fragile ecosystems along the border region. Almost all areas along the U.S./Mexico border contain essential habitat for rare species protected under the Endangered Species Act. Such species include the Sonora pronghorn antelope, lesser long nosed bat, and large cats such as the jaguar and ocelot. These species are placed in great jeopardy by JTF-6's extensive road, trail, fence and wall building; light installation; facility construction; ground operations; and overall cumulative effects from the greatly increased human presence in border regions.

Information from Border Action Network (formerly known as SWARM). www.borderaction.org

lot—where, among other things, they would receive signals of movement from the sensor buried by El Polvo. Sixteen of the remaining Marines would be deployed at four designated LP/OP sites, four soldiers per location, rotating every few days to keep the troops fresh. The following day—May 15—16 Marines were sent to their posts, officially, if secretly, inaugurating the military's 14-day mission.

¿Quién Está Manejando la Plaza?

Unit 513, stationed near El Polvo, consisted of four noncommissioned Marine corporals: Ronald Wieler, Jr.; Ray Torres, Jr.; James Matthew Blood; and the team leader, San Francisco-native Clemente Bañuelos. For the next five days, the four young men (all of them between the ages of 19 and 22) lived day and night in the mesquite brush of a county where temperatures routinely soar into the triple digits. Each wore a ghilli suit, camouflage that covered him from head to toe in stringy brown and green burlap strips, their M-16 rifles similarly obscured, with their faces darkened, so that the Marines looked like nothing so much as large blobs of foliage—or, as some would later suggest, Bigfoot. While living on military rations and sweltering in their bulky garb, they looked through their binoculars, listened to the sensor reports on their radios, and in general came to know the world of the border through the eyes and ears of trained warriors.

"Every night they saw vehicles crossing," Rodriguez told me. Of course, this wouldn't surprise Redford residents, most of whom had family on the other side and routinely crossed over themselves. Furthermore, El Polvo has long been a corridor for contrabandistas —though the goods in question tend to be clothes, electronic wares, or chickens being ferried *into* Mexico. So what, exactly, was there for the Marines to see? According to Rodriguez, one third or fourth night, Unit 513 observed the crossing of ten illegal aliens, who were subsequently apprehended by the Border Patrol. But they weren't carrying drugs, and they bore no connection to El Cubano's smuggling scheme. According to David Castañeda, the Marines never once observed any backpackers; and though El Cubano was arrested a month later, credit for his apprehension would go to the Mexican police rather than anyone on the American side of the river.

In short, Unit 513 saw and did nothing during its five-day observation period at El Polvo to fulfill anyone's notion of an anti-drug mission. But on the afternoon of Tuesday, May 20, while encamped near their "hide site" near the banks of the Río Grande, the four Marines did see someone. It was a Mexican man on horseback, across the river, gazing at America and waiting.

There is no way to know for certain whether the horseman was the same man beside a parked truck I saw 22 days later when I visited El Polvo and watched the father and brother of Esequiel Junior take the goats to the water. There is also probably no way to know for sure what he was up to. We do know that he unwittingly triggered the calamitous accident that was waiting all along to happen. The sighting of this man prompted the four Marines to move to higher ground—within view of Hernandez, who stood watch over his flock with a rickety .22 in hand, prepared to fire on the pack of wild dogs from town that had recently mutilated one of his goats.

The world of fact grows murky here. Did the teenager see the Marines? And if so, could he tell who or what they were? (Said Colonel Kelly at the press conference, "It is the team's impression that there is no mistake that they were identified as human.") Or, considering their bushy camouflage and the standard duck-walking movements of stalking Marines, did he believe them to be dogs? Border Patrol officials confirm that a Marine radioed word that they had been fired upon—twice, according to two Marines in their statements. The Marines say that they then shadowed Hernandez (for how long is unclear) and that he not only did not retreat but eventually raised his rifle to fire at one of them. The Rangers have already expressed doubt over this scenario, considering that Bañuelos shot the right-handed Hernandez in the right side, which would not have been exposed to the team leader if Hernandez had been aiming in the other Marine's direction. Instead, judging from the entry point of the single lethal bullet, one might conclude that Hernandez was turning to go back home with his goats.

Regardless, Bañuelos fired his M-16 once. According to the Marines, Hernandez staggered, then fell backward into a three-foot fire pit. That, at least, is where the Border Patrol found him 22 minutes later. The Marines made no attempt to revive Hernandez, though, as the autopsy would later establish, he bled to death; in other words, he did not die instantly. Did the Marines let him die because they were not required to save his life? Or was it in their best interests, judging by what happened at El Polvo, that Esequiel Hernandez be prevented from describing his version of the events?

We know this: the Marines at no time told him, as a lawman might, who they were and what their business was. Citing the windy conditions of that afternoon (though that, too, is a matter of dispute) that would have made verbal communications difficult, Colonel Kelly told the press, "In order to get the attention of the individual, they would've had to expose themselves. And there was no requirement under the rules of engagement about having to do that."

We also know this: though at the time of his death Esequiel Hernandez actually had a U.S. Marines recruiting poster tacked to the wall of his bedroom, he did not know that the Joint Chiefs of Staff Standing Rules of Engagement applied to the world that was in his backyard.

Here is the best of all I know. Twenty-two days after Esequiel Junior was shot to death, I sat on a rock beside El Polvo and said, "Buenas tardes" to his father as he passed me on horseback. "Buenas tardes," replied Esequiel Senior, as did Noel, and then they followed their goats uphill toward home. But the man across the river on the Mexican side continued to stand beside his truck for almost an hour. He looked at me, and I looked at him. Neither of us seemed to be in any imminent danger.

Then at about 6:30, I heard the sound of an engine coming from the north. Looking up, I saw a large vehicle slash and jiggle its way through the brush-clogged dirt road. It was a large flatbed truck, piled at least six feet high with contraband—which, I could plainly see, consisted of nothing more than some 70 automobile tires precariously tied to the bed. Slowly, inexorably, the truck advanced upon El Polvo. It plowed noisily through the river, spraying water everywhere. A minute later it was across. Only then did the lone man beside the truck move. He waved to the driver of the contraband, hopped in his own vehicle and drove off after him.

While watching the tire contrabandistas vanish into the Mexican interior that afternoon, it occurred to me that somewhere in somebody's headquarters, a sensor signal had been transmitted. Maybe somebody would hear the signal. Even if he did, the battle would be joined too late.

The Hernandez family received a $1.9 million settlement in a wrongful death claim against the government in 1998. The government admitted no fault in the death of Esequiel Hernandez Junior. The Texas Rangers, reviewing the case after the trials were over, made a public accusation of obstruction of justice. "The federal government came in and stifled the investigation," said Ranger Sgt. David Duncan. "It's really depressing. The system we hoped would work failed at the federal level." Enrique Madrid, a citizen of Redford who has studied the case at length, says, "The federal government had to obstruct justice, it had to pay off the Hernandez family, and it had to leave the border. Soldiers are meant to protect us, not to shoot us. Imagine what the morale of the military would be if those soldiers had been imprisoned—for following orders! So you can see, they had to do whatever they could, illegal or otherwise, to protect the entire military from disillusionment. This was a disaster, a true disaster."

Mexican-Americans and the Militarization of the Border

"We [Mexican-Americans] are the only ethnic group in the whole country who can claim to have a national police force we can call our very own.

"It wasn't [the Border Patrol's] choice to police us. It is policy that has placed them in the position of policing us. We are the police constituency. There's a whole folklore about it. There's songs, there's jokes, there's stories. And the jokes particularly are revealing. Sometimes the agent is the butt of the joke, sometimes it's the immigrant, sometimes it's both of them together.

"There was an old (INS) sector chief who retired in El Paso, and a reporter from Juárez told me that he asked him, 'What do you think of Mexicans?' He said 'I know them very well. I've been arresting them for 25 years.' And the same is true for us, we who have been arrested...

"I coined a phrase—the abused-community syndrome—like the battered-wife syndrome. It's gone on for so many generations that we no longer see the abuse. It's become a way of life. Part of our work is increasing public awareness that we are an abused community. This doesn't happen to other communities. Particularly the issue of U.S. citizens being stopped and questioned and detained, and sometimes even deported. It doesn't happen to Anglo-Americans, African-Americans. It happens to Americans of Mexican origin.

"When I address Mexican-American audiences, I talk to them about the fact that even in our own self-definition, if you listen to Mexican-Americans, we are the only ones who keep saying, 'Oh yeah, I'm a fourth generation, fifth generation, eighth generation American.' We are continually reinforcing our right to be here because we are constantly being questioned about our right to be here. I hear many Americans saying, 'It doesn't bother me that they stop me and ask me for my papers.' But it doesn't happen to anybody else. It's a fourth amendment violation to be stopped based on appearance.

"There's a song, a very popular salsa song. The guy proposes to the girl. He says, 'Let's live together till the INS separates us.' When I talk to agents, I say, 'That's how predominant you are in our lives. It's no longer until God do us part, it's until the INS do us part.'"

From "The Militarization of the U.S. Mexico Border: Part 1—Border Communities Respond to Militarization. An interview with María Jiménez" by Nic Paget-Clark. Originally published in *In Motion Magazine*, February 2, 1998. www.inmotionmagazine.com

María Jiménez is director of the Immigration Law Enforcement Monitoring Project (ILEMP), a project of the American Friends Service Committee. Founded in 1987, its goal is to reduce the abuse of authority in the enforcement of immigration laws.

The Border as a Looking Glass

BOBBY BYRD

The border is at the end of the world—that is, if you measure your world as the cultural, political and geographical space occupied by the United States of America. Heroes are not allowed to live here. The iconography of our culture simply does not stretch this far. Maybe it's for this reason that antiheroes—persons who seem contrary to the überculture's system of values—flourish along the border, men and women who have staked out a moral territory rooted deep in the border's geography, this sort of anti-place, like a vacuum in the collective consciousness. Like the Tohono O'odham, these antiheroes have garnered some kind of understanding here at the end of the world, understanding that can perhaps help keep afloat this cursed boat of ours that has sprung so many bloody leaks.

Enrique Madrid is one of these antiheroes. He's a big man in horn-rimmed glasses who usually packages himself inside a guayabera shirt—sometimes white, sometimes blue—that hangs comfortably over his middle-aged spread. His thick black hair is unruly, and it's turning silver at the tips. Both in his house and in his mind, books and data and artifacts surround him. He seems to be constantly sifting through information to make some sort of meaning out of the violence and confusion that happen along the border. Indeed, he has studied history through the looking glass of the border and knows deep down that something is tragically unbalanced in the way our culture perceives this world. Enrique is no optimist about the future, especially for the people along the frontera; yet, paradoxically, an hour or two spent with Enrique talking about the border and his ideas is a good salve for the anxious heart.

Enrique lives in Redford, Texas, with Ruby, his wife of 35 years and another of Redford's several antiheroes. The little community—its total population has hovered around 100 souls[1] for years—is nestled in an open spot in the Río Grande Valley as the river begins its cut into the canyons of Big Bend country. Most drivers traveling south on Farm-to-Market Road 170 from Presidio toward Terlingua and Lajitas and the Big Bend National Park hardly slow down to wonder who lives here. Enrique's family has been here over 130 years since the governor of Texas recruited Mexicans to settle the area. They fought off Apaches and carved out irrigated fields from the wilderness. They named their pueblo El Polvo (The Dust), but that got changed when the U.S. Post Office demanded an English name.

Enrique is a home-grown intellectual, "an independent scholar," as he calls himself. He could have easily been a PhD in history or anthropology at some fancy university

---

1 Enrique told me that one year, five babies were born in Redford, creating a mild population boom of 5% in a single year.

somewhere, but he walked away from his very promising education in the late 60s. The reason was the Vietnam War. "My friends," he says, "were dying. The war was decimating the Hispanic community." He fought in his own way. As a student at the University of Texas at Austin, he voluntarily refused his "student deferment" and applied for a deferment as a Conscientious Objector (C.O.). He based his objections to the war not on religious grounds but on moral and legal grounds.

His draft board was in Alpine, and in Alpine a C.O. was a coward. Or a Communist. And they knew what to do to un-American troublemakers, especially if they were Mexicans —they changed Enrique's status to 1-A. He had to decide between going to Vietnam or fighting in court and maybe even going to jail. He chose the latter.

After several years of litigation, full of financial worries for Enrique and his family, a federal judge threw the government's case out of court on a technicality. It was a hollow victory for Enrique. He wanted his victory to be based on moral issues about the war.

Enrique decided not to return to the university. More than ever, he felt that the Vietnam War was evil and that the military industrial complex was the beast that manipulated the war effort. The university, because of the largesse supplied by LBJ's Texas White House, was belly deep in the mud and feeding at the trough. He decided to return to Redford with his new wife Ruby—a young woman from East Texas who believed in his struggles against the war—and to resume his life there. He became a clerk in his father's grocery store; Ruby became a teacher. Enrique also became a self-taught scholar, with an emphasis on Border Studies, and an activist struggling to protect the environment and the archeology in his part of la frontera.

All this from a young man who grew up in one of the most unpopulated and poorest places in the United States, a place where people waded or paddled back and forth across the muddy river to visit friends and relatives, to trade and buy and sell, to visit a curandera on one side or a doctor on the other. The governments of Mexico and the United States, like the border itself, were abstractions and a hindrance to ordinary life. The other side of the river was simply the other side of the river.

Redford, of course, is the town where on May 20, 1997 (almost five years to the day as I write this), four U.S. Marines stalked and killed Esequiel Hernandez, a goatherd who had just celebrated his 18th birthday. Esequiel, an American citizen, had been watering his goats at the río after returning from school. The Marines had been bivouacked for five days in an arroyo within 200 yards from the American village. But nobody in Redford knew they were there. According to the training the Marines had received, 75% of all citizens in Redford were narcotraficantes. Thus, every citizen not in diapers was suspect, enemies of the U.S. government.

The bullet shot by squad leader Clemente Bañuelos—more than the gradual militariza-tion of the border, more than the short-sighted drug laws, more than the mishandling of immigration issues—crystallized the feelings of many of us who live on the U.S. side of the border. We finally realized that our home is not governed in the same way as the rest of the country. The border had become increasingly federalized, and martial law was more than just a whisper. The constitution and its guarantees do not exist here the way they exist, say, in St. Louis. This is what the death of Esequiel Hernandez taught us.

In February of 2002, on a Sunday afternoon, my wife Lee and I visited with Enrique and Ruby in their home, his mother and father's house, a 100-year-old adobe that sits beside FM 170. Across the road is the elementary school where Ruby teaches; down the hill 50 yards away is the Río Grande; and on the other side is Mexico. The Chihuahua desert sun was already pushing the thermometer into the high 80s, but inside the cool adobe darkness we happily discovered a wonderful clutter of books and ideas.

Our visit was intense and much more than either of us expected. We enjoyed a long rambling conversation with Enrique. He talked and we listened. Ruby sat to the side, every now and then adding important pieces of information or points of view, sometimes retrieving this or that book. We learned about history—the Native American history of Redford, the Mexican history of Redford, the history of Enrique's family in Redford, the history of the U.S. in Redford. We learned about how Esequiel died and how horror-struck his family and the community felt; we learned about what the government did and didn't do; and we learned about how Father Melvin LaFollette, another border antihero and an Episcopal priest (now retired) who has lived almost in exile from his church, organized the stunned community after Esequiel's death.

Somewhere in the midst of the conversation, I asked, "Enrique, don't you think the government will legalize drugs one of these days? They have to understand sooner or later that these laws are crazy and stupid."

Enrique grinned and shouted, "They'll never legalize drugs!"

"Why not?"

"I'll tell you in a while."

First he wanted to tell us about his mother, Lucia Rede Madrid, a Redford citizen who ("ironically," as Enrique likes to point out) was somehow blessed with the status of "hero" by the powers-that-be. When she retired from teaching, she wanted to keep her intellectual life alive. Redford didn't have a lending library, so she began one in her home with her own books and her own funds. Books were available in Spanish or English. Folks from either side of the river could come by and get a library card and check out books. It was the only library of its kind in the United States, and Lucia became famous for her work. Bush the First twice flew her to Washington to receive medals honoring her library and her spirit of volunteerism. She was one of his "points of light." Bush was also the president initially responsible for sending the Marines to guard the border, and, thus, his hands are soiled with Esequiel's blood.

When Lucia received her first award, *Parade Magazine* sent a reporter and photographer team to Redford to document Lucia's achievement. They posed her with two children who were using the library that day. One was Esequiel Hernandez, a frequent borrower of books and one of Lucia's favorite patrons.

Esequiel Hernandez as a young boy, sitting in the library with Lucia Madrid. This photo appeared in Parade Magazine, *accompanying an article about Lucia Madrid which described her efforts to start a library in the small town of Redford, Texas.*

Since 1996 Lucia has been living in a nursing home. Enrique and Ruby never told her about Esequiel's tragic death. "It would break her heart," he said. We listened to a truck roll by outside and his dog whimpering in the bedroom. Then he leaned forward in his chair and stared at us through those big horned-rimmed glasses. He said, "That is the irony. With one hand, Bush gives my mother these awards. With the other, he sends the Marines to watch us and even kill us because we fit the profile of drug-smugglers."

The conversation lulled. We talked about this and that. Enrique showed us fossils and photographs and the land grant his grandfather Secundino received in 1870. As the time came near when we had to go, I asked him again: "Why won't the government ever legalize drugs?"

Enrique smiled and pulled out more books. He started telling me about Native American spirituality, how it's based on the immediate experience of the sacred in the landscape—rocks and rivers and canyons and plants and sun and earth and wind and moon. Enrique had become excited, talking in a louder voice, his hands moving through the air as he talked

LEE BYRD

Enrique and Ruby Madrid at Esequiel Hernandez' gravesite.

about the shamans, the spiritual leaders of the Native American communities, taking drugs to induce their religious experience. "Indeed," he said, pointing to a book, "the use of drugs was at the very core of native religion."

"So?"

Enrique pulled off his glasses and a beatific smile spread across his large brown face. "The drug war," he announced, "began the minute the Pilgrims set foot on Plymouth Rock. Same thing with Columbus. The English and the Spaniards believed that God sits on a throne somewhere in the sky. In their world view, God is an abstract and rational being. He governs from on high. Like a king. Not so with the Indians. They believed that the people came up out of the earth and the gods came along with them, showing them the way. They believed that the rocks and the river and the sky are holy. They believe this because they are pagans and pagans take drugs. Christians read about God. Christians are told about God and talk about God. Christians don't take drugs.

"But Indians take drugs and they experience God. That is what they believe."

He took a deep breath and excused himself for simplifying everything. "But," he said, "that's what I believe. The War on Drugs is really about two different world views. It's a war between those world views. That's why the government will never legalize drugs. It's impossible. They'd have to change everything. They'd have to change the way they think."

How Much Does It Cost?

http://www.drugabuse.gov/Infofax/costs.html

A study prepared by The Lewin Group for the National Institute on Drug Abuse and the National Institute on Alcohol Abuse and Alcoholism estimated the total economic cost of alcohol and drug abuse to be $245.7 billion for 1992. Of this cost, $97.7 billion* was due to drug abuse. This estimate includes substance abuse treatment and prevention costs as well as other healthcare costs, costs associated with reduced job productivity or lost earnings, and other costs to society such as crime and social welfare. The study also determined that these costs are borne primarily by governments (46 percent), followed by those who abuse drugs and members of their households (44 percent).

The 1992 cost estimate has increased 50 percent over the cost estimate from 1985 data. The four primary contributors to this increase were (1) the epidemic of heavy cocaine use (2) the HIV epidemic (3) an eightfold increase in state and Federal incarcerations for drug offenses, and (4) a threefold increase in crimes attributed to drugs.

More than half of the estimated costs of drug abuse were associated with drug-related crime. These costs included lost productivity of victims and incarcerated perpetrators of drug- related crime (20.4 percent); lost legitimate production due to drug-related crime careers (19.7 percent); and other costs of drug-related crime, including Federal drug traffic control, property damage, and police, legal, and corrections services (18.4 percent). Most of the remaining costs resulted from premature deaths (14.9 percent), lost productivity due to drug-related illness (14.5 percent), and healthcare expenditures (10.2 percent).

The White House Office of National Drug Control Policy (ONDCP) conducted a study to determine how much money is spent on illegal drugs that otherwise would support legitimate spending or savings by the user in the overall economy. ONDCP found that, between 1988 and 1995, Americans spent $57.3 billion on drugs, broken down as follows: $38 billion on cocaine, $9.6 billion on heroin, $7 billion on marijuana, and $2.7 billion on other illegal drugs and on the misuse of legal drugs

* This estimate includes illicit drugs and other drugs taken for non-medical purposes. It does not include nicotine.

May Our Daughters Come Home
Nuestra hijas de regreso a casa

Since 1993 over 320 women have been killed in Ciudad, Juárez.

Why did I start the rape crisis center?
Because I am a woman, and because I have a conscience.
—Esther Chavez Cano,
director of Casa Amiga in Juárez

The Dead Women Of Juárez

SAM QUINONES

from *True Tales of Another Mexico: the Lynch Mob, the Popsicle Kings, Chalizco & the Bronx,* 1997

EDITOR'S NOTE: *This essay was published in June of 1997. The violence has continued. Nobody knows the true numbers of women killed, though it is estimated to be about 320. Latif Sharif, the Egyptian arrested for the women's murders in 1995, is still in jail. He has never been convicted.*

Seven men were already in jail in Ciudad Juárez, charged in the serial murder of 17 young women—the case apparently solved—when Sandra Juárez' body turned up on the banks of the Río Grande.

One Saturday in July of 1996, Sandra, 17, walked into Ciudad Juárez from Lagunillas, a village of 40 adobe houses, 30 miles from the nearest telephone, in a parched region of the state of Zacatecas. She was no match for the city. On Monday, she went looking for work in the maquiladoras—the assembly plants—that dominate the Juárez economy. A few days later, they found her blouse on the Mexican side of the river. She lay strangled to death on the U.S. side. Her case has not been solved. No one knows where she went, or with whom, that Monday.

For the people of Ciudad Juárez, Sandra's case, and others that turned up that summer, played havoc with some accepted beliefs. Until then, for example, they had believed that the city's first serial-murder case, which had attracted news media from across Mexico and the United States, had been put behind them. They believed that a foreigner and a group of U.S. style gang-bangers were responsible. Given the town's border location, Juarenses are used to blaming things on people from somewhere else; that 80 percent of the town's prison population is from somewhere else is an oft-quoted statistic.

But about the time Sandra Juárez died, people in town finally had to start listening to Esther Chavez. Chavez is a thin, almost frail, retired accountant who lives in a middle-class neighborhood of Juárez and would not seem the type to get involved in a serial murder case. Nor did Chavez have much history of feminist involvement when she organized a women's group known as Grupo 8 de Marzo. But, from newspaper clippings, Chavez had been keeping an informal list of cases involving dead young women ever since she noted the rape and murder of 13-year-old Esperanza Leyva on November 15, 1993. By that time the list was already 13 cases long. "We had gone to talk to the mayor," Chavez says. "He promised to get higher authorities involved. He was my very good friend, but he never did anything for us. What we were trying to get people to see was a general climate of violence against women."

The cases were notable in that the identifiable victims were usually young and working-class. A good number had worked in the maquiladoras. These were not murders of passion, taking place in a bar or bedroom. Some of the women had been raped, many had been mutilated and a good many more had been dumped like the worn-out parts to some machine in isolated spots in the deserts surrounding the city. Their killer or killers didn't even take the trouble to cover them with dirt, believing, with good reason, that the sun and the desert's scavengers would quickly wipe their corpses from the face of the earth. By the summer of 1996, Chavez had counted 86 of these cases, dating back to Esperanza Leyva in 1993. Actually, that turned out not to be a whole lot in the larger scheme of things; Juárez tallies more than 250 homicides a year, of which a good number are drug-related executions and well more than 86 are gang killings. But Juárez is also a place where, according to the Assistant Attorney General based in the city, those who aren't gang members or drug smugglers can live free of the fear of murder. So the women's deaths, finally, were notable in their number as well. By the time Sandra Juárez' body appeared on the banks of the Río Grande, people in town had to listen to Esther Chavez and consider the possibility that behind the dying women of Juárez was something even more disturbing than a lone serial murderer, something that had to do with what the town had become.

Ciudad Juárez spreads low, bleak and treeless across the valley floor south of El Paso and the Río Grande. The smell of fetid sewers is a constant companion through town, a nagging reminder that the desert is no place for a major industrial center.

Years ago Juárez thrived because it understood that beneath America's puritan rhetoric, a buck was always waiting to be made. During Prohibition, Juárez produced whiskey and beer and ran it across the border. Bars emerged along Avenida Juárez, the main drag leading to the bridge into El Paso, and have never left. "Divorce planes" brought American couples in to quickly end their marriages. To women looking for work, Juárez offered prostitution. Until the mid-1960s, Juárez was a bustling city of sin.

Then the maquiladoras arrived. Over the next three decades, the assembly plants turned dusty border outposts into major stops in the global economy, assembling televisions, telephones, appliances, clothes, calculators, car parts—all for export to the world's wealthiest market across the border. In Juárez, several maquiladoras even count America's coupons.

Mexico began allowing maquiladoras on the border in 1964. The idea was to sop up migrant workers returning after the U.S. ended the so-called "bracero" treaty, a 22-year-old agreement that allowed Mexicans to work seasonally and legally in America's fields. The maquilas began as an afterthought. But beginning in the late 1970's, the country lurched through recession after recession, and the peso steadily lost value. Many U.S. and foreign firms saw a payroll paid in a currency that always lost value as a nifty proposition. As Mexico

Mother searching alone in the desert for her missing daughter.

JULIÁN CARDONA

staggered, the maquiladora sector along the border became an increasingly important job-provider. Today, some 970,000 people—mostly unskilled and low-paid—work in more than 3,800 maquiladoras, completing in 25 years one of the most remarkable industrial transformations anywhere in the latter half of the twentieth century. Virtually all the plants are owned by foreign companies: General Motors, Ford, Hughes, Phillips, RCA, Sony, Toshiba, Dae Woo, and on down to minor candy and clothing manufacturers.

Juárez saw the twenty-first century in the maquiladora. The city always had more maquila jobs than any other city—178,000 today. As the maquila grew, so grew Juárez. The city went from 407,000 inhabitants in 1970 to what townspeople can only estimate is about 1.5 million people today, with several thousand more wandering through in any given month.

But since, in Mexico, border towns barely qualify as Mexican, Juárez was always last on the list when the central government in far-off Mexico City doled out the resources. The city couldn't provide basic municipal services for everyone the maquiladoras pulled from the interior. Urban planning was an impossibility. And on a maquiladora salary, no worker could afford much rent. So shantytowns leaped into the desert. They were without drinking water, sewers, parks, lighting or paved streets. An apocalyptic folk craft—shack-building—developed using plastic tarp and barrels, wood pallets, cardboard, wire cord, all that was maquiladora detritus. Bottle caps were used for bolts. Nor was monied development controlled. A lot of people got rich selling the desert to foreign maquilas. Meanwhile, a collection of cheesy strip malls hunkered down around town, as developers mimicked what they saw across the border.

Juárez grew rootless and cold under the desert sun, a place to make money, but not a place to love or know or drink from a faucet. Here 500 street gangs fought a war of attrition among themselves. Walking among the cars at intersections were Indians in plastic sandals hawking gum and Mennonites in overalls selling cheese. Narcos in gold chains and snake-skin boots, Chevy Suburbans and assault rifles winked again at El Norte's puritan rhetoric and used Juárez as the mainline into the American vein. Coming off the border is a gaudy collection of neon nightclubs, advertising the profiles of buxom, naked women, and cheesy curio shops that sell tequila and sarapes to day-visitors from El Paso.

As Juárez grew, an anonymity that characterizes many large U.S. cities settled on it. Police make a lot of the fact that so many of the dead women—more than half on Chavez' list—are unidentified. Nor do they have missing-persons reports matching their descriptions. No one claims these bodies. Their families in some isolated part of Mexico may believe they live somewhere in the U.S., or simply don't care where they are. This, police say, is what they're up against. One Mexican politician has suggested lowering maquiladora salaries and building a wall 50 kilometers out of town to staunch the flow of Mexico into Juárez. Meanwhile, one citizens' group now gives seminars in high schools to educate newcomers on the city's history on the theory that people won't love what they don't know. It's hard to imagine a city with more bars over its windows and doors. Even in the shantytowns, where people have little to steal, some shacks of cardboard and plywood have barred windows. Everywhere, too, is the incessant babble of gang graffiti marking Juárez as a border town—too close to the gringo is what the rest of Mexico would say.

But Juárez offered jobs and that makes it like America in the most important way. Like the U.S., Juárez attracted Mexicans from the interior who were restless and willing to risk a lot to change their lives. People from the rural states of Durango, Zacatecas and Coahuila continue to trudge into Juárez in huge numbers, figuring anything is better than the brutish life of the bankrupt Mexican campo. But unlike the U.S., which attracts mainly men, Juárez became a magnet for women, especially young women. The maquila did not, as Mexican planners hoped, employ many men returning from the U.S. Instead, the plants pulled young women to the border from deep in Mexico's countryside. In Juárez for many years, more than 80 percent of all maquila workers were women. Even today, with maquila work heavier, more than 60 percent of the maquila workforce is female. These were women with few of the skills that the industrial economy would reward. They were interchangeable and they moved frequently between jobs, which were generally similar in their monotony. Juárez thirsted for them. Many plants in Juárez have "Help Wanted" banners flying almost all year round.

Forming a line to search for bodies.

One of the women that Juárez attracted was Elizabeth Castro, a 17-year-old who had come from the state of Zacatecas. On August 10, 1995, Castro's decomposing body appeared along a highway. At the time no one thought much of it. For a few days she even remained unidentified. Then, through August and September, the bodies of more young women began showing up, several of them in Lote Bravo, a magnificent sprawl of caramel-colored desert south of the airport. The doctors autopsying the bodies said some showed signs of being raped. Several of them were too decomposed to identify. Pressure mounted and headlines became shrill. Juárez had seen a lot, but never this.

Juarenses were comforted, however temporarily, by the arrest in early October of Abdel Latif Sharif, an Egyptian chemist. Police accused him of killing the women, including Castro. (Witnesses were later found who said they'd seen Sharif and Elizabeth Castro in a club together.) Finally the case had something Juárez was used to—a foreigner with a history. Sharif had lived in Florida for a number of years and there had been convicted of a variety of sex crimes against girls and spent time in prison. When the U.S. deported him, he didn't return to Egypt. He came to Juárez.

Police claimed the 49-year-old Sharif had been prowling the downtown clubs that maquiladora workers frequented, seducing young women, then killing them. But Sharif said he was innocent, a scapegoat for police under public pressure. He predicted the bodies would continue to appear. He was right.

Lomas de Poleo is a stretch of desert west of town littered with the wind-blown trash of clandestine garbage dumpings. Within a few months of Sharif's arrest, the decomposing bodies of young women began appearing amid the debris. A goatherder found three of them.

It takes a lot to shock Juárez, but the continuing discovery of bodies did the trick. Civil patrols were now organized to protect children getting out of school and young women as they returned home from their maquila jobs. The shantytowns of Anapra and Lomas de Poleo formed squads to comb the desert areas for more corpses. The newspapers were filled with the latest news, clues and conjecture about the case. Police competence was routinely questioned.

Then, one night in April of 1996, the police raided clubs along Avenida Juárez, the bar-studded drag leading from El Paso, where officers had been working undercover. They arrested a gang called Los Rebeldes (The Rebels). The police theorized that Sharif paid Los Rebeldes to kill women while he was in jail to make it seem that the real killer was still at large. And there stood the police case.

But then came the summer of 1996. More dumped bodies showed up. They continue to be found. So while evidence points to a serial murderer in a few of the cases, what now seemed clear was that Juárez had something much larger on its hands. Indeed, since the arrests of Los Rebeldes in early 1996, the bodies of almost 50 women have turned up.

Rocio Miranda, a bar owner, was raped by 17 young men, then dumped in a vat of acid. The only parts of Miranda that remained when she was found were her hands, feet and the silicon implants that police used to identify her. Silvia Rivera, 21, was stabbed to death by her husband and buried out near the prison; she was first identified and buried as one Elizabeth Ontiveros, who'd been reported missing, until Ontiveros showed up, having run off with her boyfriend. Soledad Beltran, a stripper known as Yesenia, turned up in a drainage ditch, stabbed to death, her killers unknown. Sonia Yvette Ramirez, 13, was raped and killed and left a block from police headquarters. Her father spent two months tracking down her boyfriend, who had fled south to Chihuahua City. There he cornered him in an auto-repair shop, thrashed him and turned him over to police, who charged him with Sonia's murder.

Brenda Najera, 15, and Susana Flores, 13, were both raped, tortured and shot in the head. An autopsy showed Susana had had four heart attacks before dying. And there were more women who turned up whose identity still is unknown, leaving behind only the grimy detritus of a dime-store novel: a tattoo on the wrist, black jeans, fingernails painted dark red, green socks, white panties, a black bra and often the signs of rape. One woman was found with two brassieres lying by her side. Two others were found on a motorcycle race-track in the desert wearing slippers and bathrobes.

Worried mother.

There was no one thing—or one person or group—to pin the bodies on any more. If a serial murderer was at large, there was a lot of other horrible stuff going on as well. It came to seem as if Juárez was awash in dead women merely because it was Juárez.

Among the corpses that summer was Sandra Juárez. A lot about Sandra was typical of the young country women whose labor forms the backbone of Ciudad Juárez. As with many of them, Sandra's last little piece of the world was in a concrete-block house on the outskirts of town in a neighborhood with neither pavement nor a sewer system; electricity came only five years ago. This is where her aunts and cousins live.

You get there by heading out Avenida Tecnologico east from downtown. Amid a battalion of billboards you spot Space Burger and the last gasp of Thunderbird Motors. A little ahead is Peter Piper Pizza, where "Lunch Paquetes" can be had for 9.90 pesos. Over Wrinkled Bridge (Puente Arrugado) is the Mini-Super and a Del Rio Superette, then the Autotel, with curtains over its parking spaces for maximum privacy, next door to the Silver Fox Piano Bar. Along the way is Autos Hawaii with its "Facilidades de Pago" (Easy Payments). As you head further east you begin to see the squat maquiladoras where Sandra thought she glimpsed a future: Cadimex, FCM, the Los Fuentes Industrial Park now under construction ("Come Grow With Us").

In coming here, Sandra followed a new tradition for women in her family, indeed in most of her village. "There's no work there," says her cousin Joel Juárez, who left Lagunillas 12 years ago. "The men work part of the year in the fields. For women there's nothing. Life's hard. About 20 years ago, the first family left [for Ciudad Juárez]. They came back, told us about it and we came running."

Behind her relatives' concrete-block house are signs of the limboworld between rural and post-modernity that Sandra's family occupies: a traditional adobe bread oven, a chicken coop and a one-room shack made of pallets, cardboard and plastic tarp discarded by maquiladoras where family members have worked. Their house stands as a symbol of the wrenching social changes that Ciudad Juárez is as unprepared to address as its residents' demand for paved streets.

People here surmise that these changes are one reason why women are murdered and tossed away. On display in Juárez is the quick and brutal mashing of a rural people into an industrial work force. Thousands of women like Sandra come here hoping to be part of it. The maquiladora yanked these women from the farm with the offer of their first paycheck; they became Mexico's "Rosie the Riveter." In a matter of a few years, the maquiladora turned time-honored sex roles upside down: women became the family providers. Maquiladoras, for all the nastiness associated with them, created a new Mexican woman. Maquila workers often came to see the world, and their place in it, differently. But this same process did not create a new man.

In that regard, the case of Marcela Macias, a 35-year-old mother of four, is instructive. On June 19, Macias's decomposing body was found buried under some tires near a highway leading out of town. Two days later police arrested her husband, Ramon Ochoa, 49. Ochoa told police that his wife had become more independent since taking a job at a maquiladora and had been talking back to him. He believed she had a lover. He said he would spy on her at work and see her eating lunch with other men. She told him she was going to sit with whomever she pleased. "My sister was very independent," says Macias' half-sister, Silvia. "He was afraid of that and felt she was unfaithful." In the year since she took the job, the couple fought constantly. Ochoa said he strangled her during one such fight, buried her and reported her missing.

"This is so symptomatic of the way men respond when women begin to leave home and not be dependent on them," says María Antonietta Esparza. Community pressure surrounding the deaths of the women prompted officials to set up an office to handle reports of sex crimes and domestic violence, staffed entirely by women. It is one of only about 20 such offices in Mexico. Esparza, an attorney, is its director. She says men from rural areas are used to controlling women down to how they dress and speak. Women, once they get to the maquila, often aren't as disposed to take it as when they were down on the farm. No one

The saddest moment.

knows how many of the cases of murdered women have to do with domestic violence or a general male resentment toward uppity women. But the reports Esparza's office handles have risen steadily every month in the year since it opened and show no sign of tapering off. Says Esparza: "We don't stop being part of a culture. In some sense, men may feel unprotected in not having a woman to cook and clean for them, like a mother. This vision of women's work is what makes them feel, when the woman does work, like they're losing control."

Esparza believes the crude and quick modernization of country women going on now in Juárez has another role to play in the killings. Nothing about Mexican country life prepares a young woman for Juárez. In their villages, they are prohibited from even being out after dark; the first boy they sleep with they marry. But in Juárez all the chains come off. "They come from an atmosphere where they couldn't do anything, to one where everything is within their reach. They're easy prey," Esparza says. "They come looking for work. They don't know the city. Don't know the conditions. Perhaps all they know is what they've heard in songs: 'Ciudad Juárez is numero uno.' They go to these clubs, which are fertile fields for the commission of these kinds of crimes."

As the killings of young women progressed, police looked for reasons and thought they found one in the glut of clubs that thrived with the arrival of 178,000 maquiladora jobs. Following Sharif's arrest, detectives claimed the victims led double lives, unbeknownst to their families. After their maquila jobs, according to investigators, these women doubled as party girls in the dance halls of downtown Juárez. These claims earned the police no love among the victims' families, who vigorously denied them.

But whatever the truth of the matter and investigators' lack of tact notwithstanding, police were right about one thing: the bars and dance halls now play an essential function in maquiladora life and, for that reason, probably have something to do with the killings. "Maquila work is long and monotonous. (The women) work eight hours, plus the time they spend in buses getting to work," says Esther Chavez. "So on Fridays and Saturdays they go dancing. They're looking for affection. Men there take advantage of them. (Women) have been taught to work. But they haven't been taught to live in a violent city with problems like this one. They come here very trusting, because in rural areas customs are much different."

The clubs are likely where some women met their killers. It's not a coincidence that the clubs are also the best public display of women's new economic place in this town. Juárez is full of young women with money and the freedom to enjoy it for the first time, thirsting for an escape from tedium and willing to throw caution to the wind.

Go to Juárez' central plaza before dawn on Friday and you'll see them. At 4:30 a.m. in Plaza de Armas, the hulls of buses stand vacant and a light breeze blows the sounds of a taxi driver's radio across the square. By 5 a.m., more buses are arriving, here to take workers to the maquiladoras by starting time. And suddenly, within half an hour, the square teems with silent, scurrying people, an open-air Grand Central Station muted except for the sound of the wrenching gears of dozens of maquiladora buses. They lurch to a stop, quickly take on passengers, then move out to deliver the assembly plants their workers by 7 a.m. This is simply part of many workers' withering daily routine; to get here on time they must arise from their shanty at 4 a.m.

What makes Friday different is that many women arrive at the square as if bound for some fashionable dinner party, instead of eight hours of tedious assembly work. They're decked out in sheer black dresses, tight miniskirts, an occasional ankle-length gown shuffles by on high-heels over the cracked, gum-smeared sidewalk; hair is piled high, lips sparkling red and fingernails glittering with polish. Since many workers live in shantytowns on the edge of town, going home after work is incompatible with having fun on Friday night. So every Friday before dawn, Plaza de Armas looks vaguely like a cocktail party.

Through the day they work. Then, in the afternoon, they hit the clubs. By 4:30 p.m. on Fridays—an hour after work and well before the sun goes down—young women have packed the city's bars and dance halls, where they stay until early Saturday morning. It brings to mind a 1960s Friday night in Pittsburgh or Detroit, except the workers are usually teenage girls, not burly men in their 30s. To watch them arrive at the clubs is a remarkable and rare sight for Mexico: groups of three, four and five women at a time file in, pay their own way, order their own drinks, light their own cigarettes. "They're all looking for a man," says a bouncer at El Patio, one of the most popular dance halls with maquiladora line workers. That's true. But the other truth is that the bars that once offered women for sale to gringos now must cater to Mexican women's new economic power. At some clubs, women don't wait for men to ask, and fill the floor dancing with each other. A routine offering these days are "sexy boys" shows—male strippers. Nothing measures the cultural distance between Juárez and the isolated villages that provide it with workers like a woman who pays her own money at a club and gives a thumbs-up-thumbs-down to a man feverishly undressing on stage for her pleasure. Mexican village life leaves no room to conceive of such a thing.

One favorite place is Casino Deportivo on Avenida Juárez. Police say that Sharif was seen in this club with Elizabeth Castro. Maquiladoras do hire people in their late 20s and 30s, but they also wink at hiring kids under the legal age of 18. From Deportivo's clientele, maquila employees all, it seems that Mexico is industrializing on the backs of high school students. Under black lights, kids dance to the polkas of a norteño band and then to the thunking bass of disco. They paste their home-state identity on their clothes in letters of white gothic script: "ZAC"—Zacatecas; "COAH"—Coahuila; "DGO"—Durango.

"We work all week and on the weekend we've got to get out," says Anahy Rentería, a 22-year-old. She and her cousin, Marisela Martínez, 17, have come from the village of Canatlan in the state of Durango in the last six months. Now they're living with relatives and making television components at the Haromex plant. They are dressed identically in silver lame blouses and black jeans, with "DGO" in enormous letters spelled out down their right pants legs, each of which cost them a week's salary. At home in Canatlan, there's nothing to do and little work for women. Juárez is a funpark in comparison. "Things were so boring at home," says Martínez, "so I bugged and bugged my parents and they finally let me come here."

"Have you ever seen the film *Citizen X*?" asks Ignacio Alvarado, a reporter who has covered the murder cases for the *Diario de Juárez* newspaper, sitting in a cafeteria one morning. *Citizen X* was an HBO production starring Donald Sutherland and is based on the investigation into the first serial murder/rape case in the Soviet Union. Officials at the Attorney General's office in Juárez played the film for their detectives investigating Sharif and Los Rebeldes. How much it influenced their investigative strategies depends on who you ask. In one sense, using the film was a bold move by a department looking for any edge it could find in its first serial-murder case. But it also highlighted what Juarenses say is another factor in the continuing murder of young women: a criminal-justice system utterly unprepared for today's Juárez.

Alongside the virtually absent public-work and social-work infrastructure, the city never developed a criminal-justice infrastructure worth the name. Detectives send bodies to the local university laboratory since they don't have a morgue lab of their own. They don't have gloves with which to handle evidence, nor bags to put that evidence in. Police officers number only about 1,200—300 per shift—for a wild city of 1.5 million. The local jail was built for 800 prisoners, yet now holds 1,600. And, in a city that has depended on female labor for three decades, Esparza's sex-crimes and family violence office has only been open since August of 1996.

All this has become an issue because, besides the continuing appearance of dead women—many of whose murders are unsolved—police have had no success in their case against the one man they have caught. The Egyptian has been in jail for almost two years, but he has yet to be convicted of anything. Judges have been reluctant to find him guilty on the available evidence and just as reluctant to face public wrath by letting him go. So he exists in legal limbo, as investigators try to find enough dirt on him to convince a judge.

Police are undaunted. "Look how long it took to catch the killer in *Citizen X*," says Jorge Lopez, Assistant Attorney General. But the lack of results has simply confirmed Juarenses' fears regarding police competence. Victims' families generally feel that if they had been wealthy, police response to their daughters' deaths would have been overwhelming and more sensitive.

Astrid González sees more systemic problems, related to the city's inability to keep up with its population. Homicide detectives still receive only six months of training before they're put on the street, and then they're allowed only five gallons of gasoline per day, says González, who has organized a group known as the Citizen Committee in the Fight Against Violence. She remembers a case in which a man wanted for a long series of rapes was arrested robbing a woman. The judge, about to get off work, quickly set bail for the robbery, but ignored the other cases that, though requiring lengthy paperwork, would have kept the suspect in jail without bail. The man hasn't been seen since.

"Judges are poorly paid, too," says González. "Impunity promotes crime. People believe they can commit crime without punishment. They don't just believe it, either. They prove it."

The lack of confidence in the police has confused the case of the growing numbers of dead young women. Juárez wonders whether it's in the midst of an enormous serial murder, a variety of unrelated crimes with serial murder included or whether there's been serial murder at all and the whole thing's just been bungled by the cops.

"I'll tell you about a case that says a lot about Juárez," says Jorge Ostos, a psychologist who runs the state police academy south of town. Ostos is a young, thin, articulate man given to diagramming his ideas on paper as he speaks. At one point he took a lot of derision for suggesting that the reason for Juárez' violence was that people had stopped believing in the Virgin of Guadalupe. As a metaphor, though, the idea isn't that far-fetched. The normal ties that bind Mexicans in community don't exist much in Juárez, which is a point Ostos likes to make. "When I was a kid, the parents in the neighborhood took part in raising you," he says. "If they saw you smoking or drinking, they'd say something. But today, society is separated from itself."

The story he tells is of a 10-year-old girl, Ana-María Garcia, who left home alone to visit her father who lived a couple miles away. Getting toward dusk, she began the walk home, again unaccompanied. Near a liquor store, her path crossed that of four teenage boys who had spent the afternoon inhaling a variety of industrial solvents and were by this time quite out of their minds. They grabbed her as she walked by, put her in a car, taped her mouth, and took her to a nearby hill where they raped her and stabbed her 17 times. Her body was found a few days later.

To Ostos, the case illustrates two other problems that have accompanied Juárez on its march to modernity. One is the breakdown of the family—both the girl's family, who let her walk home alone, and the youths' families, who raised thugs. Accompanying that is the rise of drug abuse and gang activity. "I tell you this because a lot of people talk about a serial killer in Juárez. I don't discard the possibility," Ostos says. "What I'm sure of is that there are as many potential killers as there are drug addicts in this town. You've got the possibility of psychopaths on every corner. What happened [to Ana-María Garcia] could have happened in all these cases involving murdered women in the last three years. The question is, do we have a serial killer or simply a whole bunch of psychopaths roaming the streets?"

Sitting in her office at the non-profit FEMAP, Graciela de la Rosa tries to answer this question. FEMAP is a non-profit organization that educates maquila workers on workplace rights and health issues. De la Rosa, a Juárez native, is a thick woman, a well-known firebrand around town. She has watched waves of maquiladora workers arrive in town, while her city has moved out further into the desert.

"It's obvious that many of these girls went willingly with their murderers," she says. "Why do they go? Because they're young. Sex plays a role. But most important is that they don't have the psychosocial resources to understand what's happening, to ask themselves if they should go and to say no to a man.

"This is part of the collision of the migrant who's just arrived and has no resources to confront the dangers and complexities of this forced 'modernization' we have going on here.

"Children are blind before the maquila. Choosing between the village and the maquila, the maquila is better because, although you're not paid well, at least you have food. But what happens to the migrant when she arrives? She immediately enters into this process of modernization that U.S. culture and Juárez offers her, which is without any substance.

"People never thought that the city needed housing, education, artistic activities. They only saw the money to be made selling land to the maquiladoras. So they created an industrial sector in a city without water. The city center is the mirror of Juárez' crisis. It's the proof that this is a sacked city. The only thing that remains intact is the Cathedral. The church is the only value remaining in downtown. The rest is nausea. What do the businessmen do? They open their 'Juárez Moderno,' where there's cineplexes and malls.

"Meanwhile, the maquiladora is now part of the family duty. The same in France during the 1800s, when the whole family had to work in the mines because one salary wasn't

> "We families are having to do our own investigation. We can't count on the authorities, who have treated us with contempt whenever we try to find out what happened and who might have killed our daughter."
>
> *—Josefina González,*
> *mother of murder victim Claudia I. González*

enough. Here, the mother, the children, the whole family enters the maquiladora to survive. Here they're modernized through production.

"If you add to this education in crisis, institutions in crisis, government in crisis, what are you going to have? Crime, murder. The only way we're modern is in the producing.

"Crime has always existed," she says, finally. "There are many mysteries in the human heart that contribute to that. So you can understand two, three, four of these killings from that point of view. But 86 [approximately 320 in 2002]murders is really the product of the circumstances; it's a product of the social decomposition of a place. The collective madness is making itself felt."

Juárez, today, is part Dodge City, part Dicken's London, nestled at the dawn of the 21st century. The growing stack of unsolved cases of murdered women is in some twisted sense a measure of the city's growth, of the distance it's putting between itself and the Third World. "Perhaps the life that people led in Zacatecas or Durango, or in Juárez 20 years ago, is saner," says Jorge Ostos.

Perhaps that is part of what's behind these killings: that growth does not necessarily equal development or sanity, and Juárez' expansion was too quick, tore too many bonds that gave life balance. Juárez has married itself to the maquiladora for 30 years and, without an accompanying social development, these 86 women are the downside. Perhaps, too, it's that Mexico's rural young women have changed Juárez, responded to what it asked of them and now are resented for it.

What can be said with more certainty, however, is that these cases reflect Juárez' anonymity. No one knows, nor seems to care, what happened to most of the murdered women of Ciudad Juárez. The cases have a public half-life of about three days any more. They pile up, people shake their heads and the dead women are left to be remembered only by their families. "Anonima" is the word that appears frequently on Esther Chavez' list. This is what Juárez has come to accept about itself today. The murder in 1979 of one maquiladora worker generated more outrage than most of the current cases combined. Life after all is not a Hollywood mystery. There is no resolution, no evil madman to conveniently pin it all on. The perfect murder is, it turns out, unusually easy to commit, especially when the victim is no one important, an anonymous figure, and Juárez has enough of those.

All of which leaves Sandra's people up on Capulín Street with a lifetime of wondering ahead of them. "What we'd like is to know something," says her aunt, María de Jesus Vasquez, pleading, holding out her hands. "We don't know anything."

Murdered Women of Juárez
Compiled by Esther Chavez Cano

This is not an "official list" of the murdered women of Juárez. In fact, there are no official lists available from police authorities. This list was painstakingly compiled by Esther Chavez from reports found in the Juárez newspapers.

Victim's Name	Date Corpse Located	Age
Alma Chavira Farel	1/23/1993	?
Angelina Luna Villalobos	1/25/1993	16
unknown	2/17/1993	?
Jessica Lizalde Leon	3/14/1993	?
Luz de la O. Garcia	4/21/1993	?
unknown	5/5/1993	35
Elizabeth Ramos	5/8/1993	26
unknown	5/13/1993	25
Verónica Huitron Quezada	6/5/1993	?
unknown	6/11/1993	?
Guadalupe Ivonne Estrada Salas	6/15/1993	16
unknown	9/1/1993	?
Marcela Santos Garza	9/17/1993	18
Mireya Hernández Méndez	10/14/1993	20
Tomasa Salas Calderón	10/14/1993	?
Esmeralda Leyva Rodriguez	11/15/1993	13
Yolanda Tapia	12/15/1993	50
unknown	1/11/1994	25
Emilia Garcia Hernandez	2/11/1994	?
María Rocío Cordero	3/11/1994	11
Lorenza Isela González	4/25/1994	23
Donna Maurine Striplin Boggs	4/30/1994	26
Gladys Janneth Fierro	5/12/1994	12
María Agustina Hernandez	6/24/1994	33
Patricia, alias "la burra"	8/8/1994	30
unknown	10/24/1994	16
unknown	11/11/1994	30
Guillermina Hernandez	11/20/1994	15
Elizabeth Gómez	12/1995	29
Laura Ana Inere	12/1995	27
unknown	1/10/1995	?
Cristina Quezada Mauricio	1/25/1995	31
Miriam Adriana Velasquez Mendoza	2/24/1995	14
Fabiola Zamudio	4/17/1995	35
Karina Daniela Gutierrez	4/21/1995	25
Araceli Rosaura Martinez Montañés	7/4/1995	19

Victim's Name	Date Corpse Located	Age
Erica Garcia Moreno	7/16/1995	19
Gloria Olivas Morales	8/6/1995	28
Patricia Cortes Campos	8/8/1995	33
Elizabeth Castro Garcia	8/19/1995	17
Gloria Escobedo Pina	8/20/1995	20
unknown	8/22/1995	18 to 20
unknown	8/22/1995	16 to 17
Miriam de los Angeles Deras	8/27/1995	25
Silvia Elena Rivera Morales	9/2/1995	17
unknown	9/5/1995	24
unknown	9/5/1995	?
Olga Alicia Carrillo Perez	9/10/1995	13
Adriana Torres Marquez	11/2/1995	15
unknown	11/18/1995	18
Ignacia Morales Soto	11/23/1995	22
Rosa Isela Tena Quintanilla	12/15/1995	14
Aracely	10/06/1996	23
Francisca Epigmenia Hernández	2/1996	30
unknown	7/1996	?
unknown	3/9/1996	10
unknown	3/12/1996	16 to 17
unknown	3/19/1996	16
unknown	3/23/1996	16
Verónica Guadalupe Castro Pando	3/29/1996	16
unknown	3/29/1996	18
Rosario García Leal	4/8/1996	18
unknown	4/28/1996	28
unknown	6/10/1996	17
Silvia Rivera Salas	6/26/1996	21
unknown	7/8/1996	15 to 16
Sandra Luz Juárez Vasquez	7/10/1996	17
Rocio Miranda Agüero	7/30/1996	28
Sonia Ivette Ramírez	8/10/1996	13
Alma Patricia o Leticia Palafox Zamora	8/15/1996	17
Soledad Beltrán	8/15/1996	24
unknown	8/19/1996	17
Victoria Elaine Parker Hopking	9/30/1996	30
Perla Parker Hopking	9/30/1996	48
unknown	10/31/1996	?
Leticia de la Cruz Bañuelos	11/2/1996	30
Leticia García Rosales	11/14/1996	35
unknown	11/18/1996	20 to 25
Brenda Lizeth Najera	12/7/1996	15
Susana Flores Flores	12/7/1996	13

Victim's Name	Date Corpse Located	Age
Rocio Rincon	3/1997	?
Verónica Beltrán Maynez	6/1997	15
Cinthia Rocío Acosta Alvarado	3/11/1997	10
Ana María Gardea Villalobos	3/14/1997	11
unknown	3/21/1997	16
Maribel Palomino Arvizo	3/21/1997	18
Silvia Guadalupe Díaz	3/29/1997	22
Miriam Aguilar Rodriguez	4/12/1997	16
unknown	5/16/1997	28 to 33
Amelia Lucio Borjas	5/29/1997	18
Marcela Hernandez Macias	6/19/1997	35
unknown	7/10/1997	22 to 25
Martha Gutiérrez García	9/9/1997	18
María Irma Plancarte	9/28/1997	25 to 30
unknown	10/3/1997	15 to 17
María Esther Luna Alfaro	10/13/1997	?
Virginia Rodriguez Beltrán	10/14/1997	?
Juana Iñiguez Mares	10/23/1997	38
unknown	11/7/1997	?
Norma Julissa Ramos	11/8/1997	21
Erendira Buendía Muñoz	11/17/1997	19
Teresa Renteria	11/30/1997	32
Aracely Núñez Santos	12/1/1997	18 to 20
Amalia Saucedo Díaz de Leon	12/2/1997	33
Rosa Margarita Arellanes Garcia	12/9/1997	24
unknown	12/21/1997	16 to 17
Gabriela Edith Marquez Calvillo	5/1998	15
Olga González López	8/1998	23
Jessica Martínez Morales	1/3/1998	13
Martha Esmerelda Veloz Vasquez	1/25/1998	20
María Isela Núñez Herrera	1/26/1998	33
Silvia Gabriela Luna Cruz	1/27/1998	16
Ana Hipólito Campos	2/3/1998	38
unknown	2/16/1998	?
unknown	2/16/1998	?
Raquel Lechuga Macias	2/16/1998	?
unknown	2/16/1998	?
Clara Zepeda Alvarez	2/17/1998	17
Perla Patricia Sáenz Díaz	2/19/1998	25
unknown	2/21/1998	?
unknown	3/18/1998	20 to 25
Argelia Irene Salazar Crispín	4/17/1998	24
unknown	4/20/1998	16
María Sagrario González Flores	4/30/1998	17

Victim's Name	Date Corpse Located	Age	
unknown	5/24/1998	?	
Patricia Meléndez Vásquez	6/27/1998	15	Brenda
Araceli Lozano Bolanos	8/5/1998	24	
Araceli Gómez Martínez	8/19/1998	24	
Erendira Ivonne Ponce	8/31/1998	17	
Rocio Barraza Gallegos	9/21/1998	23	
Hester Van Nierop	9/21/1998	?	
María Eugenia Mendoza Arias	10/4/1998	32	
Elizabeth Soto Flores	10/26/1998	?	
Zenaida Bermúdez Campa	11/17/1998	48	
Francisca Sanchez Gutierrez	12/4/1998	51	
Celia Guadalupe Gómez de la Cruz	12/10/1998	13	
Paulina Leon	1/1999	?	
María Del Refugio Núñez Lopez	10/1999	23	
unknown	2/1999	18 to 20	
Ma.Estela Martínez Valdez	1/11/1999	33	
Patricia Monroy Torres	1/14/1999	27	
Elsa America Arrequin Mendoza	2/15/1999	22	
Irma Angélica Rosales Lozano	2/17/1999	13	
Helena Garcia Alvarado	3/4/1999	33	
Gladys Lizeth Ramos Escárcega	3/15/1999	24	
unknown	3/22/1999	?	
María Santos Ramírez	4/19/1999	60	
Irene Castillo	6/6/1999	70	
Elizabeth Flores Sanchez	6/7/1999	17	
María Elba Chávez	7/6/1999	60	
Rosa María Rivera	7/7/1999	29	
Bertha Luz Briones	8/2/1999	41	
unknown	8/10/1999	?	
Vanessa Horcasitas	8/22/1999	17	
unknown	10/16/1999	50	
Blanca Estela Vázquez Valenzuela	10/20/1999	44	
Nelly América Gómez Holguín	10/25/1999	22	
unknown	11/20/1999	18 to 20	
unknown	1/2000	28 to 30	
Elva Hernandez Martínez	9/2000	40	
María Santos Rangel Flores	1/5/2000	40 to 45	
Juana González	1/6/2000	37	
María Isabel Nava Vázquez	1/27/2000	18	
María Elena Salcido Meraz	1/27/2000	33	
Cecilia Sáenz Parra	1/31/2000	20	
Ines Silvia Marchant	2/15/2000	23	
unknown	3/8/2000	?	

Victim's Name	Date Corpse Located	Age
Perla del Castillo Holguín	3/11/2000	36
unknown	3/11/2000	22
Amparo Guzmán	4/2/2000	16
unknown	4/8/2000	65
Martha Francisca Hernandez	6/6/2000	29
Martha Alicia Esquivel Garcia	6/17/2000	33
Sandra Henry Monreal	6/17/2000	38
unknown	6/29/2000	20 to 25
Liliana Holguín de Santiago	6/29/2000	15
Aida Carrillo	7/8/2000	24
Irma Marquez	7/27/2000	37
Elodia Payan Núñez	8/5/2000	40 to 45
Leticia Armendáriz	8/8/2000	40
Sonia Yareli Torres Torres	8/14/2000	19
Otilia Santos Trujillo	10/5/2000	70
Adriana Saucedo Juárez	10/19/2000	17
María Elena Caldera	10/24/2000	15
María Verónica Santillanes Najera	11/5/2000	22
"Child, unknown"	11/7/2000	1
María Isabel Chávez Gonzalez	11/8/2000	37
Woman's skull	12/2001	?
Woman's skull	12/2001	20 or 21?
Skull	12/2001	39
Laura Georgina Vargas	1/3/2001	40
Susana Enriquez Enríquez	1/14/2001	29
Elvira Carrillo de la Fuente	1/18/2001	72
Brisa Nevarez Santos	1/27/2001	20
Lilia Alejandra Garcia A.	2/21/2001	17
Reina Sarriá Lara Lucero	2/21/2001	3
María Saturnina de Leon	2/27/2001	50
Norma Leticia Quintero M.	4/5/2001	22
Julia Luna Vera	4/10/2001	36
Laura Alondra Marquez	5/1/2001	16
Flor Idalia Marquez	5/1/2001	18
Irma Rebeca Fuentes	5/13/2001	18
Lourdes Gutierrez Rosales	6/13/2001	30
unknown	6/22/2001	4
unknown	6/23/2001	?
Rosa María Hernandez de Corral	7/17/2001	?
Leticia Vargas Flores	7/20/2001	35
unknown	7/25/2001	25 to 30
Paloma Rodríguez Rodríguez	7/25/2001	17
unknown	9/23/2001	3
María Victoria Arrellano Zubiate	10/7/2001	42

Victim's Name	Date Corpse Located	Age
unknown	11/5/2001	40
Brenda Herrera	11/6/2001	15
unknown	11/6/2001	?
Claudia Ivette Gonzalez	11/6/2001	20
unknown	11/7/2001	?
unknown	11/7/2001	?
unknown	11/7/2001	?
unknown	11/7/2001	?
unknown	11/7/2001	?
Berta Claudia Pizarro Velasco	11/13/2001	20
unknown	11/20/2001	25-30
Francisca Torres Casillas	12/6/2001	80
Natividad Monclova Moreno	12/7/2001	39
María Luisa Carsoli Berumen	12/21/2001	32
Susana Torres Valdivia	12/24/2001	20
Merced Ramirez Morales	1/25/2002	32
María Lopez Torres	1/1/2002	22
Alma Garcia	1/8/2002	30
Hilda Rodriguez Nunez	1/12/2002	28
Lourdes Ivette Lucero Campos	1/19/2002	26
unknown	1/22/2002	40
unknown	1/2002	30
Carmen Estrada Marquez	2/2002	26
Clara Hernandez Martinez	2/28/2002	32
Leticia Caldera Alvidrez	3/7/2002	20
Alicia Cerrera	3/20/002	73
Carolina Carrera	3/20/002	18
Gloria Escalante Rodríguez de Gómez	3/27/2002	73
Miriam Soledad Sáenz Acosta	3/28/2002	14
María Luisa Estrada	4/9/2002	24
Cintia Portillo de González	4/9/2002	24
Rosa Ícela de la Cruz Madrigal	4/13/2002	19
María del Rosario Ríos	2002	40
Petra de la Rosa Viuda de Mesa	2002	55
Irma Valdez Sánchez	2002	35
Zulema Olivia Alvarado Torres	5/21/2002	13
Gloria Betances Rodríguez	5/29/2002	34
Lucila Silva Dávalos	6/3/2002	30

Lawyer for Suspect in Killings in Juárez Slain

Diana Washington Valdez

El Paso Times, February 7, 2002

A Juárez lawyer for one suspect in the slayings of eight women was shot and killed by Chihuahua state police in a high-speed chase Tuesday night [February 5, 2002].

Officials said Wednesday that Mario Escobedo Jr., 29, died from a gunshot wound to the head. He was killed a week after he and his father, Mario Escobedo Sr., were interviewed by ABC's *20/20 Downtown* about women slain in Juárez.

Both Escobedos said they had received death threats for their aggressive defense of Gustavo González Meza, who along with Victor García Uríbe is accused of killing eight women whose bodies were found in November. The lawyers say the men are innocent and were tortured into confessing. Authorities deny that allegation.

The senior Escobedo said his son called him on the cell phone Tuesday night, pleading for help.

"Help me; I'm being followed. They're trying to kill me," the younger man said, according to his father. "The next thing I heard were shots and a loud crash," Escobedo Sr. said. "I was supposed to meet him to arrange for the rest of the bail money for one of our clients."

In separate statements, Chihuahua State Attorney General Jesús "Chito" Solis said Escobedo Jr. was pursued by state police when he tried to pass himself off as Francisco Estrada, a fugitive wanted in the killing of a state policeman. State officials said Escobedo Jr. shot at police and they shot back. In another statement, state Deputy Attorney General José Ortega Aceves said state police mistook Ecobedo Jr. for the fugitive.

Marco A. Moreno, spokesman for Chihuahua state police, said officers "were tipped off that (Estrada) was heading toward this part of the border in a pickup truck that looked like the one Escobedo was driving. He refused to stop when officers asked him to pull over, and then he shot at them. Our officers returned fire."

Escobedo Sr. said his son had a handgun in his truck but never used it. He said it was impossible for him to shoot while driving at a high speed and talking on the cell phone. He said no one knew the pursuers were police until witnesses saw them get out of the Jeep wearing their police logos. His son's pickup had about 15 bullet holes.

Editor's Note: In mid-2002, Chihuahua state Judge María del Carmen Verdugo Bayona ruled that the state policemen accused in the February 5 shooting death of lawyer Mario Escobedo Jr. acted in self-defense.

Juárez Center Fights for Forgotten Women
Advocate Wants Justice for Scores of Slain Females

TESSIE BORDEN

The Arizona Republic, **February 26, 2002**

JUÁREZ, MEXICO—It's 9:30 a.m., and Esther Chavez Cano's daily personal war with the unwanted problems of this largest of the border cities has begun.

She rushes into her office at Casa Amiga, the rape crisis center that grew out of the violence that has claimed the lives of more than 200[1] young women here in the past nine years. Close behind is a staff member describing this morning's emergency: a neighbor found two girls, 8 and 10, wandering in the city's El Chamizal park the previous night. They told the woman they were running away from their father's beatings.

Chavez Cano immediately calls the local district attorney's office, and one gets the feeling she has done this hundreds of times. In a firm but friendly tone, she calls on the attorneys there to take charge of the children and investigate what they say. "The authorities just don't do anything," she whispers while on hold. Chavez Cano's Casa Amiga is the only center of its kind on the Mexican side of the 1,950-mile line that separates the country from the United States. Established in February 1999, it receives funding from both U.S. and Mexican organizations.

Chavez Cano, 66, a diminutive, retired accountant whose mild manner causes listeners to lean in just to hear her, is perhaps the most outspoken and militant voice here on violence against women.

In 1993, she noticed a trend among crimes committed in Juárez: dozens of young women were turning up slain in the surrounding desert. The bodies showed evidence of beatings, rape and strangulation. Many of the women fit a distinct profile: tall and thin, with long, dark hair and medium skin, between ages 11 and 25. Often, they came from the ranks of workers who yearly swell Juárez' population from other parts of rural Mexico to work at border assembly plants, or maquiladoras.

Prodding the police

"They try to pretend these are not serial crimes," Chavez Cano said of the local authorities. "It just brings your rage out. It makes you boil."

---

1 No one know the true numbers of women killed, though it is estimated to be about 320 at the end of 2002.

Esther Chavez, director of Casa Amiga, the only rape crisis center in Mexico along the 1,950 mile border. When asked how the police felt about her work with women at Casa Amiga, she said that the police hated her. Questioned further about whether they simply ignored her, she replied, "The police don't ignore me. No. I would like it if they WOULD ignore me. They have begun a campaign against me, to silence me."

Chavez Cano and others formed the Grupo 8 de Marzo, an awareness group that collected data about the slayings and prodded police to give the murder investigations high priority—often by picketing the police station, holding crosses bearing names of victims.

No one agrees on the exact number of killings that are related.

Chavez Cano says about 230 women have been found in the past nine years, the most recent in November when eight bodies were discovered in a shallow pit. Some slayings have been traced to jealous husbands or drug traffickers. But a large number share characteristics that make investigators believe a serial killer and perhaps copycats are at work.

After raising awareness of the problem to a national level, Chavez Cano decided someone should work to prevent the deaths, rather than just clean up after the murderers.

Help from Elsewhere

With start-up money from the Maryland-based International Trauma Resource Center, the Texas Attorney General's Office and the Mexican Federation of Private Health and Community Development Associations, Chavez Cano opened Casa Amiga near the city center. A paid staff of four and an army of volunteers served 318 clients in Casa Amiga's first year, providing a 24-hour hotline, counseling and group therapy.

A poster in the waiting room at Casa Amiga.

Last year, the center added three staff members and served 5,803 clients, of which 1,172 were new cases.

Chavez Cano now worries about a troubling side issue: child sexual abuse and incest. Fifty-seven of her clients in the first year were raped children. So among her most successful programs is a puppet show that teaches children about "bad" touching and instructs them, in a gentle way, to respect their bodies.

The center takes most of her attention, but Chavez Cano does not let the police off easy when it comes to the slayings of women in the desert. They, in turn, have lashed out at her.

An Attitude of Disdain

Arturo Chavez Rascón, Chihuahua state's former attorney general, came in for some of her sharpest barbs because of his comments implying the victims contributed to their own deaths through their dress or lifestyle. It's an attitude shared by police officers on the beat, who Chavez Cano says discourage families from associating with Casa Amiga. The center used to receive about $3,000 a month from Juárez for rent and salaries, but that stipend has been cut, Cano said. Now, the center relies on money it gets from donations and showings around Mexico of the hit play *The Vagina Monologues.*

Tragedy Close to Home

Recently, the center suffered a blow of a different kind. In December, María Luisa Carsoli Berumen, an abused mother who had become a client and then a staff member at the center, was killed in front of Casa Amiga, witnesses say, by her husband, Ricardo Medina Acosta. The two had had a long and violent history that led to Carsoli Berumen leaving him. A court granted custody of their four children to Medina Acosta. She stayed in town, planning to wait until after the Christmas holidays to resume the custody fight.

On the morning of December 21, the pair argued and struggled outside the center, and she was stabbed twice in the chest as she tried to flee. A black bow at the door expresses the staff's grief. No one has been in arrested in Carsoli Berumen's death.[1]

Fighting for Respect

"The death of María Luisa forces us to work more intensely to instill respect in children, men and women, and to sensitize the authorities to the grave risk for families and all of society that domestic violence represents," Chavez Cano wrote in a column in the local newspaper.

"Rest in peace, María Luisa, and watch over your children so they remain united and sheltered by your loved ones who lament your absence."

---

1 In an interview since this article was published, Esther Chavez Cano stated that the police had arrested Medina Acosta. Despite the fact that he was in jail for murdering his wife, he retains custody of his children.

Women on the Border

compiled by www.womenontheborder.org

Women in Maquiladora Work Wages in Relation to Cost of Living

FOOD	HOURS OF WORK REQUIRED TO PURCHASE
Beans, 1 kg	4 Hrs
Rice, 1 kg	1 hr, 26 min.
Corn Tortillas, 1 kg	40 min.
Chile peppers, 1/8 kg	1 hr, 15 min.
Tomatoes, 1 kg	1 hr, 35 min,
Beef, 1 kg	8 hrs
Chicken	3 hrs
Eggs, 1 doz.	2 hrs, 24 min.
Vegetable Oil, 1 liter	2 hrs, 24 min.
Limes, 1 kg	1 hr, 20 min.
Milk, 1 gal	4 hrs, 17 min.
Toilet paper, 1 roll	43 min.
Detergent, 1 kg	2 hrs
Diapers, box of 30	11 hrs, 30 min
Shampoo, 10 oz	2 hrs, 25 min.
Elem. School uniform	57-86 hrs
Roundtrip bus fare	1-3 hrs
Cooking gas, 1 tank	20 hrs
Aspirin, bottle of 20	2 hrs, 25 min.

Note: Figures based on average prices in Tijuana, B.Calif., for an assembly line worker earning 26 Mexican pesos a day ($3.57). 1kg. is = to U.S. 2.2 lbs.

Sample of U.S. Companies Operating as Maquiladoras in Mexico

Canon Business Machines	Casio Manufacturing	Daewoo
Ertl Company	Fisher Price	JVC
Kendall Healthcare Products	Kyocera	Hasbro
Hitachi Home Electronics	Honeywell, Inc.	Hughes Aircraft
Hyundai	Precision America	International Rectifier
Leviton Manufacturing Co.	Matsushita	Mattel toys
Maxell Corporation Mitsubishi	Electronics Corp.	Nellcor Puritan Bennet
NSK Autolive	Pioneer Speakers	Samsung
Sanyo North America	SMK Electronics	Sony Electronics

- A female worker is never free from the fear of sexual harassment.
- A female worker must submit to mandatory pregnancy tests.
- Spontaneous abortions due to exposure to toxic chemicals are a common reality.

Double Standards

Notes for a Border Screenplay

DEBBIE NATHAN
The Texas Observer, June 6, 1997

Part I: Negative Hallucinations

The case had been settled only minutes ago, and now jurors for *Mendoza v. Contico* were seated in a room outfitted with movie theater chairs and plugs for devices like VCRs. They were in the "Ceremonial Court" in El Paso, where victorious lawyers often hold post-trial press conferences. In any other place, at any other time, what happened next would have been bad *Geraldo.* But here it wasn't—not after the horror that had come out during the past two weeks at trial. "Ladies and gentlemen, some of you may have weak stomachs," lawyer Jim Sherr intoned as reporters poised their pens and tried to look cynical. "If so, close your eyes, or leave the room." He popped a videotape into a TV with an outsized screen.

Mexican police had recorded the tape. It opened with nighttime shots of the desert outside Ciudad Juárez—jumpy, silvery, and spooky, like NASA footage of landings on the moon. Suddenly a wrecked car loomed out of the dark, its chassis blackened by fire and the bodywork torched to bubbles. The muffled soundtrack was policemen's Spanish: monotonous and forensically throwaway until the tape showed the cop's hand prying the trunk open with a screwdriver. Then you could hear the policemen gasping.

Inside the burned-out trunk was plaintiff Mendoza. Lorena Mendoza—and an enlarged portrait propped near the TV showed what she had looked like before she ended up in the car. She'd been 27 years old, petite and wiry, fair-skinned for a Mexican, partial to bright red lipstick, possessed of an insouciant smile and not shy about angling her body to the camera and tossing her hair. That was in life. Now, in the video, a man wearing surgical gloves gingerly lifted a rib-cage from the trunk, and a skull. They were charred and compacted like logs on a cold campfire, and when the man picked them up, chunks of Lorena Mendoza thudded to the ground.

Jurors began weeping. The press looked tearful too, even reporters from local papers and stations whose editors had ignored the two-week trial proceedings, perhaps so as not to ruffle local industries like Contico International, the defendant.

Contico is based in St. Louis, but it is also owner of Continental Sprayers of El Paso, which has as its subsidiary Continental Sprayers de México. The last is in Ciudad Juárez, right across the border from El Paso. Look under your sink at your bottle of window cleaner or in your garage at the bug killer, and there is a good chance that the trigger gizmo you push to dispense the liquid says "Continental Mfg. Co.-Mexico." Sprayers are what the company makes, and they do it in Juárez because the wages there are $24 a week for 48 hours of work.[1]

Up and down the border, more than 2,500 mostly American-owned manufacturers have been taking advantage of similar low wages for a generation. The companies are called maquiladoras; in the United States lately much has been written about their effects on the economy and workers of this country. Less has been said about how they affect standards of living in Mexico, and still less about how that country's 800,000 maquiladora laborers are impacted by working conditions and safety standards—which are often inferior to those in U.S. factories owned by the same companies.

While the $24 weekly wage is technically no secret, Americans confronted with the figure often react with what psychologists call a "negative hallucination"—they blot it from consciousness, or mentally reconfigure it to $24 *a day*. Safety conditions are even more deeply occluded in the U.S. mind. On the border, one constantly hears accounts from poor Mexicans about relatives and friends injured and killed in maquiladoras. But the stories virtually never make the U.S. media, or the Mexican press—in part because negligence suits in Mexico are practically unheard of, and when they are filed, plaintiffs seldom prevail. Meanwhile, international labor rights activists have a hard time monitoring maquiladora safety conditions because plant managers are notoriously unwilling to open their plants to careful inspection.

On the few occasions they have, gringos like Martha Mimms have spotted egregious double standards. Mimms is a glass worker at a Ford Motor Company plant in Nashville that makes automobile windshields and windows. In 1994, while on a transborder worker solidarity tour with the Tennessee Industrial Renewal Network, she visited Autovidrios, a Ford maquiladora in Juárez that manufactures the same products that her Nashville plant does, and at the time even employed American supervisors who once had given orders at Mimms' workplace. At Autovidrios, Mimms saw conditions that are thoroughly outlawed in U.S. factories: conveyor belts with no guard pieces; tables, where workers were eating snacks and lunch, covered with toxic lead paint waste; workers laboring next to robots slinging sharp glass and which, in U.S. factories, are always separated from humans with bars and gates. Autovidrios is the same factory in which—four years before Mimms' visit—a 16-year-old worker named Julio César Macías died after getting caught in a dangerous conveyor belt. In Nashville, the type of area he was assigned to is deemed so risky that two workers must be present at all times to monitor each other. Julio was by himself at the Autovidrios conveyor belt when he was crushed to death.

---

1 In 1997, when this article was written, the weekly minimum wage for maquila workers in Juarez was $24, but back when Lorena Mendoza was alive in 1990, it was $35. The weekly wage in 2002 is close to $20 a week. Weekly maquila wages fluctuate constantly, increasing or decreasing, partly because of the peso's devaluation or inflation.

The fate of Lorena Mendoza—the protagonist of *Mendoza v. Contico*—was even worse. As a bookkeeper for Continental Sprayers de México, she was charged with transporting cash wages for 70 workers down an 80-mile, two-lane highway to Palomas, an abject border pueblo where the company had opened yet another plant. The route is desolate and infamous for drug trafficking and vehicle hijackings. In its U.S. operations, Contico uses Brinks trucks to transport payroll. Such services are readily available in Mexico. Yet Lorena Mendoza and other bookkeepers and unarmed security guards carried money from Juárez to Palomas in a private car every other Friday, always at the same hour. Under such circumstances, Mendoza's survivors and their attorneys said, it was a foregone conclusion that eventually she would be attacked.

Her death, the lawyers said, was an American company's fault, and therefore the company should be subject to U.S. tort laws. The principle might sound elementary, but when El Paso Judge Jack Ferguson ruled three years ago that Mendoza's family could have its day in a Texas court, he helped set a national and international precedent. Since 1993, when the Legislature closed the door on foreign plaintiffs after a group of Costa Rican farmworkers sued a Texas chemical company whose product had rendered them sterile, it has been extremely rare for foreign plaintiffs to be allowed standing in Texas courts. When the case against Contico opened in El Paso in late March of 1997, it was the first time a maquiladora had ever been put on trial in America for negligence in Mexico. That made it the first time that the day-to-day details of maquiladora exploitation were described in sworn, on-the-record testimony that anyone could hear, simply by going down to the courthouse and walking past the shoeshine boys.

"The maquiladoras, or maquilas for short, attracted large numbers of jobless people to cities that did not have the house or infrastructure to support them. This situation was especially true in Nogales where an estimated 80 percent of the workers were new arrivals. Between the early 1980s and the mid-1990s, the population of Nogales, Sonora, tripled to some 350,000—at least fifteen times the population of Nogales, Arizona, which remained steady at about 20,000. More than half the entire workforce of Nogales, Sonora, toiled in the factories, a higher percentage than in any other city on the border. Most of those coming to work were teenagers and young adults from southern Sonora and the nearby state of Sinaloa. They found that though maquiladora jobs were plentiful, salaries were so low—about $35 to $45 for a 48-hour week—and costs so high that they could not afford to pay rent or utilities. They lived, for the most part, as squatters in shacks constructed from tin, wood pallets, plastic sheets, and cardboard boxes salvaged from the factories and the dump. Few had indoor plumbing; some had no water or electricity. Crime, disease, and family breakdown were rampant in the squatters' camps. But it was a reflection of the depth of the poverty in Mexico that most of these workers felt they were better off in Nogales that they were in their hometowns."

From *Lives on the Line,
Dispatches from the U.S.-Mexico Border*
by Miriam Davidson

Moving Pictures

But there were few spectators at the two-week proceedings, and except for the *El Paso Herald-Post*,[2] the media hardly appeared either (the national press stayed away entirely). Cross-border labor rights activists nonetheless assumed the case would generate a published record. They figured that whoever lost would appeal, and an appeal means that tape-recorded trial proceedings are sent to higher court judges in the form of transcripts that the public can also read. But there will be no transcripts, because a verdict was never reached. As the case was wrapping up, an 11th-hour, out-of-court settlement left the Lorena Mendoza family with $1.75 million, and the jurors at a press conference video horror show. The settlement occurred on April 4, 1997. Since then, the Mendoza family's lead attorney, Jim Scherr, has been talking with Hollywood agents about turning the case into a Steven Spielberg script.

Indeed, *Mendoza v. Contico* is movie material. That's my opinion after attending the entire trial. I'm not one to write screenplays, but for anyone who wants to take a stab at it, here are my *Cliffs Notes*. (With the exception of the preliminary background scenes, which are my observations after living several years in El Paso, all facts and quotations come from trial testimony and police records.)

Exposition, Scene One: Interstate-10 traveling east, into El Paso. A double image. Just off to your left, the local campus of the University of Texas: substantial, sun-drenched and sparkling. To your right, a vast, dust-ridden maw of cinderblock warrens and cardboard shacks. This is the northwest side of Ciudad Juárez, Chihuahua, Mexico, and the only part of Mexico plainly visible to El Pasoans. To make sure we all understand that this immense slum is not America and thus not our problem, an I-10 highway sign says "International Boundary 1/4 mile"—despite the fact that there is no exit anywhere nearby. Nor is there cultural entrance into this world of Mexico's working poor. Virtually all El Pasoans who venture to Juárez confine themselves to tightly-limned tourist areas, and most El Pasoans never go to Juárez at all. Neither does the press. It is as though, for Americans, the city and its people are negative hallucinations.

EXPOSITION, SCENE TWO: *Another double image. Julio's, a Juárez restaurant that American maquiladora executives favor for lunch.*[3] Mexicans go there as well, and there are two menus, one in English and the other in Spanish. A meal in English goes heavy on avocado and squash blossoms, the desserts have eggs and cream, and the cost is about $5. A Spanish meal costs $3 and consists of mushy pasta and dessert with a cornstarch base. The maquiladora executives always receive the English menu. They don't know the Spanish one exists.

---

2 The *El Paso Herald-Post,* one of two daily papers in El Paso, is no longer in business.
3 Julio's is no longer open in Juárez.

SCENE ONE: *The Gateway Arch in St. Louis; cut to a circa 1980s corporate office.*
Inside we see Lester Miller, a businessman who would also have fit precisely into the previous restaurant scene. Miller is the owner of Contico International, maker of trigger sprayers, of plastic boxes with dozens of little compartments for filing nuts and bolts, and other honest, everyday products you can buy at Wal-Mart and Home Depot. Fiftyish and heavily tanned from vacations on his yacht, Miller speaks brusquely and confidently, with a Big Apple outer-borough accent. He is on a long distance call to El Paso.

At the other end is Victor Gándara, manager of Continental Sprayers of El Paso and Continental Sprayers de México. An electrical engineer and Juárez native, Gándara is pushing forty, olive-skinned, moustachioed and natty in an elegant gray suit. He's been working so long for Miller that he is fluent in English corporate idioms like "It's a team effort, sir." But when he says "manager" it comes out "*manayer,*" and his "guys" still rhymes with "lice." We hear Miller telling Gándara that the Mexico plant needs to increase its production of trigger sprayers.

That will be difficult, Gándara says, because there's a labor shortage in Juárez. His personnel people have advertised in the papers. They've posted signs at the bus station where destitute newcomers arrive daily from Mexico's interior. They've roamed the ramshackle colonias with sound trucks and bullhorns, yelling, "¡Trabajos! ¡Trabajos!" They've even thought of putting a factory in virgin maquiladora territory: outlying farm towns where, if workers were to develop beefs about wages or working conditions, they couldn't hopscotch to other companies, like they do in Juárez' big industrial parks. But no one has answered the ads or the bullhorns. And the farm towns look too sullen, too graffiti-stricken—in short, too close to the labor problems of the city.

What to do? How about increasing the $35 a week wages a few dollars?[4] But that is impossible. Not only would it temporarily erode Contico's competitiveness, it would also start a bidding war for workers and disrupt the wage structure of the entire maquiladora sector, not to mention Mexican industrial relations in general. What to do?

SCENE TWO: *Main Street, Palomas, Chihuahua.*
A town of 12,000 inhabitants that lies just across the international line from Columbus, New Mexico, a miniscule burg whose one claim to fame is that Pancho Villa burned it down during the Mexican Revolution. On the south side of the boundary, Palomas is your stereotypically sun-bleached, enervated and beat-to-shit border dump. Not even the main street is paved, so the townspeople's cars are universally covered with dust. A handful of Americans in bermuda shorts wanders near the international bridge, but tourism here is so half-hearted that the liquor stores don't even stock Kahlua. Yet, the main drag has a surprising number of fleabag hotels. They make you wonder why so many people would come here from far away, and what their business could be.

---

4 In 1990, the minimum wage was $35 a week.

SCENE THREE: *Exterior, outskirts of Palomas.*

Victor Gándara and a gaggle of Continental Sprayers de México staff—personnel managers and bookkeepers in sports pants and nice dresses and bright makeup—enter Palomas from the two-lane highway leading to town. Their dust-free car makes them stick out like sore thumbs. They stick out even more when they pull out the bullhorn and boom about jobs. They do this because they have already reconnoitered Palomas and decided that it's a good town for their new plant. Gándara has found a site for the factory, a brand new building originally intended to house a supermarket, but which he has now rehabbed for assembly lines. The landlord of this new maquiladora is a man named Fabián Sándoval. Besides the new Continental Sprayers building, Sándoval owns a hardware store. He is well-known about town as a property owner and rancher. He is also, according to allegations in court-room testimony, well-known as a drug dealer.

Soon the sprayer maquiladora is up and running, with a work force of about 70 line operators. All are younger than 20 years old, and—even though the minimum work age in Mexico is 16—several are 15 and at least one is 14. In U.S. dollars, they make $32 a week. That is 10 percent less than what Continental's Juárez employees earn, but Mexico is divided into federal minimum-wage zones, and the Palomas zone pays less than Juárez. The workers can't do much about the inequity. Unions are almost unheard of in either place, and of the few that do exist, virtually all work hand-in-glove with the companies. In Juárez, workers "bargain" with bosses by quitting, and looking for something better at another of the city's hundreds of plants. But in Palomas, there is only one maquiladora besides Continental Sprayers. Hardly a seller's market for labor, and that is how Continental Sprayers wants it. Everything seems under control.

There is, of course, the matter of the payroll. Maquiladora workers earn so little money that hardly any have checking accounts, so they customarily receive their bimonthly pay in cash. For Contico, the question is: how to turn dollars from St. Louis to pesos in Palomas?

Theoretically, the company has two options that would follow its practice in both Juárez and in St. Louis. The first is for Contico to wire the money from a bank in St. Louis to one in Palomas—where the biggest bank is Bancomer, Mexico's version of Citibank. Throughout Mexico, Bancomer branches provide payroll services to business customers, meaning that bank personnel will put each worker's pay into a separate envelope and even deliver and distribute it, under armed guard. The second option is for St. Louis to send the money to Juárez, then forward it to Palomas in an armored Brinks-style truck.

There is also a third option, one completely outside the bounds of U.S. business practice: to drive the money from Juárez to Palomas in a private, unarmed car. This is the method many Mexican companies use. It is the one authorized by plant manager Victor Gándara, and it is employed for seventy weeks, from the time the Palomas maquila opens until the day Mendoza is murdered. Why is the payroll handled in Mexican and not American style? That question will be the legal crux of *Mendoza v. Contico*. It will not be addressed until we come to trial.

Executive award ceremony in Juárez, Mexico.

SCENE FOUR: *Interior—a small apartment in Juárez.*
The tenant is Lorena Mendoza, with her red lipstick, her smile, her 27 years. San Juana, one of Lorena's many older sisters, is with her. They are laughing as they reminisce about the last job Lorena had before she worked for Continental Sprayers de México as an accountant for a local TV station. One time back then, San Juana called Lorena and invited her to the movies after work. When San Juana got to the TV station, it was already after hours but Lorena was completely absorbed in the company books, trying to find the reason for a 20-peso shortage in the balance. At the time, it took 3,000 pesos to make a U.S. dollar. San Juana thought Lorena was crazy. "Come on," she said, "I'll just give you the 20 pesos so we can get out of here." Lorena refused, and worked for several more hours until she reconciled the twenty pesos. She missed the movie.

She is always like that: extraordinarily hardworking, punctilious and loyal. As a Continental Sprayers accountant, she now makes $166 (U.S.) a week. She is proud to be associated with an American company. Her biggest ambitions in life are to learn English, open an accounting business in the United States and take her niece to Disneyland.

SCENE FIVE: *Palomas Highway.*

Lorena, in a shiny rental car with a Continental Sprayers security guard, a young man named Montes. They are driving the $2,000 payroll to Palomas, and the road is mostly devoid of civilization. Miles pass without highway signs, gas stations, restaurants or other cars. There is only cactus, dust—and hidden under the car seat, the cash payroll for seventy workers. It's a relief to finally arrive in Palomas and distribute the money.

Afterwards, Montes and a plant supervisor cross the street to Fabián Sándoval's hardware store to cash a check. They have hardly entered when they are seized by several men brandishing machine guns, rifles and pistols. Two more arrive, wearing black and yellow T-shirts with the initials of the Mexican Federal Police. "You assholes!" says one of the first group. "Take off the T-shirts, because the whole town knows we're here by now." The armed men are waiting for Sándoval, Continental Sprayers' landlord—the reputed drug dealer. The two Continental employees are not sure whether the federal police are here to intercept Sándoval in a narcotics deal or to transact one with him. But they know they have interrupted something, and hours go by while the two men are held prisoner. Finally, with no explanation, the men are released. Montes returns to the plant, picks up Lorena and they drive back to Juárez. In a statement after her death, Montes will recall that she was nervous about what had happened, and said she didn't want to take the payroll to Palomas anymore. Yet she continued to do so, because she was a good worker and very loyal.

SCENE SIX: *Interior, Continental Sprayers factory, Palomas.*

More ominous, creepy chaos at the Palomas maquiladora. Not long after the hardware store incident, on a hot summer day in July, almost half the workers stage a wildcat strike by walking off the line, gathering in the cafeteria, and demanding an $11.66 bonus per week, in U.S. dollars, if they achieve perfect attendance. The bonus would raise their wages to about $44 for 45 hours of work. Management refuses to negotiate and summarily fires all the strikers. Among the workers in the factory and in the town, there is bitterness towards Continental Sprayers.

One worker not involved in the strike is Dario Figueroa, a 23-year-old ne'er-do-well and leader of a gang of ranch robbers and car thieves who operate in both Mexico and New Mexico. Figueroa and his cronies live near Palomas, and shortly before the strike, he applied for a job at Continental Sprayers. He was hired, no questions asked, and for three days he assembled trigger sprayers. We see him on his last day of work—a payday. Figueroa watches how the shiny car comes into Palomas and the envelopes of money come out. Then he quits.

In St. Louis, the Contico executives remain blissfully unaware of the hardware store, the wildcat strike, or Dario Figueroa's interest in the company's payroll habits.

SCENE SEVEN: *Exterior, Palomas Highway, near Palomas.*

August 3, 1990, a few days after Figueroa has quit his job at Continental. Lorena Mendoza and Continental Sprayers de México security guard Alfonso Jurado are making the Friday payroll run. It is late morning. They are driving a bright blue 1988 Celebrity and they have almost arrived in Palomas. But they never make it, because at a turnoff not far from town, the road is blocked by a white Buick Regal and a black Trans Am. Dario Figueroa's gang commandeers the Continental Sprayers car and drives Mendoza and Jurado to a desolate site off the main road. One of the gang members is a 19-year-old nicknamed "El Tibis." He sports a .38 Super, has been smoking marijuana and decides he wants to rape Mendoza. Jurado tries to interfere. The two scuffle, and El Tibis shoots Jurado in the chest. Mendoza starts to scream and El Tibis pistol-whips her in the head. Then the gang members stuff her and Jurado into the trunk of the Celebrity and drive them to a dump. On arriving, El Tibis waves around some soft drink cans filled with gasoline. Stoned, he dances about the car and pours the fuel all over it. Someone lights a match. The rest is in the police video, filmed two days later when authorities find the car with Mendoza and coworker Jurado—both of them lumps of charcoal.

Maquiladora Labor Costs in Mexico Average Hourly Wages (U.S. Dollars)

Year	Director Technicians Administrative Labor	Direct Labor
1990	$1.78	$1.25
1991	$2.05	$1.44
1992	$2.31	$1.81
1993	$2.52	$1.78
1994	$2.54	$1.80
1995	$1.69	$1.18
1996	$1.78	$1.21
1997	$1.98	$1.33
1998	$1.93	$1.32

From "Snapshot of the Emerging Border Economy," the U.S. Labor Dept.; Mexican National Institute of Statistics, Geography, and Informatics; Renezenteno: Quadral Group; BW Estimates.
http://www.corpwatch.org/

Part II: Cultural Differences

SCENE ONE: *Interior, El Paso County Court of Law.*

Six-and-a-half years later. It is March 1997, and *Mendoza v. Contico* is about to open in the El Paso County Court of Law No. 3. Lorena's mother and father, Elia and Lorenzo Mendoza, huddle at the plaintiff's table with a translator. Both are shrunken, gray-haired and dressed in the clean but dated clothes of the elderly Mexican poor. They look spent, and for good reason.

Shortly after Lorena's death in 1990, the Mendozas went looking for a U.S. lawyer to sue Contico. They searched throughout El Paso and the rest of the country but could not find anyone willing to take the case. It's hopeless, they were told over and over: U.S. law doesn't apply, and even if that were to change, it's impossible to subpoena witnesses from Mexico. Your case could never be proved.

The Mendozas look bent and meek, but in reality they are ferociously single-minded. For two years they persisted in their search, and finally found El Paso personal injury lawyers Jim Sherr and Sam Legate. Scherr is a bantam-sized man with longish hair and wire-rim glasses. His family has been on the border since his Jewish grandfather immigrated to the Rio Grande to farm cotton and run a store. Scherr is also ferociously single-minded. At age 24, he ran for El Paso City Council and ended up serving three terms. At age 22, he was the youngest lawyer in Texas. Before that, he was a self-described highschool hell-raiser, particularly when he helped organize legal challenges to rules against long hair. Scherr's partner Legate hails from Presidio, where he was a sometime lawyer, sometime schoolteacher, and sometime dropout who left everything behind to hang out in Guatemala and study Spanish.

When they met the Mendozas in 1992 and heard what had happened to their daughter, Scherr and Legate were infuriated at what they call the maquiladora industry's double standard for American and Mexican workers. They vowed to explore international tort law and figure out a way to take Contico to court. In 1994, they recruited international law expert Russell Weintraub of the University of Texas to testify that U.S. law should apply in the Mendoza case and in that of Alfonso Jurado, the dead security guard (the Mendozas also convinced Jurado's wife to file her suit). The judge who heard the arguments agreed. But three more years went by as Contico's lawyers bargained with Jurado's wife—who had small children and overdue house payments—and eventually settled with her for $500,000. Contico also spent that time working to get Scherr taken off the Mendoza case. He stayed on, and now, just before Easter of 1997, Scherr and Legate are starting the jury selection process.

SCENE TWO: *Interior, El Paso Courtroom, jury selection.*
Seventy people are led in by a bailiff. They are the salt of El Paso's earth, maybe a fourth Anglo or black, but the rest various shades and surnames of what people around here call "Hispanic." Legate starts by asking how many have ever lived outside El Paso. Hardly any raise their hands. He then inquires about whether any think that Mexicans "love their children any less" than Americans, or "hurt any less when something bad happens to them." No one moves a muscle. Legate then excoriates maquiladoras: "They want cheap labor," he says. "Thirty dollars a week as opposed to $40 a day." Scherr, however, is quick to stress that the search for cheap wages is simply "business, ladies and gentlemen." Companies "are entitled to make a profit," he adds, "and we're not here to contest that decision." After all, this is the border, and Scherr's family has been on it for generations. With those generations come practical and material ties to prominent people on both sides of the international line. People in business, in politics, on charity boards and cultural committees. People—and some of them have kin working in Scherr's office—who own maquiladoras or maquiladora stock, or who make a living doing paperwork and hiring labor for companies deep in America who want to come south and make money.

Contico's lead attorney, John McChristian—a thin man with a big moustache and fine, tapered hands—has also lived in El Paso long enough to know about these prominent people. And though none is on the prospective panel, he wants what they say and think to be heard and believed by the people the bailiff brings in. When Contico puts on its case, he tells the would-be jurors, "You're going to have an opportunity to become acquainted with the maquiladora industry." It is a wonderful industry, McChristian says, because while Mexico is "still the Third World," maquiladoras are "bringing people into the 20th century." The proof? Plants have air-conditioning, lunchrooms, and nurses' stations "as nice as any place in the United States."

Furthermore, McChristian points out, *Mendoza v. Contico* is not about double standards. Yes, Continental Sprayers de México transported its payroll differently from how it's done in El Paso or St. Louis. But that's because Mexican managers in Mexico—and not Americans in America—did things the Mexican way, and we must respect "Mexican culture." Besides, how were the Mexican managers to know that carrying money in an unarmed vehicle was dangerous? Until August 3, 1990, no payroll delivery people had ever been robbed or burned to death on the Palomas highway. And who can say that money was really the motive for Lorena Mendoza's death? After all, if there were five gang members robbing $2,000, that's only $400 apiece, and who in their right mind would murder for $400? Not to mention the fact that lots of melted coins were found in the burned-out car. So, if it wasn't money, what *was* the motive? There was none, McChristian implies. The murderers were random psychopaths—or, as he puts it, "savage monsters in Mexico." Like earthquakes, these deadly fiends are natural, unpredictable and not something Contico could have foreseen.

That, in sum, is Contico's defense. But as the trial progresses, the jury buys it less and less. Some arguments are easily dispensed with. Take the melted coins. By the time McChristian mentions them, the jury has already heard so much about worthless Mexican wages and money that they understand immediately when attorney Scherr points out that in Mexico in 1990—when it took 3,000 pesos to buy a dollar—carrying off coins was about as profitable as carrying off mud. As for people not bothering to murder for $400, after they realize that this sum represents several months' wages to a Mexican, the jury is ready to think anything.

The crazy psychopath argument also dies after Scherr and Legate bring to the witness stand the former head of the CIA in Mexico City. He is Morton "Pete" Palmer, and currently he runs a security firm that advises multinational companies south of the border on how to prevent robberies and protect their executives from kidnapping. Palmer has an old cop's bulldog face, a spook's steely unflappability and a trove of information about crime in Mexico. Bank and payroll robberies are common there, he says, even for small amounts of money. And though vehicle hijackings in Mexico tend to be nonviolent compared to the United States, the whole situation changes when the perpetrators are high on drugs—or when a female is involved. In fact, to hear Palmer tell it, the stupidest and most dangerous thing Contico could possibly have done was follow the Mexican practice of sending their money in a private car—and with a young, attractive woman to boot. Given these habits, he testifies, something horrible was bound to befall Lorena Mendoza. Contico, he concludes, was grossly negligent.

Finally, there is the defense's "cultural differences" card—which turns out to be an object lesson in the extent to which U.S. companies doing business in repressive, corrupt states often decide, "When in Rome, do as the Romans do."

The preface to this lesson is the question of whether Continental Sprayers de México was really *de* México—as Contico would have the jury believe—or merely *en* México. Nominally, maquiladoras are Mexican corporations. But as the Mendoza attorneys demonstrate, it's quite possible for a plant to be wholly owned by Americans, as long as at least five own stock. In Contico's case, the five-owner requirement was a problem, because the American company's stock is all held by one man, the Big-Apple-voiced Lester Miller. Contico's solution was to have Miller buy about a quarter of the Continental de México shares and farm out the remainder to various Contico executives. Some didn't really own stock, however, except in name. None made corporate decisions for the Mexican plants or even bothered visiting them except for an hour or two on tourist junkets. Nor did Miller take any interest in the day-to-day operations of his maquiladoras. Instead, he delegated all management tasks to Victor Gándara, the nattily-suited man who spoke business English yet was a Mexican.

Even so, Gándara's office in 1990 was not in Juárez or Palomas, but at the Continental Sprayers plant in El Paso—which again puts the onus for Lorena Mendoza's death on an American company. So Contico's lawyers try to convince the jury that Gándara didn't really call the shots in Juárez and Palomas. Instead, the attorneys say, it was his Mexican underlings who decided things like how to transport money. As witnesses, they call a series of anxious-looking women—Continental Sprayers de México's personnel people, accountants and other management types. One by one the women testify that they made all the company's decisions and only later sought approval from Ingeniero Gándara, who rubber-stamped their wishes.

But this is now, and then was something else. The Mendoza family's attorneys produce reams of depositions from months and years past, in which the same women state that it was not they but Gándara who decided things like whether to use a rental car or a Brinks truck. The implication—that the Mexican employees have been cowed into changing their

Within the U.S., the domestic impact of globalization has led to economic, social and environmental changes that mirror international patterns. Median hourly wages have steadily fallen as the economy has become more "globalized," and domestic policies focus on reducing social and environmental protections for the most vulnerable—while creating conditions ripe for corporations to consolidate their power. The disparity between those at the top of the economic strata and those at the bottom is increasing exponentially—in 1999, it was estimated that 84.6% of the nation's wealth was held in the hands of the top 20% of the U.S. population. Meanwhile, the bottom 20% held just 0.5% of the wealth.

(taken from the National Network for Immigration and Refugee Rights' Bridge Curriculum) testimony—is bolstered when ex-CIA agent Palmer tells the court that in Mexican companies, "The head man has incredible power, much more than presidents of companies do here…decision making doesn't flow down." It is bolstered again when one woman leaves the stand after testifying and is approached by Gándara, who opens his wallet and pulls out a bill. "That's okay," a Contico lawyer interjects. "*I'll* give her money for a phone call." For the jury, the damage is done.

So if it was Gándara who sent his staff to Palomas with the payroll instead of hiring a Brinks truck, why did he do it? His first excuse is that armored trucks didn't make the trip. His second is that the Palomas bank didn't do payrolls. Both claims are belied by a former bank manager and a former armored car company supervisor who tell the jury their companies would have been glad to do the work.

So why, then? Surely not to save money. Gándara himself testifies that it costs $55 a day to rent a car in Juárez, not including wages for the two employees who made the trip. The total: some $90, compared to an armored-car-service fee of $60. Why waste the money? Ex-CIA agent Palmer has suggested one possibility: that this is how it's usually done by Mexican companies. A related and more insidious reason emerges when Mendoza attorneys hold up car rental receipts provided by Continental Sprayers. One is for more than a million pesos—the U.S. equivalent of $500—for one day's rental. Another is for yet more money. "Could it be…?" the Mendoza lawyers ask, and though Contico's attorneys jump to object, the implication is that Gándara had a deal going with the rental car company to pad Contico's bill and split the proceeds.

This implication, with its pesos and dollars and whispers of sleaze, is a cheap souvenir from the culture of business in Mexico: a culture based on grotesque inequality between owners and laborers, on exploitation, intimidation, corruption, and on endemic larceny, from petit to grand. An American company that "respects" this culture—as Contico's lawyers put it—partakes of things far more sinister than Maríachi music and homemade corn tortillas. This fact is not lost on the jury, especially when the Mendoza lawyers mention the Mexican police investigator who found the car-thief gang and got one member to confess that his friends torched Mendoza and her coworker. The man has since retracted his statement, and the rest of the gang has disappeared into Mexico's interior. Meanwhile, the Mexican police investigator is no longer a police investigator. Now he is working for Contico as a consultant. This means that the official who knows most about what happened to Lorena Mendoza cannot be subpoenaed to testify regarding anything he has learned since he took his new "job."

What We're Not Talking About

After days of such testimony, anti-Contico sentiment is starting to show on the jury's faces. It gets more intense when Mendoza family members take the stand. A sister, San Juana (who once invited Lorena to the movies), is a doctor, and she sends shivers through the courtroom as she talks of visiting the morgue—she wanted to examine the body to prove it wasn't really Lorena's. On arriving, she was petrified to find that there was no body, only a plastic bag of bones and ashes, from which she extracted a womb, an ovary, and some molars whose fillings she ascertained were her sister's. Afterwards she closed the bag, returned home and assured her mother that yes, she combed Lorena's hair, and yes, bought a lovely dress to bury her in.

The mother is sworn in, downcast, and her old husband, half deaf, with a hearing aid like a wad of bubble gum in his ear. After seven years, both clearly are still in mourning for their youngest daughter's cheery disposition, her beauty, her dreams of life in the United States; and they stolidly describe how they haven't eaten right since she died, or slept or been able to maintain normal blood pressure. When they finish, the jury glares at everybody and everything related to Contico. The panel's growing animus is obvious to the company's lawyers, and just before closing arguments, they offer the Mendozas $1.75 million to settle out of court. The family's lawyers approve the deal, because although the jury will later tell the judge that they unanimously wanted to convict Contico and award the Mendozas up to $27 million, Contico has vowed to appeal. The Mendoza attorneys know the higher Texas courts have turned markedly pro-business since the early 1990s. Not only would they probably overturn an anti-Contico verdict, they would also nullify local Judge Ferguson's 1994 ruling allowing a Texas company's wrongdoing in Mexico to be tried in this state. If they were to make that ruling, no international cases like *Mendoza v. Contico* would ever get into court in Texas.

So the Mendozas take Contico's offer, along with the company's promise to build a statue of Lorena in Juárez dedicated to employee safety and to establish a maquiladora worker scholarship fund in her name. Then everyone troops to Ceremonial Court for the press conference and its chilling videotape. Lawyer Scherr tells the jurors to teach their friends and family the lesson of *Mendoza v. Contico*: that when it comes to workers' safety, double standards between the United States and Mexico are intolerable.

"Of course, we're not talking about wages," Scherr repeats, which is ironic given the post-trial comments of jurors. Donna Ricci is one; she is middle-aged and a longtime El Pasoan. Yet, Ricci tells me, until she sat through *Mendoza v. Contico,* she had no idea how meager maquiladora pay is (and the figures used at trial were from seven years ago: since the 1994 peso devaluation, they're down from $35 to $25 per week). Twenty-year-old Vanessa Rodarte has lived here all her life but until the trial she had never heard of maquiladoras— period—much less what they pay. When she and the other jurors went out for lunch, Rodarte says, they would talk about "how we were getting paid $6 a day for jury duty—a total joke—and we'd go to a restaurant and blow it all on a meal, and maquiladora workers don't make $6 in a whole day!"

Wages *are* what *Mendoza v. Contico* was about. These days it hardly takes Karl Marx to understand that the global stampede for bargain-basement Third World labor is what leads to discounted safety standards and the kind of fire-sale ethics that put Lorena Mendoza on a highway to her death. Susan Mika, the San Antonio-based coordinator of Coalition for Justice in the Maquiladoras, refuses to concede the question of wages, as she makes a short but eloquent speech at the Ceremonial Court press conference. When she finishes, the audience breaks into applause.

Mika has just spent the past two weeks in court, furiously typing testimony into a laptop. Now she prepares to leave the border with her hard drive, but—because the case was settled—without the official transcripts she'd hoped to distribute to the world. The Mendozas return to Juárez and are immediately terrorized by unknown men who torch a family car. On the front seat they leave a burned coin, apparently part of the evidence collected seven years ago when Lorena's body was retrieved. The family goes to the Juárez police station for help. When they arrive, they see the same men who'd burned the car—walking around the office as though they worked there. Afraid for their lives, the Mendozas petition the U.S. government for refugee status.

It remains to be seen whether they will win asylum,[5] and if they do, whether they will ever see a statue of their daughter in Juárez. As for their case, perhaps it will go down as a footnote to later trials that raise the same issues of maquiladora double standards, but succeed in producing a verdict and a written record.

For now, *Mendoza v. Contico* is nothing more than potential: notes for a screenplay; a sheaf of grim scenes; glimmerings of worker consciousness; a primer on maquiladoras for norteamericanos. Modest hope for the future.

---

5 The Mendoza family, reached through a family friend, declined to update the editors of *Puro Border* on the outcome of their asylum petition because of fears for their personal safety.

U.S.-Mexico Border Economics

compiled by George Kourous, Interhemispheric Resource Center (www.irc-online.org)

Number of maquiladoras located in Mexico in 1965: 12

By January 1993, one year before NAFTA took effect: 2,078
As of January 2000: 4000+

Percentage of maquiladoras located in Mexico's border zone: 80%

Percent of U.S. border population living below poverty level: 33%

Percent of total U.S. population living below poverty level: 12%

Percent of households in Tijuana living below poverty level: 50%

Percent of Tijuana's households whose income depends on maquiladora employment: 42%

Percent of maquiladora workers interviewed for a 1997 American Journal of
Industrial Medicine article who reported exposure to toxic dusts and vapors: 44%

Percentage of workers interviewed for a similar 1996 study by a union organization
in Tijuana who reported chronic upper airway irritation: 58%

Percent who reported chronic sore throats: 57%

Percent reporting skin rashes: 62%

Estimated annual health costs resulting from air pollution in the
binational border zone: $1 billion

Metric tons of hazardous waste shipped from Mexico to the United States in 1997,
according to Mexican government figures: 5,943

Tons shipped from the United States to Mexico: 230,417

Current number hazardous waste disposal facilities in Mexico: 1

Cost of meeting water, wastewater, and solid waste needs in the border zone
for 1994-2003, according to Sierra Club: $7.02 billion

For 2000 alone, according to the U.S. General Accounting office: $3.25 billion

For 2000-2005 period, according to the NAFTA-created North American
Development Bank: $1.913 billion

Number of commercial trucks that crossed the border in 1999: 4.2 million

Number of trucks crossing just at the border's busiest port of entry on the border,
Laredo, Texas, during 1999: 2.2 million

Percent of roads in Nogales, Sonora, that are unpaved: 90%
In Agua Prieta: 85%   In Cd. Juárez: 55%

Estimated cost of paving just 42 miles of Cd. Juárez roads,
according to city planners: $295 million

Total Cd. Juárez municipal budget, 2001: $150 million

Percent of that budget spent on public works: 33%

Rasquachismo

*To be rasquache is to posit a bawdy, spunky consciousness,
to seek to subvert and turn ruling paradigms upside down.
It is a witty, irreverent and impertinent posture that
recodes and moves outside established boundaries . . .
It is a way of putting yourself together or creating
an environment replete with color, texture and pattern;
a rampant decorative sense whose basic axiom
might be "too much is not enough."*
— Tomás Ybarra-Frausto

Ropa Usada

Cecilia Ballí

She met him up in the clouds, on their way to Houston. Shuffling up the aisle in a gray fedora, the old white man with ruddy cheeks and tiny pearly teeth took the seat beside her.

He wanted to know where she was going. In her broken English, she replied: "I go to California for the graduación de my daughter from Stanford University." It was Spring 1998, and with frequent flyer miles I'd chalked up on trips home, my mother was flying to my college graduation.

Her answer impressed the old man. Stanford, he said, is a very good school. But she has never needed much encouragement when it comes to bragging about her daughters, so she went on: Just last month, she said, she had flown to New York because her other daughter had graduated from Cornell, the one who had studied industrial relations and labor law. She mentioned, too, that I wanted to be a journalist, and that at one time I had written for *The Brownsville Herald* and been an intern at the *Los Angeles Times*.

The *Los Angeles Times*? His pink face lit up. The *Los Angeles Times* once wrote a story about him and the ropa usada stores he owned in Brownsville, he said proudly.

My mother stared at the old man's face, her forehead beginning to crumple with surprise. It would be too much of a coincidence, but then again…"You *Jonson*?!"

He flashed her that broad, delighted smile he gets when people recognize him. "I'm Jim Johnson."

For more than a decade, Jim Johnson had been a brand name in my family. Back in the '80s, a whole crew of Hinojosas worked inside the dilapidated warehouse he owned in Brownsville, where hundreds of pounds of used clothing were shipped in from throughout the country, sorted into high, speckled heaps of fabric and then pounded back together and spit out to the farthest reaches of the globe. For the endless piles of rags they sifted through daily, my aunts called the place la garra, the rag.

My cousins, and to some extent my sisters and me, were raised rather well dressed. Between Leti, Velia, Lela, Juanita and Raquel and Marta, the Hinojosa sisters memorized every family member's clothing size and unusual body dimensions—who had, for instance, the small waist but huge hips, or the long torso but short legs. As they dug through mounds of used clothes they were allowed to set aside some of the prettier items for themselves, which they dumped on a scale before they clocked out for the day and bought for just $3 a pound. And so they always came home with some unexpected treat: a flowery church dress, a flirtatious jean skirt or some other garment that anyone in the family, from the 40-year-old mom to the six-month-old baby, might put to use.

It was not just that shopping at the mall was more expensive. This was *good* stuff. It was brand-name clothes that often arrived intact, price tags and all. Or maybe they had been worn once or twice by some fickle rich girl up north. Who cared? If someone in the family complimented you on a nice skirt, you'd stick out your hip and declare playfully, imitating your mother's bad pronunciation: "Jeem Jonson, Ropa Usada." If the girls at school asked—which they always did—where you had bought your stretchy Guess jeans, you simply gave them, nose slightly lifted, the well-rehearsed Brownsville answer: "I don't know, my mom got them for me."

From the outside, the warehouse was a thrilling mystery. Since my family didn't live too far from it, and because my mother was one of the few Hinojosas who didn't work there, we often drove to the secret cavern through the thickness of warm South Texas nights and waited in the car until the loud bell rang inside, signaling the end of the night shift. Slowly, they would begin to emerge from the building: one woman, then two, then droves of them. Some of them young and coy and all dolled up for work, others old as grandmothers in flowery skirts. There was hardly any lighting outside, so my sisters and I strained our eyes until we spotted the women with the tightest jeans and the prettiest curly hair. Those were the Hinojosas.

Family gatherings always morphed into story-telling sessions about la garra. Leti the impersonator told the best ones by far. Her specialty was imitating her boss' passes at Marta, which usually went something like a blunt "tú casarte conmigo," or recounting the times the foreign buyers came by the warehouse and she kidded with them in mock Japanese and Italian. A whole way of life evolved in that enormous corrugated metal shed tucked away anonymously behind the Golden Corral Family Steak House on Boca Chica Boulevard. Fledging entrepreneurship. (Marta nearly earns a teacher's salary selling Mexican gold jewelry to her co-workers.) Romance. (Juanita met her hardworking husband there, and has been happily married since.) And always, in huge, juicy doses, workplace drama.

There were tales of Jim Johnson's authoritarian rules and of his explosive temper. Any worker who walked by a piece of clothing that had fallen to the ground and did not pick it up would face his wrath—once, he even threw a rag at a woman's face and made her weep. But there were also stories about Jim Johnson's generosity. About the way he bought each of his best workers a bottle of her favorite perfume for Christmas. About the times he invited his best employees to his house and prepared great feasts of fish and chips, the women eating shyly in the same room as Mr. Johnson's politician friends while their squirmy kids dunked their little bodies in the boss' pool.

Until my mother met him that spring morning, great clothes and stories were the only way the rest of us had ever known this Jim Johnson.

The old man is rambling on with some New York businessman named Randy, talking about me as I sit patiently in his brown wood-paneled office. The sentences spill out fast, chasing each other as if he were boasting about his own children.

"And she's studying at Rice University and she's going to get her Ph.D. in six weeks. I met her momma when she was flying to her college graduation at Stanford and she was sitting next to me and she asked, 'Are you Jim Johnson?' Six of her sisters work for me, you see. And her mom said last week she went to New York where her other girl graduated from Cornell. Now, isn't that *something*?"

I don't bother correcting Jim Johnson's minor mistakes—pointing out that it is going to take me five more years to get the Ph.D., or that my twin sister graduated a month, not a week, before me. It's been three years since he met my mother. And truth is, I'd rather have Jim Johnson discuss my resumé than anything else. The first

Downtown Brownsville.

thing out of his mouth when he met me today, after he'd looked me up and down: "You look like the whole bunch out there, but you're prettier than they are."

He was, of course, referring to the Hinojosas, four of whom still work for him (#5 went to night school and became a hairdresser, #6 an acclaimed cake decorator). I try to keep this in mind as I stroll his used-clothing kingdom with my reporter's notepad and my critical eye. He was so happy when I called and told him I wanted to write about his business. He remembered my college graduation.

Today the warehouse looks like a tired sweatshop with its piles of old rags and its swarms of dark-skinned women. Perhaps it was always this dark and this shabby. Something about childhood makes small things look grand. But Jim Johnson appears rather upbeat as he tells me about his multimillion-dollar business and the road that took him there: the tree-studded East Texas wilderness where his family grew cotton and corn; the $300 his

Mexican neighbors lent him to go to college and study agriculture; the job he took selling Firestone tires until he decided he was tired of peddling rubber and a friend talked him into trying an interesting little business.

If they obtained a charter to form a non-profit organization, the state would allow them to take surplus bales of used clothing from Goodwill Industries and the Salvation Army, sell them, and keep half of the profits, sending the rest to senior citizen centers. "I got my first week of bidness right here, Cecilia," he says to me proudly, and he opens one of his desk drawers and pulls out an old black ledger with neat, handwritten print. His total expenses in July 1964 were $422.13, including the cost of the store. He sold $164.27.

Yet, there was a genius to Jim Johnson's success, and it was this: as time passed, he figured out that if he sorted all of the used clothes just the way his customers wanted to buy and wear them, he could sell every last dingy sock. So he began drafting little mismatched lists that evolved over the years, separating yarn sweaters from bulky sweaters, Wranglers from Levi's, corduroy jackets from tweed jackets, real fur from synthetic fur, white shirts from polyester shirts from athletic shirts. There were other odd categories too, such as "hippie" and "tropical" and "remnants." His employees learned cotton and rayon and polyester, and they learned denim, silk, yarn, wool, flannel, leather, velvet, lace, chenille, cashmere and suede. Bales upon bales of used clothes arrived each day and were sorted into more than 100 classifications that only made sense to the workers, ranging from form to function to a curious mixture of both.

And so there were Levi's and 70s-era t-shirts for the Japanese, cashmere sweaters and corduroy pants for the Italians, Tommy Hilfiger button-downs and baby clothes for the Mexicans. And for the Africans and the Cambodians and the Pakistanis there were— "Don't write this down," Joe the plant manager says, pointing at my notebook—"Number 2 grades," a politically correct way of saying that the clothes might be faded or dotted with pinholes, since that's what the masses of those countries can afford.

But even as he expanded his global trade, Jim Johnson's best customer remained next door. For just on the other side of a toll booth and maybe a few sniffing dogs was a wily businessman's dream: the largest informal economy one could hope for. It's not merely that Mexicans were willing to take their neighbor's discards. Rather, they recognized the potential for turning a profit where Americans saw waste. The chiveras, as they called the Mexican women who came directly to his nine ropa usada stores in downtown Brownsville, paid $250 for each bale they picked apart, then lugged their best finds back to the international bridge and snuck them across, since importing used clothes for retail is against Mexican law.

The rest—the clothes that were too torn or too stained or otherwise bent out of shape— lost buttons and zippers, and got shredded into cleaning rags for maintenance workers. Leftover cardboard boxes were flattened and sold to dealers. Mounds of useless bale wire were crunched into tall bundles and recycled for money. In the old days, even zippers and buttons proved their value. They were processed into the stuff used to make roofing shingles, so that

Jim Johnson's workers elegantly referred to them in the collective as rufi.

By 1978, the Corpus Christi paper reported that Johnson International Materials, Inc. had generated $6 million that year. It was, without a doubt, the most efficient recycling system you've ever seen. And on the concrete floor of an otherwise insignificant storehouse on the U.S. / Mexico border, a crew of fashion experts had brilliantly recreated the social distinctions of the world in iridescent piles of fabric that reached up to the sky.

It wasn't the best job but it was the most convenient, is what my aunts used to say. Sure, it wasn't easy to spend endless hours hunched over a heap of rags, surrounded by a multicolored sea of 100-gallon plastic trash cans, crunching each garment into a ball and tossing it toward the proper container like basketball players. They called it clasear, a Tex-Mex verb that seemed conceived precisely for

"Our Lady of Ropa Usada"—used clothing stores are ubiquitous along the U.S./Mexican Border.

this kind of work. Other women spent equally droning shifts pulling garments from a mountain of cotton and slipping them under the humming razor of a gray Eastman cutting machine, magically transforming old t-shirts into wiping rags. Yes, it was hard to meet the demanding quotas sketched in lead on a sheet of notebook paper taped to the wall, and, yes, it was irritating to go home at the end of the day with your fingernails packed tightly with grime. But there were perks, too.

Where else could you skip a day's work without getting fired if a child got sick? Where else could you run off to McDonald's for a sausage biscuit and large coffee if you got the morning munchies? And, as my cousin Lucha put it rather succinctly, where else could you land a job without any formal education or language skills or physical attributes other than a strong back? "Aquí no te piden inglés ni matemáticas—aquí nomás chíngale," she pointed out. If you busted your ass, so to speak, you were good.

That's why the women came, searching for work, from both sides of the border. Most of them already knew someone who worked for Jim Johnson, and if they'd been forewarned, they'd return after the cranky old man said in his gringo Spanish, "No hay trabajo." And then return again, until he was convinced that they really wanted to work for him. Deep down, their labor philosophy appealed to him: give me a chance and I'll work really hard to repay you. In times of bad business, a group of the "girls" (as he referred to them) even huddled under a tree during lunchtime, locked hands and spoke to God on the boss' behalf.

The benefits of the job were swiftly forgotten with the arrival of a particularly miserable pack of ropa usada. In one case, a can of dog food had accidentally landed in a bale when it was packed. By the time it arrived at Jim Johnson's warehouse, the lump had gotten squashed and rotted, so that the clothes reeked unbelievably. Then there was the bale in which, according to la garra lore, a sorter discovered an aborted baby in a plastic bag.

Yet, good days could deliver nice cash bonuses. They made their appearance in small bundles of bills, tight wads of cash some poor fool or careless drunk had left folded in a jean pocket, stuffed in a sock or pinned to her underpants. The odds of finding them were highest when the bales came from New York. The excited announcement would be made— "Viene paca buena porque viene de Nueva York!"—and the women would sort its contents as carefully as if they were cleaning beans.

There is the story of the day Juanita fished out $500 from a pair of pants, and of how Raquel spotted $480 hidden in a blouse. And then there was the time my cousin Mairé was working at Jim Johnson's to pay her college tuition and a woman nearby lifted a pair of pants.

"Mira, mija, ¿te queda este pantalón?" she asked Mairé, tossing the jeans in her direction.

"N'ombre, no me queda," said Mairé, nose wrinkled. She tossed them back.

"Sí te queda. Llévatelo," the woman insisted, tossing them again.

Mairé gave in. "Bueno." And when she inspected the jeans thoroughly, she was rewarded with $150.

Then, of course, there were clothing benefits. A woman who worked for Jim Johnson could dress an elementary school with the same amount of money someone else might spend on a couple of back-to-school outfits. The more children or nieces one had, the better the deal became. One year alone, Velia paid her boss $1,000 for clothing but took home some 350 pounds of low-rise jeans and glittery tops and expensive dance leotards for her daughters. You could mix and match with clothes you had bought at the department stores, though sometimes Jim Johnson's stuff was even better. And when your house got over-stuffed with rags because you had bought them so cheap, you simply organized the most fabulous garage sale the block had ever witnessed and recouped some of the money.

That's why the women stayed—some of them years, some of them decades, until there were generations of mothers and daughters and aunts and cousins all working together in

Cecilia Ballí and Jim Johnson

that metal warehouse. They became comadres or enemies but always passed around the collection basket when somebody needed extra help. They sold tamales to each other, gossiped about the woman whose head had gotten too big since she started losing weight, studied together for the U.S. citizenship exam. They watched each other's kids have babies and graduate from college and move on to better lives in better parts of town. For Jim Johnson's birthday, they showed their appreciation by throwing a big bash or pitching in to buy him a huge gift basket.

Jim Johnson smiled in the pictures they took at his parties and hung them from his dresser mirror. He glowed over each new college degree and each newborn grandchild. And sometimes, he thought to himself how blessed he was to have found this good little business and these loyal workers in this far-flung corner of the world.

"¿Cuánto es?" the old man demands to know from the bleached blonde who manages one of his downtown stores.

Every afternoon at roughly the same hour with the same expectations, Jim Johnson shuffles into each of his nine shops, drops a blue Texas State Bank zippered pouch on the counter and asks to know how much each of his saleswomen sold that day. In brown polyester pants, an orange-and-red plaid shirt and a green camouflage cap, he looks more like a senior citizen on his way to a neighborhood association meeting than a man who owns a ranch in East Texas, cabins in the wilderness and half-a-million worth of cattle. Or someone who manages a business that now sells about $8 million in leftovers a year.

The woman smiles bashfully at me and then answers him meekly, apologetically: "Muy poquito, Jim. Docientos trece."

The boss huffs and shouts: "¡Necesito frío!"

Not that anybody in the room can do anything about it. Cold weather will draw steady streams of customers in search of extra layers, but Brownsville's temperature is as unexciting as warm milk this Halloween afternoon. "We had a really good day the other day," he laments, "but this weather's killing us." He takes the bills and rolls of coins and mutters on his way out: "This girl's kinda slow." At night he will sit alone at his dinner table counting pennies, nickels, dimes.

Jim Johnson was 73 years that October afternoon. His life had become routine. He reported to his warehouse early, treated his plant manager to lunch, exchanged a shrimp (or slice of tomato) for good luck. Then he worked again, took a quick afternoon snooze, made his downtown rounds and counted his earnings. But unlike other men his age, this one still had an empire to defend. "We got that cat down in Mexico we need to collect from," he told his manager Joe as we lunched at the Oyster Bar. "Call him and tell him you're going to put your abogado on it." And he had wild stories to tell—of the day he met Miss Florida down in Mexico, of the time a Hawaiian woman came to meet him after she saw him featured on network television and he took her out for a fine dinner in Matamoros.

We had spent an entire day talking. Though he had been a faceless figure in my life—sometimes a generous boss, sometimes, when I began to see the warehouse and the world differently, a labor exploiter—today he ceased being "Jeem Jonson, Ropa Usada," and became, simply, Jim.

When we reached the last of his stores, which my aunt Marta now runs, I thanked him for the tour and asked him if I could take his picture. But he protested. Why just take a shot with Marta? How about one with me?

The old man grabbed my waist and looked into the camera with his big, pearly grin.

Rasquachismo

An Aesthetic of the Underclass

TOMÁS YBARRA-FRAUSTO

from *CARA—Chicano Art: Resistance and Affirmation*

To be rasquache is to posit a bawdy, spunky consciousness, to seek to subvert and turn ruling paradigms upside down. It is a witty, irreverent and impertinent posture that recodes and moves outside established boundaries.

To be rasquache is to be down, but not out, fregado pero no jodido. Responding to a direct relationship with the material level of existence or subsistence is what engenders a rasquache attitude of survival and inventiveness.

In an environment always on the edge of coming apart (the car, the job, the toilet), things are held together with spit, grit and movidas. Movidas are the coping strategies you use to gain time, to make options, to retain hope. Rasquachismo is a compendium of all the movidas deployed in immediate, day-to-day living. Resilience at hand, hacer rendir las cosas. This use of available resources engenders hybridization, juxtaposition and integration. Rasquachismo is a sensibility attuned to mixtures and confluence, preferring communion over purity.

Pulling through and making do are no guarantee of security, so things that are rasquache possess an ephemeral quality, a sense of temporality and impermanence—here today and gone tomorrow. While things might be created al troche y moche, slapdash, using whatever is at hand, attention is always given to nuances and details. Appearance and form take precedence over function.

Rasquachismo is a vernacular system of taste that is intuitive and sincere, not thought out and self-conscious. It is a way of putting yourself together or creating an environment replete with color, texture and pattern; a rampant decorative sense whose basic axiom might be "too much is not enough." Rasquachismo draws its essence within the world of the tattered, shattered and broken: lo remendado (stitched together).

The visual artist Ramses Noriega recalls a barrio character from the border who exemplifies this attitude:

"Around the years of 1949-54 in Mexicali, a small bordertown at that time,
there lived a man who would walk through the impoverished neighborhood of

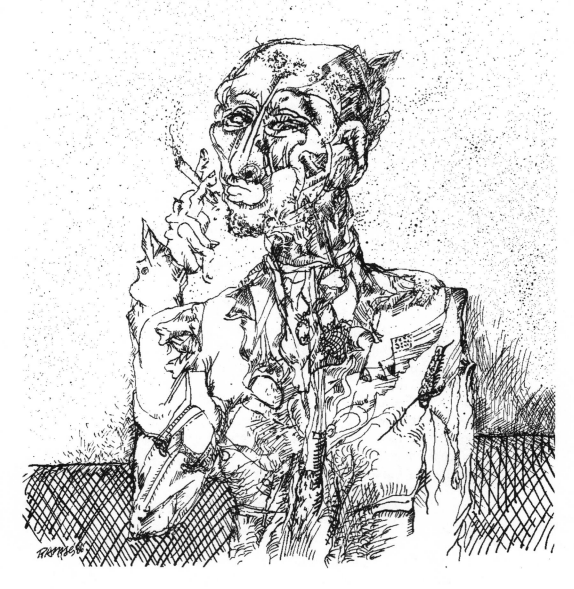

"Don Rasquache," by Ramses Noriega.

RASQUACHISMO

Barrio Loma Linda. He dressed in a tuxedo, used a cane and wore a hat of the type that Charlie Chaplin used in his films. He was a sight to see, not so much for the tuxedo he wore but for the material he used to sew it together. This man collected small pieces of colorful cloth he found at the local dump, sewed them together with a thread and needle, and created a unique patch quilt effect over an old coat and pants someone had thrown away.

"Don Rasquache, as we called this man in the barrio, walked like a true gentleman of wealthy nobility, you might say. He never talked—and there was no need to either. He lived, people said, in one of the caves in the wall of a 20-foot precipice of the canyon that intersects Mexicali."[1]

1 Letter from Ramses to Rudy Gugliano of Phoenix, Arizona (February 11, 1988), explaining the source of his painting "Don Rasquache."

Shooting the Border

BRUCE BERMAN

Going to work: unloading fake ponies for the tourists in front of the cathedral in downtown Juárez.

You know you're lost when a photo editor at *The New York Times* asks you to shoot pictures for a story on the border and asks you to shoot The Contrast. He breathes the phrase into the mouthpiece. I am glad he is in New York and not in front of me, here in El Paso, because sooner or later we'd come to blows. But I need money, so I go to work. I shoot around for a few days showing donkeys blasting past beautiful girls on Juárez streets, a legless guy selling CD players on the Bridge, a shot of El Paso's downtown, taken from a mountain cemetery in Juárez. And on and on.

He keeps rejecting my shots.

Finally, I say, "Hey, José, let's get real! What, exactly, do you want to see in this picture?"

"The gleaming towers of El Paso with the slums of Juárez in the foreground," he replies.

Ah yes, I think, *The Wonderful of Us* versus *The Depravity of Them.* Judged by our cultural standard, of course.

I ask, "Do you realize that 'the gleaming towers of El Paso' are those old 14-story bank buildings from the 60s? And those 'slums' you're talking about are those little casitas that tens of thousands of immigrants have built and invested their dreams in?"

"Yes," he replies, no guile in his voice whatsoever. "So what's your point?"

The heat rises up in my head. I cannot help myself. I begin to rant: "Because if you want me to shoot the pictures on the basis of what I have learned here and come to know after shooting this border for all these years, then you're asking me to take the wrong pictures. I really got to tell you that the mentality in those old bank buildings is all about poverty and what's never going to be done in this goddamned valley. Those so-called skyscrapers are about keeping a lid on the energy of this place and giving as little as you can get away with and about managing exploitation. And, by the way, those 'gleaming towers' are now way tarnished and weren't too good in the first place. And those little cabanas—that obviously offend you or you wouldn't be calling them 'slums'—have repeatedly been my only source of hope in this world because, over and over, coming back from assignments and private wanderings, I have seen uncountable acts of kindness, unlimited doses of hope and optimism and pure faith and been offered the hand of love and friendship. I have always left those 'little slums' a rich man. Like someone had rammed gold into my pockets."

So, I say this to my editor and he gets angry. He tells me he used to be a photographer in Texas. He thinks I don't get it.

And maybe I don't.

BRUCE BERMAN

THIS IS THE DAY 'OLD BLUE EYES' DIED, 15 MAY 1998 —*His name is Chaplin. Lives in El Paso. 80. Virile. Mexican, but lost in the border long ago. He sits on his couch. This is the room that had been the bar room in the brothel he'd bartended. He had a day job, too. Bought the building. Lives in this room now. His friends lodge here. Some are years behind in rent. One in particular, The Muralist, is Chaplin's spiritual heir. The Muralist has brought me to meet The Man. Chaplin's girl comes to visit him every Wednesday, at noon. She comes from Juárez. Originally she came for the money, but now there's more to the relationship. He visits her over there, too. Dinner. Dancing. Loving. He walks back across the bridge in his shiny shoes, the Lodging house, five blocks from the border. White light out that window, but it's worse. There's gentry movin' in. A bar has infiltrated. Thirtyish. Boozy. Desperate. Devouring texture and soul and, inevitably, the world of Chaplin. His world is shrinking. He's O.K, though. Strong. A man, a life lived fully. Virile. 80.* —Bruce Berman

RASQUACHISMO

Nothing to Declare: Welcome to Tijuana

Juan Villoro
Translated by Antonio Garza
Letras Libres, May 2000

EDITOR'S NOTE: *The original impulse for* Puro Border *was to bring together the best writing by people who live on either side of the U.S./Mexico border. We weren't about to let an 'outlander' in! But Juan Villoro, a native of Mexico City (a ¡chilango!) now living in Spain, won us over with his overwhelming fronterizo sensibilities.*

North-by-Northwest

In one of their best parodies, Adolfo Bioy Cásares and Jorge Luis Borges invented a writer so caught up in his own internal reality that he could only describe what was happening on the north-northeast corner of his desk. Being less sensible than that character, I agreed to write about Tijuana in the north-northwest corner of Mexico.

The biggest disadvantage of being from Mexico City is that your origins are obvious to everyone. Chilangos are so disparaged in the rest of the country that we should perhaps stay in our own area. In fact, Tijuana is the place where journalist El Gato Félix began a "Chilangos, Go Home" campaign before he was assassinated—not by one of us, as far as we know.

In my defense, I should say that the Great Customs House of Baja California Norte dispels all provincialism. It is the most crossed border in the world, where the city limits of the Global Village change landscape as if by remote control. It's the duty-free store that traffics reality and dreams. For anthropologist Néstor García Canclini, it is one of the largest laboratories of the post-modern experience. For Tijuana writer Luis Humberto Crosthwaite, "It's an invented city, malleable and with many faces."

One of the typical products of this Mecca of syncretic culture is the Caesar Salad. Mexicans who make their pilgrimages to the Vatican are usually surprised that nobody offers them the antipasto we assume to be an Italian favorite. The answer to this mystery is simple—the Cesar for whom the salad was named was not one of the Roman Caesars, but was César Cardini, a Tijuana restaurateur disposed to culture smuggling.

As Mexico's most cosmopolitan of cities, Tijuana is the primary point of contact we have with the most powerful nation in the world, and this complexity requires multifaceted investigation. On the flight there, I thumbed through Aeroméxico's in-flight magazine to find the usual map of Mexico. It made me think of an ancient atlas with Aeolus, his puffed-out cheeks representing the directions of the winds, and an inscription that signaled the end of the world—*Hic sunt leones / There are lions here.* It showed an unexplored horizon that promised wild beasts. Now that lions yawn for a living at the circus, we must look for other animals to represent the unknown. What animal embodies the borderline condition of Tijuana? Through my headphones I hear Manu Chao's voice:

> Welcome to Tijuana
> tequila, sexo y mariguana
> con el coyote no hay aduana.

The lyrics advertise my travel destination as a City of Vice for sinners on a budget. In this deeply mythical folklore, the coyote is omnipresent. The problem is that it's about a person corrupted into a beast—a being who pronounces marvelously the two languages he speaks poorly and who has access to the secret passageways that let Mexicans enter into the United States. The coyotes have sent so many Oaxacans to San Diego that the city is now often called Oaxacalifornia.

Another creature that might symbolize this border-area is the seal, an animal torn between sea and land. It's no accident that Federicio Campbell chose to analogize his villagers to seals in the novel *Everything about the Seals (Todo lo de Focas)*. All these creatures aside, nothing compares to the hybridized farm animal Tijuana dreamed up—burros painted like zebras. For reasons I can't understand, tourists love getting their picture taken next to this veterinary perversion.

The first thing a visitor sees upon landing in this city where donkeys masquerade as zebras is a metal wall, the same metal wall that the U.S. Army used as a road to advance in the dunes during Desert Storm. Placed here as a means of control, the wall is ridiculous. It has slits that act as rungs, and the wall isn't very high. Wade Graham in *Harper's* magazine compares this symbolic wall to Christo's installation work.

Running a fence along the border that extends 30 meters into the ocean doesn't stop the illegals, but it does warn them that they *will* be stopped. The worthless scrap iron functions merely as advertising. It foretells the horrors that the adventurous may suffer. It's no coincidence that the landscape is ugly. Since October 1994, when Operation Gatekeeper was implemented, approximately 400 Mexicans have died trying to reach that temporary heaven we call el otro lado (the other side).

The Invisible Chinese

According to Crosthwaite, "President López de Santa Ana was the largest real estate agent in history." Thanks to him, we Mexicans lost half of our land; the border dropped down to Tijuana and it was attacked by little Century 21 signs. Land value is measured by its proximity to the empire. The city has grown so far north that it rubs up against the barbed wire fence where that which is Mexican becomes suspect. But on the American side, San Diego has its back to the border and its houses face the Pacific Ocean.

What could possibly unite these two disparate cultures? Before my trip, I talked to Daniel Sada, a writer from Mexicali who'd just finished his invigorating contribution to the Mexican novel, *Porque parece mentira la verdad nunca se sabe (Because It Looks Like Lying, the Truth is Never Known).* Daniel took me out to a Chinese restaurant on Bucareli Street in Mexico City. The restaurant belongs to Lin May. She's the Amazonian woman with breast implants who did stripteases at the Esperanza Iris Theater. Although the place was empty, and the décor was nightclub-esque, a Chinese waiter handed us lunch menus. We ate our chop suey by the dance stage like gangsters out of a Scorcese movie who had just shut down the place so they could chow down on some noodles.

"Do you know what culture brings Mexico and the United States together?" Daniel half-shut his eyes like a pitcher on the mound and hurled his answer—"Chinese food."

Mexicali was founded in a basin below sea level, in the middle of the desert. The Chinese were welcome there because the terrain was considered uninhabitable. With the secretiveness of a people used to living in kitchens, they spread throughout the border. The nights in Mexamerica are aglow with neon Chinese characters. In Tijuana, there are almost 300 Chinese restaurants and a consulate which keeps up with the immigration paperwork of this populous but invisible people who cook so much food.

In the movie "Pulp Fiction," set in Los Angeles, a criminal holds up a cafeteria by shouting, "Get the Mexicans out of the kitchen!" If the scene had occurred a few miles south, he would have shouted, "Get the Chinese out!" This would have permitted us to see them for the first time.

In Tijuana, Luis Humberto Crosthwaite also took me to an amazing restaurant that serves the local cuisine, Chinese food. Because he's lived in Tijuana since his birth in 1962, he knows many people, including some Chinese folks who hide amid the steam of their pots. This liking for secrecy has led them to open little clandestine cafes where their customers arrive like guests invited to a home. Luis Humberto made me try shrimp glazed in coconut and other Tijuanan marvels, delicacies that surely Marco Polo tasted as he traveled along the Great Wall. But he didn't consider me worthy of membership in that fraternity of people who hide in order to eat glazed duck. Only those who already know some of these people-in-hiding can belong to the brotherhood. I don't know the exact number of people you need to know. All I know is that I don't yet qualify.

These invisible Chinese restaurants are as interesting as other forms of local commerce. The informal economy in Mexico has produced strange merchandise, but someone seems to be buying it. You see masks of the former president Salinas de Gortari. Before the border toll booths, cars stop to buy even weirder handicrafts. This is the only place in the Western world where plaster sculptures of Bart Simpson, the size of dorm refrigerators, are considered decoration. You can choose from Power Rangers, Pocahontas or Aladdin. These artisans keep up with Hollywood trends. Currently they're engrossed in Tarzan. The rough mold will be painted with acrylic paints thus ensuring the result will be grotesque. And yes, it's a complete success. You even see people walking across who buy them and then carry them home piggyback.

Tijuana has the greatest concentration of pharmacies on the planet. That says two things about Americans: either they're very sick people or very self-indulgent hypochondriacs. Prescription drugs so vigilantly controlled in the U.S. can be bought here without a prescription.

Dentists, dermatologists and plastic surgeons are the biggest beneficiaries of the border's cheap unregulated medicine. On a good day, you'll bump into a pack of clinical tourists. And if you're lucky, you'll see these humanoids with cherry-red faces fresh off the plastic surgeon's table.

From greyhound races to lobster tacos, the mercado that is Tijuana has it all in stock. In this emporium of transactions, the poet Robert L. Jones proudly boasts of having crossed the bridge carrying "one undocumented rose." But of course, love isn't the only motivation for such lyricism. Above a border toll crossing you can see a billboard that reveals the consequences of this international commerce: *Herpes? Call 800-336-CURE.*

Erotic Matinee

The Mexican Consulate in San Diego and the Colegio de la Frontera Norte organized a field trip for a group of writers and journalists so we could see the real Tijuana. There were to be no pictures of sightseers with brooms in hand standing next to striped burros. We had to take an interactive tour as participatory as the one taken by the head of the Colegio, Jorge Bustamante. He experienced the reality of the border by crossing the border just like a wetback.

As soon as I got into the school's minibus, a professor started railing against an unexpected byproduct of capital-chauvinism.

"Have you ever noticed that the weather man on chilango-TV points out the weather for places in central Mexico, and the whole time his head is covering the entire peninsula of Baja California?"

"No, uh, I hadn't noticed *that.*"

"That's how cruel centralization can be."

I sat there shamefacedly keeping quiet until we got to our first stop: an enormous statue of a nude woman. It was so large that it was up there with the largest statue of Lenin in the old Soviet Union. The size of this giant wasn't as significant as the fact that the sculptor lived inside of her. It was oddly oedipal; he can look onto the world from a balcony that comes out of his loved one's stomach. And he has hung out a FOR SALE sign.

After contemplating the statue, simultaneously womb and condo, we traveled along the Mexican side of the border. Our colleagues from the Colegio referred to it as la línea—the line.

The closer you get to the U.S., the poorer the city becomes. Half of the construction is made of the ever-present tire. Houses are erected on top of tire pillars, like beach huts on piers. On hills of loose soil often visited by earthquakes, these tires act as both a foundation and a shock absorber.

I saw walls, swings and bricks made from tires. In this refuge for nomads, the tire, the emblem of mobility, is stationary.

It was 11 in the morning when our van went in an unexpected direction—Coahuila Street. It was late for many things, but it was a bit too early to visit a night club.

"The greatest inconvenience of being executed is that it's always done at dawn." I thought of this line by Carlos Fuentes as we entered the cabaret with people from the Colegio. The darkness of the place created a sense of suspended time, an eternal midnight which regulars in Las Vegas and at Hugh Hefner's mansion know well.

I sat down between two academics to contemplate this erotic failure. A woman stripped on the catwalk, fondled by drug-laden eyes. Down front, two customers in cowboy hats stared at the bottles covering their table. It seemed like they'd been in that position for a week.

There are people who go to strip joints to get turned on, and there are others who go to get excited by those who are turned on. "You've got to go to El Bambi," a friend tells me, "and you can see soldiers kissing each other." This reporter is not as engrossed by the exposed breasts as much as he is by the reactions of audience members. Sticking bills of money in a woman's g-string is commercialized eroticism, but it's no less sordid being a nosy observer.

The woman on my right pointed at the stripper getting off amid thin applause: "Don't worry, the other girls are better. What would you like them to do to you?"

My purple chair turned out to be a great spot for fretting. It felt like Tijuana time was standing still at 11 o'clock. My companion was disturbing me more that the dancers. A harsh announcer called out the next victim—Yadira or Yasmine or Yesina, something like that. The professor sitting next to me crossed her legs. OK, I haven't said this before, but she was wearing very short shorts and was sporting an ankle bracelet, attire not so uncommon in this 100-degree border heat, but unthinkable on a university campus in Mexico City. My neighbor asked for a double shot of tequila, but what they brought her looked more like a triple. She took a looong drink. I could see the tequila enter her throat, and I knew I saw too much. I asked my other colleague something, the one who hates the meteorologists blocking Baja California. She could not explain reality without statistics. By the time I took a sip from my tequila, the short shorts professor had already finished hers. The woman on my right was talking as if her suffering were linguistic. She explained the women's routines, what men got off on, what American's tastes were. She neither condemned nor celebrated the sex industry. That was life, hard, broken and monotonous. There was something irresistible in her impartiality in the face of everyone else's frenzy. I quit looking at the stage. I could only see the woman who was checking out the stage.

"Do you want a dance?" she asked.

It was at a Tijuana matinee. The stripper was moving towards my table or my lap.

I asked for the check.

We got back to sun-baked Coahuila Street. The professors were refreshed and glowed as if we had just had some invigorating juices.

I was reminded of another trip I once took to Tijuana. I went with my wife and I asked a taxi driver to drive us around for an hour. We circled around statues of different heroes, a planetarium decorated by a model of a small dinosaur and a place where an impresario built a miniature model of Mexico. It had been closed because of a dearth of visitors.

"People aren't very patriotic," complained the driver.

I wondered if the desire to see a shriveled motherland was a test of patriotism, but I couldn't keep up my train of thought: we were on Coahuila Street and the driver was pointing out the whores.

"Here come some cheap hookers. Poor girls." He turned to my wife: "Sorry ma'am, but you told me to drive around for an hour, and, well, after twenty minutes we're bound to bump into some hookers."

I got back into the Colegio van. Time went back to normal. It wasn't 11 o'clock anymore, the hour held back for desire. Where were we going? I'd find out in twenty minutes.

The Bad Weed

After the Cold War, the U.S. was unable to tout its virtues without reference to an archetypal enemy. The Latino drug lord replaced the devouring communists. Drug trafficking prospers throughout the continent because of organized crime networks. Of these networks, very little is known of the drug lords who operate on the northern side of the American continent. By contrast, unrelenting propaganda keeps us up to date with the intimate lives and detailed misdeeds of each and every Latin American drug cartel.

The most crossed border in the world is an irresistible magnet for the drug traffickers who have built their homes along the border. They are part banking fortresses and part arabesque mansions full of megalomaniacal grandeur.

In 1994 Luis Donaldo Colosio, the PRI presidential candidate, was assassinated in the Tijuana suburb of Lomas Taurinas. In his book, *Sorpresas te da la vida (Life Hands You Surprises)*, Jorge G. Castaneda offers an explanation for the crime. President Salinas, he argues, broke his non-aggression pact with the narcotraficantes by signing the NAFTA agreement with the U.S. and Canada, so the regional cartel took matters into their own hand.

Most Mexicans know about Lomas Taurinas from TV footage. We saw a dusty valley filled with party faithful in jackets and a sad crowd where Colosio was finished off point blank. The sequence become the oracle that we could watch a thousand times without finding a single clue.

By now, the crime scene qualifies as a "place of interest." The city government has touched up the gorge. A little memorial commemorates the assassination and a few offices put in enough energy to erect a pistachio-green wall, but none was able to fill the wall with something of value.

In its civic poverty, Lomas Taurinas shows the uneven battle between the legal authorities and the audacious lawbreakers. To say that the crime was because of drug traffickers is almost like saying, "It was in the hands of God." Organized crime is impenetrable and the losses it incurs come only from inside the organizations. Like suddenly a drug lord (or his double) dies on the operating table while undergoing liposuction, or he's found dead in the trunk of a car with enough stab wounds to insure the job was done right. Only someone in the Brotherhood can get close to those colorful Versace shirts and the golden spoons that hang from around their necks.

These famous ghosts incriminate themselves in the pursuit of pleasure with certain kinds of cars, certain restaurants, and a specific type of woman: Grand Marquis, seafood from Los (N)Arcos Restaurant, women in spandex with flaming red hair.

The most important cultural manifestation of narcotraficantes is heard in the songs which have changed the repertoire of norteño bands. Although not all members of this norteño New Wave pay their respects to Camelia la Texana in these drug epics, rhythmic accordion plays still churn out the narco hit parade, singing about Cessnas on hidden air fields, farm workers who pack AK-47s and drugs being smuggled to the U.S. The city of the Caesar Salad hasn't produced as many narcocorridos as Culicán, the real Motown of this music craze, but Tijuana does its part:

> Unos perros rastreadores
> Encontraron a Yolanda
> Con tres kilos de heroína
> Bien atados a la espalda

> Drug-sniffing dogs
> Found Yolanda
> With the kilos of heroin
> Tied tight on her back

So sing the Los Incomparables de Tijuana. Also singing their share are Los Aduanales (The Customs Agents):

> Salieron de San Isidro
> Procedentes de Tijuana
> Traían las llantas del carro
> Repletas de hierba mala

They left San Isidro
Coming out of Tijuana
Their car tires
Stuffed with the baddest weed

Aliens

It's summer and on the empire's terraces, they are serving three-colored noodles and fragrant cappuccinos. In these areas of controlled enjoyment—where cigarette smoke sets off fire alarms—wine enjoys an excellent reputation. North Americans need pleasures that are medically certified. And this alcoholic grape regulates hypertension.

Each bottle of California wine has a label which chronicles its epicurean attributes. But those who raise wine glasses in support of Napa Valley red wine overlook the work it took to produce it.

It all begins in the burning Mexican desert. Near the Tijuana border crossing, plaster heads of Bart Simpson are stored in whitewashed stalls. Not far from there, in the nearby dry hills, other figures stick out. Men are waiting for the perfect moment. Unmoving, crouched down, they wait to advance. Their posture is a testimony to the heritage of their poverty—no Mexican of Spanish blood could "rest" in such a hunkered position.

I imagined it would be hard to talk to them, but on the Mexican riverbank, before being spotlighted by helicopters, these undocumented ones talk incessantly.

A 50-year-old man wearing a baseball cap and sneakers begins to tell me, "I have my three children on the other side. I was also there but I had to go back to Oaxaca for the youngest one."

The border is an enormous depository of stories. These accounts prove that crossing is possible. The fact that Rubén, Chucho, Carmen and Ramona are already working in strawberry fields and grape orchards means that they have dodged the helicopters which they call "mosquitoes" and a heat-sensing device they refer to as "the eye of the tiger." Soon, one of them will be a happy alien in the U.S.

But pessimism is also plentiful. "I have been bounced back more than 30 times," said one young man who seemed to have been born trying to cross.

The trick is perseverance. Sooner or later, the tide cannot be contained. The migra can only send out 20 men on searches. If they send you back to Mexico, you must endure one more day of hunger with blistering noon heat and cutting wind at daybreak—one more try. On the other side, after a 20-minute walk, yellow taxis are there ready to give you a ride down Interstate 5, on the yellow brick road to jobs.

"The motherfucking government can go fuck itself," yells a strong 20-something man. He is wearing a black t-shirt with a gothic logo of some rock group. "We need another Pancho Villa." He kicks some rocks. "Does it seem right that I can get time for begging? It's okay to lock me up for robbing but not for panhandling. They're fucks."

Apparently, Mexican police stop people from begging near the Immigration Office. Others look at him, fed up with his loud mouth.

"What we need is democracy and justice," an old man explained.

"And a fucking gun to kill those assholes," added the fanatic.

I wondered how the old men were going to jump the barricades and run, but they didn't seem worried. It was worse to stay where they were. All of them came from far away—Zacatecas, Morelos, Aguascalientes.

At night, the waiting men suck on tequila-soaked oranges to keep warm. They cover themselves with cardboard boxes, and when they wake up, they burn the boxes.

"Why?"

"Because it's the law," they answer.

Mexamerica is a country with its own rules. For $700, a coyote will take you to San Francisco, a crazy expense for immigrants who are trying to avoid the $27 passport fee. They might as well be renting a limo with that money.

In 1991, 65.5 million people crossed through the Otay Point of Entry by legal means. Near by in San Ysidro, 40,000 cars cross daily. No one keeps statistics for those illegals who were successful in crossing. Only the rejected are counted—1,700 a day in the San Diego area.

The rules of Mexamerica are absurd. On the other side, jobs are waiting but the manual laborers must go through initiation rites to satisfy the most demanding of tribes.

In this theatre of bilateral posturing, the U.S. government strengthens its stance to win the racist vote (including any Chicanos who already have the proper paperwork). In turn, the Mexican government makes good use of the harassment to carry out its own foreign policy, to do what it cannot do in Mexico. Our countrymen suffocate in boxcars, their bones found under brush; others die from the xenophobic actions of the Los Angeles Police Department. These events permit even the most undemocratic of countries to protest in the name of human rights.

While people are drinking summer wine on terraces in the U.S., Mexicans are picking grapes in the Napa Valley. Not far from there, in a Hollywood basement, the *Alien* movie poster preserves a cool glowing message: "In outer space, no one can hear you scream."

Coda

On my final passage through customs back to Mexico, I take the line marked NADA QUE DECLARAR. This slogan shields those journeying with legal baggage. But it also protects those who are returning filled with confusion.

Johnny Tecate Crosses the Border Looking Sort of Muslim

Roberto Castillo Udiarte

Translated by Antonio Garza
Letras Libres, 2001

Johnny Tecate wants to cross into San Diego with his new *visa laser* and a few bucks to buy himself some CDs at the used record shop. But with the growing gringo panic from the Taliban threat, crossing this border has become complicated. It's already been militarized with G.I. Joes and the National Guard. The tension belongs to them, Johnny thinks, but they do a good job of spreading it to tijuanenses through their looks, gestures, attitudes, dogs and bossy voices.

And there's Johnny in his old Ford, waiting in line with cars manned by executives; families in pickups, with mothers who are taking their rowdy kids to school; young women taking their lingerie to be washed in cleaner waters; sinaloenses in black pickup trucks with tinted windows; VW Bugs filled with students sporting locks of blue and red hair; shuttle vans carrying ladies who are going to spend their dollars at the mall; and gringos coming back from morning surfing trips in Baja. There are workers crossing on bicycle—the new way of dodging the never-ending lines—because these past few weeks the car lines have grown as much as the waiting time to cross. Ever since the run-in with the Taliban, time to cross has doubled from two hours to four, and on some days, up to six hours. All of this means that more stuff is being sold by street peddlers who walk between the gridlocked cars: t-shirts that say WANTED followed by a picture of Osama Bin Laden and carts with tons of munchies, banana and mamey smoothies. They peddle orange juice for people's impatience, sodas for anxiety, chocolate milk for the wait, machaca and egg burritos for anguish, egg and chorizo tortas for the discomfort, pico de gallo for one's exasperation, and little U.S. flags for injured patriotism, along with the sale of local and national newspapers, and magazines like *Proceso* and *Vanidades.*

Johnny thinks that drivers and passengers have put on some pounds these past few weeks, but to balance things out they've also dedicated more time to reading.

After three and a half hours in line, Johnny gets to the customs official's booth where the agent's gringo eyes scrutinize the *visa laser*. With a Spanish learned from Taco Bell and McDonald's ads, the agent asks:

You Johnny Tecate?

Johnny answers: Yes, I am.

You live Tijuana?

Yes, I live Tijuana.

You go secondary inspection.

Just as Johnny gets to the inspection station in his old gray car with peeling paint he is surrounded by drooling dogs that have never taken a drug test; the three agents have the same traits. The dogs sniff the dog pee from the freshly urinated-on tires. The agents look at Johnny, then turn to look at his *visa laser*, then back to Johnny.

Where go you?

His question seems more of a demand. To buy CDs.

Afghan Whigs CDs?

I dunno, depends.

Your beard look longer than in the picture. Why?

For comfort.

You have Muslim family?

No.

You think to have cornershop in San Diego?

Not yet, anyway.

How many women you have in household?

Five.

Five?

Yes, my wife and four daughters.

The customs inspectors turn to a portable Japanese computer screen; they stare into it without blinking, consulting it in silence. They hide their emotions like cowboy heroes from old Westerns. One looks like John Wayne; the other, the one with the computer, could be Clint Eastwood; the third one, Charles Bronson. The guy who looks like Clint types on his new laptop and shows the screen to the older one, Wayne. After scanning the screen, he turns quickly to Johnny, and with a raspy voice he asks:

You have Middle East friends?

Yes.

How they named?

Edu Arel and Al Tam di Bela.

Where do they live?

In the desert.

Are they terrorists?

No, they are my compadres.

What do they do for a living?

One's a teacher, the other's an electrician.

Do you know how to fly a plane?

No, they scare me.

Do you know Osama Bin Laden?

No.

Do you like belly dancing?

Of course.

The three agents fire another series of questions.

Have you Afghan hounds? You read Koran? Speak Aramaic? Know you Three Mustafas? Have you read *Arabian Nights*? Know you Ali Baba? Mohammad Ali?

Johnny answers automatically with no. Meanwhile he looks at the old FBI poster that offers a two million dollar reward for any information leading to the capture of the Arellano-Felix brothers. Johnny asks himself when it was that the Arellano-Felix brothers slipped from their position as Public Enemies Number One.

Have you ever traveled to Middle East?

No.

Johnny Tecate now imagines himself along Highway 5, right around the shopping centers in Chula Vista, one of the many shopping centers that are more and more empty (as if they had been infected with anthrax) with merchandise discounted as much as 50% off. And he fantasizes that he's at the wonderful Music Trader to buy some CDs of Badi Assad, Nusrat Fateh Ali Khan, Rabih Abou-Khalil, Omar Faruk Tekbilek, or the Uzbeks.

Have you ever contemplated becoming a terrorist some summer afternoon?

"..."

The Graveyards are the Witnesses

Five Snapshots of the Corrido Norteño

Julian Herbert

Translated by John William Byrd and Antonio Garza

One: A beer road

Just as Homer created the epic poem to demonstrate that the ocean and wine are the same color, the Mexican troubadours invented the corrido norteño so that men would have an eternal thirst for beer. A few verses of "Lamberto Quintero" distills the essence of this metaphysical thirst:

> Un día 28 de enero,
> cómo me duele esa fecha,
> a don Lamberto Quintero
> lo seguía una camioneta.
> Iban con rumbo a El Salado
> nomás a dar una vuelta.
>
> On the 28th of January
> —how that day pains me—
> a truck followed behind
> Don Lamberto Quintero.
> They were cruising to El Salado
> just to take a spin.
>
> Pasaron El Carrizal.
> Iban tomando cerveza.
> Su compañero le dice:
> — Nos sigue una camioneta.
> Lamberto sonriendo dice:
> — ¿Pa qué son las metralletas?

They passed by El Carrizal.
They were drinking beer.
His buddy says to him,
 "Hey, a truck is following us."
Lamberto smiles and says,
 "What do we have the machine guns for?"

The smile in the face of danger, the rhyme between "cerveza," "camioneta" and "metralleta," the carelessness of being ready to die "just to take a spin"—these few lines sketch out the perfect norteño vato.

But, you've got to finish the list of attributes.

Resistol-brand cowboy hat. Cheyenne truck with squealing brakes. Pioneer stereo bought black-market hot from the hometown customs house. A Marlboro between the teeth and a can of Tecate resting against his nuts. This is the anonymous norteño hero who travels the highways from Baja to Sonora, from Chihuahua to Durango, from Coahuila to Tamaulipas, unifying the most vast and lonely territory of Mexico into a cold drink of beer. This is a man who travels—at 80 miles per hour—the dream of living and dying in this land where violence is happy and prosperous and a little gaudy. Where the young ladies only agree to dance with the bravest men. And where, with the help of the accordion and the bajo sexto, you can swallow the bitter gulp of lost dollars more easily.

Two: I'm doing what I'm doing because I don't want to steal

I spent my childhood in a small town in Coahuila, Ciudad Frontera. My family was poor, so when I was nine years old I had to look for work. I found it quickly—singer on the bus. My brother Saíd and I formed a group. The stage was the aisle of a Transportes Anáhuac bus smelling of sweat and corroded metal. We sang old norteño boleros and, of course, corridos: "El Asesino," "Pistoleros famosos," "El polvo maldito." We sang in voices that were high-pitched but full of bravado, because when you sing corridos about drug runners full of bullet holes you can't come off like little fairies: the characters of the songs infuse your voice with brave energy. After two or three songs, we collected our earnings and got off at the next stop. We would find another bus and a new clientele, not caring if the ride carried us closer or farther from our house.

Ciudad Frontera is the center of an archipelago of ghost towns—San Buenaventura, Lamadrid, Nadadores, Sacramento. Every 10 minutes a whitewashed shack, a plaza with a gazebo riddled by bullets or a town square where you could shelter yourself from dust storms would appear in front of the bus. From ranch to ranch, from two in the afternoon to nine at night, Saíd and I got to know the world and celebrated the life and death of its heroes. Afterwards, we would return home with our pockets full of one-peso and five-peso coins.

One time, on a bus for employees of a steel mill, a worker gave me a 100-peso bill and told me, "Hey. Sing the corrido of Laurita Garza." Another time, we got in a fight with two kids who tried to rob us in the middle of a field. I guess we won because, deep down, we knew that the spirit of the gunfighter Gerardo González was fighting on our side.

Three: Laurita Garza

Lalo Mora—the king of a thousand crowns, founder of Los Invasores de Nuevo León and composer of songs that fall in the same canon of drunken sadness as the songs of Cornelio Reyna and Hank Williams—is also the author of "Laurita Garza," a corrido norteño that can lay claim to the title, Masterpiece of the Popular Mexican Narrative. Here is the complete text:

> A orillas del río Bravo,
> en una hacienda escondida,
> Laurita mató a su novio
> porque ya no la quería
> y con otra iba a casarse
> nomás porque las podía.

> On the banks of the Rio Grande
> in a hidden hacienda.
> Laurita killed her lover
> because he didn't love her anymore
> and was going to marry another
> just because he could.

> Hallaron dos cuerpos muertos
> al fondo de una parcela.
> Uno era el de Emilio Guerra,
> el prometido de Estela.
> El otro el de Laura Garza,
> la maestra de la escuela.

> They found two dead bodies
> at the bottom of a field.
> One was Emilio Guerra
> the fiancée of Estela.
> The other was Laura Garza,
> the teacher at the school.

El día que iba a casarse,
ella lo mandó llamar:
—Cariño del alma mía,
tú no te puedes casar.
¿No decías que me amabas,
que era cuestión de esperar?

The day he was going to marry
she asked that he come call.
"Love of my life,
you can't get married.
Didn't you say you loved me,
That it was only a matter of waiting?

"Tú no puedes hacerme esto,
¿qué pensará mi familia?
No puedes abandonarme
después que te di mi vida.
No digas que no me quieres
como antes sí me querías."

"You can't do this to me,
what will my family think?
You can't abandon me
after I gave you my life.
Don't say that you don't love me
like you used to love me."

—Sólo vine a despedirme —
Emilio le contestó.
—Tengo a mi novia pedida,
lo nuestro al fin se acabó.
Que te sirva de experiencia
lo que esta vez te pasó.

"I only came to say goodbye,"
Emilio answered her.
"I have my lovely fiancée,
Our love is finally finished.
I hope that the experience
of what happened teaches you something."

No sabía que estaba armada
Y su muerte muy cerquita;
de la bolsa de su abrigo
sacó una escuadra cortita.
Con ella le dio seis tiros.
Luego se mató Laurita.

He didn't know that she was armed
and that his death was very close.
From the pocket of her jacket
she pulled out a short pistol.
She shot him six times,
then Laurita killed herself.

It isn't difficult to find an echo of the traditional in the first two verses: it gently approximates the "In a village of La Mancha" that starts *Don Quixote*—a formula that was in turn based on an almost unknown romance collected by Luis de Medina in Toledo in 1596, according to the research of the academic Martín de Riquer. Also, it must be noted, this beginning coincides with the detailed geographic imprecision that characterizes almost all the stories from the folktale genre.

In the manner of some historical romances and in a journalistic tone, but also in the manner of contemporary novels that compete to be the narrative *tour de force*, like *Chronicle of a Death Foretold* or *The Baron in the Tree*, what the corrido relates resolves itself immediately, even in the first stanza: Laurita killed her lover because he didn't love her anymore.

In the second stanza we discover something seemingly irrelevant, but which instead fuels the tension and verisimilitude: Laura Garza was a schoolteacher. This fact, which speaks of a certain level of education, joined with the diminutive "Laurita," explains why Emilio wasn't afraid of meeting her in secret, even if just to cut her loose. This verbal economy permits us to imagine the personality of both characters, giving greater dramatic effect to the dialogue that follows.

Verses three, four and five recount the painful exchange of love and contempt between the distraught girl and the faithless lover. This part of the corrido is pretty simple, and I will not expand on its traditional and folkloric roots.

In contrast, the final stanza turns out to be explosive: each line describes concrete details like the coat pocket, the size of the pistol or the number of bullets that Emilio receives. This precision, which breaks with the general tone of the story, forces the scene to move at a faster pace. The violence becomes greater—and ironic, thanks to the three diminutives: la muerta cerquita, la escuadra cortita and Laurita killing herself.

If we overlook the puritanical styling, we could, to a certain point, catalog the text of *Laurita Garza* as "conceptualist": its poetic virtues do not stem from metaphor, but in the suggestive combination of narrative details and verbal accidents.

Finally, I think that it is of little importance if the author knowingly created this humble jewel: it is enough to examine it thoroughly to appreciate its brilliance.

Four: The graveyards are the witnesses

In their role as sagas or narratives of heroic exploits, corridos norteños represent a chaotic, but meticulous, cultural thread. They all have sequels, obscure origins, antagonistic responses and historic correlations. They are like cross fire, a frontier where different planes of reality mix. An Aleph made by gunshots.

In the '70s, Ramón Ayala and his Bravos del Norte recorded the corrido "Gerardo González," the story of a gunslinger executed by the police. It starts like this:

> Ya todos sabían que era pistolero,
> ya todos sabían que era muy valiente,
> por eso las leyes ni tiempo le dieron
> el día que a mansalva
> y cobardemente
> le dieron la muerte.

> Everybody already knew he was a gunslinger,
> everybody already knew he was very brave,
> that's why the lawmen didn't give him any more time
> —full of cowardice
> and without any warning—
> they killed him dead.

Years later, in the '80s, the same Ramón recorded "El federal de Caminos" which relates the assassination of a "legal" hero—Javier Peña, officer of the Mexican Federal Highway Patrol. This is the last verse:

Norteño musicians, Juárez, Mexico

Javier su deber cumplía.
Cómo poder olvidarlo
cuando sonriendo decía
(da tristeza recordarlo):
— Que me canten los Bravos del Norte
el corrido de Gerardo.

Javier was doing his duty.
How could I forget it,
when smiling he said,
(it's sad to remember this)
"I hope the Bravos del Norte
sing me the corrido de Gerardo."

The corrido norteño has given birth to the metacorrido: if someone says that among the drug traffickers he is "the boss of all bosses," someone will respond that he is a chicken who wants to be a rooster; if Lino Quintana smuggles his product in a red car, Pedro Márquez goes shopping in Acapulco in a gray truck; if Emilio Varela gets seven bullets in Los Angeles, his sons and grandsons and great-grandsons will return to Tijuana and San Ysidro to fuck or to kill or, if that is not possible, to take Camelia the Texan's daughters and granddaughters dancing. The historical reality of some of the characters is left behind because of the public's ardent desire for the second and third installments in the series.

The sheer number of names and events associated with the genre creates a situation — just like what happens in contemporary fantasy literature—which makes it necessary to compile catalogues, summaries and guides: that is to say, corridos that are compendiums of corridos.

As such, the first—and to date the best—of these catalogues is "Pistoleros famosos":

> Cayeron Dimas de León,
> Generoso Garza Cano
> y los hermanos Del Fierro
> y uno que otro americano.
> A todos los más valientes
> a traición los han matado.

> These are the ones who are fallen—
> Dimas de León,
> Generoso Garza Cano
> and the del Fierro brothers,
> and some American.
> All the bravest,
> treachery has murdered them.

> Liquidaron a Esequiel
> por el año del 40
> José López en Linares
> siguió aumentando la cuenta
> y Arturo Garza Treviño
> allá en el once sesenta.

> They offed Esequiel
> in the year1940.
> José López at Linares
> added to the list.
> And Arturo Garza Treviño
> there out at highway marker 1170.

"Pistoleros famosos" realizes the great aspiration of all epics—it encompasses the world in the name of a hero. It's just that, for the corrido norteño, there is no heroism greater than dying. A man can be judged good and without fault because he mocks the gringo authorities from his little plane, because he tries again and again to cross illegally into the U.S., because he drinks his beer with a blonde for company, kills federal agents, is a good friend, doesn't forgive insults, exports packages of kilos or, more simply, keeps alive the Mexican tradition of living just to raise a lot of hell.[1] But there is no heroism greater than to let yourself die in a hail of bullets. And if it is on the border, even better. One of the last verses of "Pistoleros Famosos" says it clearly:

> Los pistoleros de fama
> una ofensa no la olvidan
> y se mueren en la raya;
> no les importa la vida.
> Los panteones son testigos,
> es cierto, no son mentiras.

> The famous gunslingers
> never forget an insult
> and die at the limit;
> they didn't care about living.
> The graveyards are the witnesses,
> and, for sure, this isn't a lie.

This self-destructive occupation—which awakens in us our affection for the antiheroes, the drug runners, the enemies of the status quo—is justified from the same root as epic sentiment. Jorge Luis Borges has said that the true heroes of the *Iliad* are, for almost every reader, the Trojans, because there is more dignity and beauty in defeat than in victory. Fans who monitor the corrido norteño know that, by analogy, it is our turn to play the role of the Trojans in the cultural war that springs from Mexico's northern border.

Five: And with this, I say goodbye

You can recognize a good cantina by three essential traits: there is sawdust on the floor, the beer is iced and the jukebox has the best records by Los Tigres del Norte, Los Invasores de Nuevo León and Los Cadetes de Linares.

---

1 The Spanish reads "no más pa' chingar" which literally means "only to fuck" or "only to rape," an idiomatic Mexican expression that is one of the many children of the verb "chingar." Some of its other children mean well. To be "chingón" can be a positive superlative. As expected, the verb has many bad children, as in this instance, where the direct object is understood—the world.

Just like the Celts and the Roman legionnaires, just like the Three Musketeers and the Elizabethan groundlings, just like the cowboys and the Marines, the inhabitant of northern Mexico drinks his beer slowly as a shelter from spirits both lethal and kind: suicidal drug-runners, incorruptible captains, charitable coyotes, neurotic bodyguards and infantile police who kill their narco-fathers in oedipal police operations.

A host of saints comfort people along the border, Juan Soldado ("Soldier John") prominent among them. This figure in Mexico's border history, a soldier killed by a death squad in 1938 after he was unjustly accused of raping and killing an eight-year-old girl, has become the unofficial saint for illegal immigrants—for those who feel scorned, unjustly blamed and victimized. Every June 24, people celebrate Juan Soldado's sainthood by visiting his shrine, located in the Tijuana cemetery where he was murdered. The little girl he was accused of killing lies buried not far from his grave but people seldom visit her.

The bar is the plaza of the minstrels, the meeting around the ancient campfire, the almost legendary territory where, from time to time, the heroes drop in. With the heat of the drinks, the accordions and nasal voices from a good jukebox, the norteño restores the savagery that is so emotionally draining, and—in an era completely post-Salinas and dominated by NAFTA—is destroyed by the proliferation of the skeptical flowers of the Mall,[2] antiseptic franchises and an exotic succession of new traffic laws that are of little use in a country full of potholes and police. There is a petrified essence, between sordid and mineral, which makes a good bar resemble a cave or a grotto.

If beer and corridos are best enjoyed on desert highways and in cave-like bars, it is because in the confluence between these two environments there is a happiness almost Apache in nature. And even though none (or almost none) of the blood of the nomadic Indians survives in ours, we have made from the landscape a form of destiny.

Wallace Stevens wrote once, "No man is a hero to anyone who knows him." We—who see our face in the mirror every morning, and hear about the news via satellite or internet, and have contemplated our own entrails with the help of fiber optic cables—we know ourselves too well. But the three minutes that a corrido lasts are enough to restore in our mind an ancient passion: to have been—in infancy, in a blurred movie of a night of hell-raising, in the communal memory, in the bed of a thin, dark-skinned woman—a famous gunslinger, a warrior who with his sword runs through a bland century of hamburgers and canned sodas.

And it is this distant dream that makes us sing.

2 In Spanish the text reads, "flores de Mall" which is a pun on Baudelaire's "flors du mal," or "flowers of evil."

RASQUACHISMO

The Place of Wilderness

*As O'odham, we know the desert is the place of wilderness.
It is the place of dreams for those who must dream those kinds
of dreams, and it is the place of songs for those who must sing
those kinds of songs. But it is also the place where nightmares
hide, nightmares so fierce that one can believe one has seen
a guardian angel. For the O'odham, the desert is certainly
a place of power. Because we know this essence of the desert,
although sometimes we do not fully understand it,
we are able to live in it.*
—OFELIA ZEPEDA

Where the Wilderness Begins

OFELIA ZEPEDA

Isle: Interdisciplinary Studies in Literature and Environment, Spring 1977

Perhaps, when it really was not necessary, since there was no one else around when the Creator formed the shape of the first human and was about to place him on the ground, he ran his hand across the spot where the human was going to be put. Perhaps the place cleared was only the size of the human's feet, or perhaps the space was the size of the state of Texas; surely he must have signified a space.

As children we have done the same. I remember playing on the cool earth floor on a hot summer day, and even though the dirt surface that was our yard and play area had been designated by our mother, we defined it further. Her signal to the space was to sprinkle it with water and sweep it every morning in order to keep the surface firm and dust free. The dirt floor was hard as cement. Once we sat down on it, whether we were playing jacks, dolls, or cars, we further ran our hands over a certain spot on this floor, clearing it and designating it as where we would play. We cleared a small space for the rag dolls to sleep. We cleared further spaces that featured roads or served as places for houses and other childhood toys. We redefined space that was already ours.

Living in the desert, we have all done the same. We have marked the space within the space that is already ours. This space, I say, is already ours, ours in the sense that this is our habitat: we are the ones who were put here to live. And even though we live here, we continue to re-mark it, create boundaries. We fence in, and out. We know where the "wild" desert ends and the "other space" begins. Now because we know where the desert ends, we also know *what* is in that desert. Sometimes we know these things firsthand, sometimes not. As O'odham,[1] we know the desert is the place of wilderness. It is the place of dreams for those who must dream those kinds of dreams, and it is the place of songs for those who must sing those kinds of songs. But it is also the place where nightmares hide, nightmares so fierce that one can believe one has seen a guardian angel. For the O'odham, the desert is certainly a place of power. Because we know this essence of the desert, although sometimes we do not fully understand it, we are able to live in it.

In talking about living in the desert, I will hold some of the perspective of the Tohono O'odham, the Desert People, a tribe indigenous to the southern Arizona desert. I will pull

---

1 O'odham means simply the People, or Tohono O'odham, the Desert People. Their roots in the Sonora Desert extend for thousands of years into pre-history. Because of the Gadsden Purchase in 1854, the U.S./Mexico Border bifurcates their homeland, which now lies in southern Arizona and northern Sonora. "We didn't cross the border," say the O'odham, "the border crossed us."

from what I know personally, some of it certainly gained along the way from family. Other things that I say are bits of other O'odham people's stories.

As a child, I grew up knowing two communities, communities that complemented each other very well. Much of my childhood was spent in the place I was born, Stanfield, Arizona. Stanfield was a cotton-farming community up until the early '70s. This community was a desert region, but with a new façade, a façade of greenery pushed up from the ground artificially. Despite its appearance, this place still had limited rainfall with the regular urgency of summer monsoons. The temperatures were extreme, the air dry and clear. The winters were the same as in any desert, mildly cold and tolerable.

The other place was a village just inside the Mexican border, which was my mother's traditional home. When I was a child, our family spent time there, too. This place was also an agricultural region of sorts. It was noted for its numerous natural springs and, at that time, its large surface ponds. We planted fields mostly of corn, melon, squash and beans. There were also orchards of pomegranates and figs. This village was an oasis, and so special, it was considered by some as a sacred place. From these two homelands in the desert, I grew up familiar with it and knowing how to live in it. Even though both places were clearly defined by their water and agricultural boundaries, in both places one did not need to look too far to see where the "wild desert" began.

It began at the end of the cotton fields or just over a low hill. It was beyond these places, the ends of fields and over desert hills, that we as children knew not to venture too far. I remember adults telling us, "something is going to get you" should we venture toward those desert regions. These threats were not false threats of the bogeyman; no, they were real. It was the case then, as it is now, that members of society who do not fit elsewhere oftentimes find themselves on the edges of communities, in the desert, existing as well as they can. It was these people that adults warned us against. Another thing to fear is something that we cannot see but believe exists.

"Something is going to get you" sometimes referred not to anything physical, but to something psychological or spiritual. O'odham believe that one can be met by a being, a spirit, at almost any time. These meetings can happen in the most mundane places, but they can also occur in more mystical wilderness areas like the desert. And unless one actually ventures out for such a meeting because one is supposed to, it is best to keep one's chances low by avoiding the mystical places, the wilderness spaces, whenever possible.

There is a story about a male relative who, after a night of partying and drinking, ended up having to walk home the next day. His walk put him in the midst of dry, wild desert for a considerable stretch. The story goes that he suffered dehydration, not to mention mild sunstroke coupled with hangover, and in this state he had a meeting with a spirit animal. The animal he claims to have met was the bear who gave him his songs. My mother tells this story with some humor. She asks, Where would a bear come from? It does not live in the desert. Nonetheless, this relative had the songs. Unfortunately, he did not live very long, and,

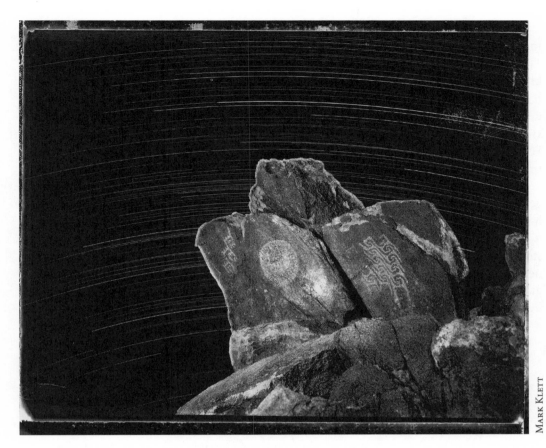

MARK KLETT

"Caborca," Tohono O'Odham rock-carving and stars

as far as anyone knows, never had a single opportunity to take advantage of his curing power on anyone suffering sickness caused by the bear—perhaps it was just as well.

There are many accounts of O'odham men who have been called to go out in the desert for such meetings. These meetings are for gaining knowledge about a variety of traditional ways, including curing rituals, songs, and finding solutions to various major concerns, either for themselves or for the group. As children we were kept vaguely informed about such goings-on. On occasion if we asked too many questions, we were simply given the explanation that so-and-so went hunting and that was the reason for being gone for several days at a time. Even in our cotton field town, we knew of men who went out into the desert because they were supposed to. I remember watching them walk down the road alongside the cotton field, come to the end of the field, turn away and disappear into the desert. The desert does hold all sorts of power, much of it not accessible to everyone, most of it harmless.

There are other stories from out of the desert that have nearly become folklore among many O'odham. One such story tells of something that exists in certain parts of the desert. This thing they speak of is not a physical being, and it has been ascertained by those knowledgeable that it is not a spiritual being either. And the features of this thing? Well, it has none, none yet described by anyone, since no one has really seen it. Those who have experienced this phenomenon claim it is an air, a feeling, and when one gets too close to such a place, one experiences the basest, most visceral fear an evolved human is capable of. People tell how a horse will not go near an area that manifests this thing; they sense a fear unlike any other, according to those who know horses. This is a phenomenon that some people like to tell about with much relish and exaggerated detail. Some dismiss it as the bogeyman syndrome, while others are convinced this thing is truly a manifestation of Satan himself. Whether any of this is true is still in question.

Those who do not believe might perhaps think differently when they hear Mrs. Antone's story. What she saw caused her to be overcome by such fear that the only thing that saved her from being scared out of her wits was a beautiful vision of what she believed to be a guardian angel. This experience led her to relocate to a bigger cleared space in the desert, become a born-again Christian and join the Assembly of God Church.

She tells her story:

"I had just gotten married. I married a Mexican man. We were both young. This was around 1940, back when there was not [sic] electricity in the desert. Anyway, he took me to his home. It was just a little shack out in the middle of the desert. There were not [sic] other houses near us. We were alone except for a few of his cows. It was nighttime when we got to his place, and it was really dark, no moon. We had only been there a short time when he suddenly said he had to leave. I didn't want him to leave because I didn't want to stay there alone. He told me, 'Take this and you will be all right.' He handed me his .22 and left. I didn't know what to do. I started to go about the little house and straighten up, trying to keep my mind off being alone. Suddenly, I heard something outside. At first it was like a breeze blowing through, maybe a little dust devil. But when I quickly looked outside, none of the tree limbs were moving. As I stood in the middle of that little house, I felt this thing move the walls of the house just slightly, and as suddenly as it had begun, it stopped.

"And then I had a sensation something was inside the house with me. It was like cold, wet air. It seemed to permeate my being. I don't know how to explain it. I know it seemed to possess me because it seemed it was holding me not the same way a man or a woman would hold another with the arms, but it held me on the inside of my body, by my backbone. I couldn't move, I couldn't feel my skin, I couldn't breathe even though I was alive. Have you ever seen someone take their last breath before they die and their blood stops running through their body? I think I felt my blood stop running. I felt dry, not wet and alive the way a human is supposed to. I stood there and just held my .22 rifle to my chest.

"My mind, I don't know what my mind was doing. It was either not working or it was working too fast to be of any use. Thoughts were running all around, too many, too quickly, like a bag full of marbles spilled on a concrete floor. I searched quickly, my mind. The only thing I recall was something that told me to pray. That is all. So I did. I prayed and prayed and prayed for what seemed like an eternity. That was all my mind could do. Finally, *It* released me. I felt my fingers warm up with the rush of blood. I could move. The first thing I did was look out this little hole in the door into the blackness and I saw something floating. It was white. It floated above the house and upward until I couldn't see it anymore. It was like one of those beautiful angels I used to see in the books. Then I understood what it was—my guardian angel. It was my guardian angel who had come and saved me from that thing. I just know this is what happened."

"The O'odham lived successfully in the Sonoran Desert for thousands of years but now find themselves at this border: they have the lowest per capita income of all U.S. reservations ($3,113), 70 percent unemployment and the highest school drop-out rate of all Native American tribes. Fewer than half of the adults have completed high school. The homicide rate among the O'odham is three times the national average and twice that of all Native American communities."

—from "Desert Walk,"
Howard Mansfield,
DoubleTake Magazine

When Mrs. Antone told me her story, she was living in a small Arizona town, which of course was in the desert but had been altered by underground water, irrigated fields and copper mining.

I began by stating that O'odham, to a certain extent, know how to live in the desert because, to a certain extent, they know what is in that desert. Some of it is good, and some not. Some of it is real, and some perhaps manufactured by active imaginations. Regardless, contemporary O'odham have available to them various insurance options they can "purchase" in order to protect the space they have set up as their homes within the desert. One option is a cleared yard and a fence, which primarily acts as a deterrent to medium-sized wild animals. The cleared yard is often a meeting ground for uninvited animals, where their host has the option of redirecting the animal back to its original trail. The fence and yard, though, are no match for the more spirit-formed intruder. The option in this case for many O'odham is to invite the local medicine man over to "clean" the house and space. This cleaning protects the building and space from nonphysical intrusions. And for many O'odham who may also happen to be Catholic, a double dose of spiritual protection can come in the form of the local padre who can, following the medicine man, "bless" the space and the house. Finally, some families may have a fiesta at their home. Part of the fiesta might include ritual dancing by the neighboring Yoeme—either Matachine dancing or, even better, Deer Dancing. This dancing offers protection insurance because wherever the Matachines dance, the ground becomes sacred; the same is true for the Deer Dancer, but with the Deer Dancer is the additional bonus of the holy water from the gourd drum. Once the celebration is completed, the water from the drum is sprinkled all about and the place is holy—to some, sacred. I have a friend who does not allow cars in the parking space next to his house because that is where the dancers danced. Even he has to park his truck out on the street.

So there we are. To live in the desert is to know the desert as well as possible, and if that is not the case, then there certainly are ways to protect oneself.

U.S.-Mexico Border Environment by the Numbers

compiled by George Kourous
Interhemispheric Resource Center (www.irc-online.org)

Water

Percent of Colorado River allotted to Mexico by treaty: 10%

Reduction in the biological productivity of the Colorado River delta, located in Mexico, since the river began to be dammed upstream in the United States in the 1930s: 95%

Number of years that drought emergencies have been regularly declared in northern Mexican states: 9

Percent of Cd. Juárez water estimated to be lost to leaks: 30%

Estimated rural water loss due to seepage or evaporation in all of Mexico, nationwide: 55%

Percent of water used by agriculture on both sides of the border: 85-90%

Amount by which the Brownsville Irrigation District was able to reduce water use after implementing modern conservation techniques: 33%

Estimated cost of upgrading Mexico's water infrastructure over the next 10 years: $60 billion

Amount by which the 2001 budget of Mexico's National Water Commission was slashed after the U.S. economic slowdown sparked a recession south of the border: $27.5 million

Number of Mexican cities facing a "severe water crisis," according to that country's National Water Commission: 38

Number of Mexicans without regular access to drinking water: 12 million

Percent of municipal drinking water imported by San Diego County and Tijuana, respectively: 90% and 95%

Year that the Hueco Bolson aquifer, the main source of groundwater for El Paso and Cd. Juárez, is expected to run out of potable water: 2030.

First time in its known history that the Río Grande failed to reach the ocean: February 2001

Average per capita consumption for water in Mexican border communities: 100 gallons/capita/day

Average per capita consumption of water in Albuquerque: 200 gallons/capita/day
In Laredo, Texas: 220 gallons/capita/day
In El Paso: 170 gallons/capita/day

Biodiversity

Number of endemic plant and animal species found in the border area: 450

Number of migratory species found in the border area: 700

Percentage of all species listed as threatened or endangered by the Department of the Interior (DOI) that are found in the borderlands: 31%

Number of plant and animal species in danger of extinction on the Mexican side of the border: 85

Energy development plans

Increase in Mexico's electrical generation capacity between now and 2007 planned by that country's Federal Electrical Commission (FEC): 15,000 megawatts

Percent of that expansion to be cited in Mexico's northern states: 65%

Number of existing power plants in U.S. border states: 3; in Mexico: 10

Number of new power plants recently approved for U.S. border states: 4; for Mexico: 12

Number of future power plants proposed for U.S. border states: 11; for Mexico: 10

Money matters

Increase in average annual amounts of soil erosion, solid waste generation and air pollution in Mexico since 1988, according to government figures: 63%

Estimated financial costs of this environmental degradation: $36 billion per year

Value of Mexico's economic growth annually over same period: $14 billion per year

Estimated cost of environmental degradation in Mexico in 1999: $47 billion

Decline in real spending on environmental protection in Mexico since 1994: 45%

Average annual spending on the border environment by the Mexican government, 1997-2000: $34 million

Average annual spending on the border environment by the U.S. government, 1997-2000: $130 million

THE PLACE OF WILDERNESS

COUNTING SHEEP

DOUG PEACOCK

from *Counting Sheep: 20 Ways of Seeing Bighorn,* 1993

> I think the slain
> Care little if they sleep or rise again;
> And we, the living, wherefore should we ache
> With counting our lost ones?
>
> AESCHYLUS, *Prometheus Bound*

Insomnia has been the central dysfunction of my adult life, and I go into the desert to sleep. I figure I have spent almost two years of my life sleeping under the stars among the cactus of the American Southwest or, on rare stormy nights, in a tent on the desert shore of the Sea of Cortez. My favorite desert for sleeping, however, is the great expanse of country embracing the border of southwestern Arizona and Mexico, the uninhabited desert ranges and valleys of the Cabeza Prieta—one of the best places on earth to get a good night's sleep.

Cabeza Prieta is the name of a block of mountainous hills within an area of the same name now designated as a national wildlife refuge. This refuge is surrounded by similar wastelands managed by the National Park Service or the Bureau of Land Management, or used as a bombing range by the U.S. Marine Corps and U.S. Air Force. It's all great country. The only paved road is Mexican Highway 2 just south of the border, on the northern edge of the Pinacate Protected Zone. I pay no attention whatsoever to these cultural, governmental and otherwise artificial boundaries and have democratically thrown down my sleeping bag on about 220 different nights in washes on all sides of the fence.

The soporific device of counting sheep in order to fall asleep has never worked for me. Instead, I tend to log the constellations with a star chart or read by a tiny ironwood fire until I'm drowsy. Some nights I just watch the celestial clock unfurl or think about a girl I used to know. Sheep never cross my mind until just around daybreak when, sometimes, the clatter of real desert bighorn sheep startles me fully awake.

This doesn't happen very often, of course: four times, my notebooks say. Four mountain sheep on four mornings spread over three decades. Desert bighorns aren't the kind of animals I see in the flesh very often, although I run across their tracks nearly every time I visit the Cabeza Prieta. The sheep I see I invariably hear first. One of the best times for this is in the morning, from your sleeping bag, though you can also hear them moving about on the scree and rocks toward evening.

The first bighorn to cross my path was north of Buck Tank along a low spine of a granitic hill running north into the bajada. It was daybreak on Christmas Day 1979. I was still in the bag, warming my fingers over the ironwood ashes of the previous night's fire, when the sound of rocks clattering on the ridge startled me. I reached for my field glasses and scanned the ridge for movement. The slope was bare except for a few creosote and elephant trees dotting the hillside. I couldn't see anything moving. Suddenly I heard more racket and caught movement coming over the saddle.

It was then that I saw what looked like a ghostly gray grizzly coming toward me. The animal's head had a curl of corrugated horn. The bear was a sheep, a ram with a full curl. I dropped the glasses, and the bighorn caught the movement; he stopped and looked at me from 20 yards. As sunlight capped the tops of the highest peaks, he turned and ambled back across the crest of the ridge.

The reason I sleep well in the desert is probably because I walk so much out there. Traveling over the land on foot is absolutely the best way to see the country—to scent its fragrance, feel its heat and get to know its plants and animals; this simple activity is the great instructor of my life. I do my best thinking while walking—saving me countless thousands of dollars in occupational counseling, legal fees and behavioral therapy. The Cabeza Prieta is my favorite place in the world to walk.

I didn't always do so much walking out on the Cabeza Prieta. My first trips out there, beginning in the late 1960s, were made in the usual fashion, driving a pickup across the Devil's Highway or easing a jeep up the sandy tracks of the spur roads. Most of these trips, and 90 percent of my several dozen nonsolo visits to the Cabeza Prieta, I made with two close friends named Ed: Ed Gage and Ed Abbey.

Later, when truck camping seemed tame and I needed a bit of adventure in my life, I decided to try to walk across the Cabeza Prieta alone. I would cover 120 to 165 miles each trip, depending on the route I took. Taking it easy, I could usually make the trip in about 11 days—10 nights free from insomnia, 10 great nights of untroubled sleep.

In all, I've made seven of these trips, solo backpacking the area from Welton, Tacna, or the Tinajas Altas to Ajo, Organ Pipe, or Quitobaquito, and sometimes vice versa, always by different routes, crossing all the big valleys. Adding in my trips by vehicle, this means I've spent more than 200 nights of my life sleeping out there.

On these desert treks I average from about 12 to 20 miles per day. The mileage I can cover depends on the terrain, on whether I am fasting or low on food, and if I'm walking during daylight or by moonlight. Anything over 20 miles tends to rub raw spots into my aging body or bruise my feet, especially when I'm carrying my full load of water: three and one-half gallons on the longer dry legs of the journey between the Sierra Pinta and Charlie Bell or Papago Well. My exact daily distance is whatever it takes to ensure the fatigue that banishes insomnia. Night walking is more exhausting because you need to brace yourself against injury; for instance, you have to lock your knees and ankles by tensing your quadriceps whenever you break through the honeycombed earth of rodent colonies under the creosote of the bajadas.

I keep crude journal notes of all this and record such things as tracks and sightings of bighorn sheep—a very big deal to me. Actually, on my walks I've seen few bighorn sheep, but then, as everyone knows, the best way to see sheep is to sit quietly, not to walk with your nose at the level of the creosote. I have, however, seen a lot of tracks.

What little I know of desert bighorn sheep is mostly inferred from these tracks and the few sheep sightings I've lucked into: to be exact, 34 bighorn sheep scattered through the desert ranges of the Cabeza Prieta during the past two decades. Ed Gage saw the first one just north of Cabeza Prieta Tanks back in the winter of 1972, one of our first trips together. He had been sitting on a ridgetop reading Kazantzakis when he heard rocks clattering on the slope above him. Gage looked up and saw a magnificent ram with a full curl amble down the ridge away from him, big scrotum swinging from side to side, he said, so he knew it was a ram (he had never seen a sheep before). The bighorn passed down the slope and disappeared below him.

My sheep count began in 1972 (I didn't see any the first three years) and ended in March 1992. Except for the ones I glimpsed from my sleeping bag, I saw all these sheep in precipitous terrain much like that of Gage's ram. My biggest count was a mixed herd of seven ewes and younger sheep one mile east of Half Way Tank in the Cabeza Prieta Mountains. Once I saw four rams bedded together and facing out in the four directions on a spur ridge running off the Sierra Pinta into the Tule Desert north of Sunday Pass. I've seen pairs of desert bighorns three times—in the Growler, the Agua Dulce and the Cabeza Prieta Mountains—and once I startled a group of three ewes near an outlier hill south of the Aguila Mountains. The rest of my sightings have all been of single animals.

The tracks are a different story. My field notes indicate behavior I have never witnessed: sheep crossing the big valleys and using the creosote-covered bajadas. I found sheep tracks crossing and recrossing the Tule Desert using the same route, from the mouth of Smoke Tree Wash east to Isla Pinta, during three different years. One of these crossings was made by a mixed herd of four or five ewes and two young ones. Other odd crossings include a ram from just south of Bean Pass trekking nonstop west along the Devil Hills to the north end of the Cabeza Prieta; a single sheep from the Agua Dulce by way of O'Neill Hills into the Pinta Sands; and two sets of bighorn tracks starting from an old, man-made pile of rocks, perhaps marking a very large grave, on the mideastern flank of the Granite Mountains across the Growler Valley and disappearing in the basaltic cobbles of the Growlers just north of Charlie Bell.

You would think bighorn sheep would be nervous out in these flats and open areas where they are vulnerable to predators. I've seen circumstantial sign of sheep predation only twice, and both times it involved mountain lions. Lions are not common in the low desert because their preferred prey, deer, come down here only infrequently. The first time I saw a lion sign was on a trip with Ed Gage back in 1973 near one of the higher tanks of the Tinajas

Altas; it consisted only of a recent lion track near a much older, disarticulated bighorn skeleton. The other, seen while I was visiting Ed Abbey in 1990, was a dismembered carcass of a young sheep; there was indirect evidence that the bighorn had been cached, and I found lion scat and scraping nearby.

The only times I've run into—actually I heard them—desert bighorns at night have been when the moon was big. Twice I was sitting quietly, and the other time I was backpacking by the light of the nearly full moon. One such night, at the southern tip of the Copper Mountains, I heard the clatter of rolling rocks and the dull clank of hooves high on the slope. This racket had to be sheep moving on the hillside. What else could it be?

Sometimes I wonder how anybody ever manages to study desert sheep; I have enough trouble just seeing them. When I'm up north—in Montana, British Columbia or Alaska—I see bighorn sheep all the time. I see them in the spring down low in the valleys when snow still clogs the passes and slopes. Later in the year I watch them feeding and bedding on grassy ridges and avalanche chutes above the timberline. Twice I've found sheep carcasses buried by grizzlies, and, though I have never seen a grizzly bear successfully chase and kill a bighorn, I once followed a big male grizzly in Glacier National Park who charged a herd of rams, scattering them up the scree and on up the cliffs behind Haystack Butte, where the bear turned back. Even as late as November, I sometimes linger in grizzly country and watch the big rams clash, the clank of their hollow horns resounding through the absorbent air of the snow-filled basins of the Rocky Mountain Front near Many Glacier.

I've never seen that sort of thing in the desert. One March, from a great distance, I watched a three-quarter-curl ram south of Growler Peak, probably browsing on lupine brush. At any rate, he was feeding; I couldn't be sure on what. During the spring of 1973, Ed Abbey and I found agave flowers in the Agua Dulce chewed off by sheep and the remains of smashed barrel cactus near Sunday Pass with sheep tracks all around. But what desert bighorns eat from day to day remains a mystery to me.

All this sheep lore doesn't add up to much when it's spread over 30 years. To me, the sudden appearance of desert bighorn sheep has always been a mystery, a blessing, sometimes a specter bearing just the edge of fear. Despite my cryptic field notes, my memory of sheep over the last three decades shrivels to those who roused me from my sleeping bag and startled me on the brilliant nights of the full moon. Those sheep, it seems, I had to earn.

Even sheep sign can be a gift. It has been more than 20 years since Ed Gage and I found a sheep track outside a mine shaft southeast of Papago Well. Inside the 50-year-old hole was an old case of dynamite, the nitroglycerin all sweated out and dangerously unstable. Nearby, at Bassarisc Tank, we found more sheep tracks and the paw print of a lion; suddenly, the entire desert was imbued with unseen power and danger.

During December 1974, Ed Abbey and I drove my pickup into the Cabeza Prieta. Ed and I were unattached and without families at the time. We had spent a sniffling, lonely Christmas Eve at a topless bar in Tucson drinking whiskey. Thinking we could improve on that, we packed up and drove 150 miles west over Charlie Bell Pass into the Cabeza Prieta. We sipped beer all the way from Three Forks and were a tad plastered by the time we hit Charlie Bell Pass. We got my 1966 Ford truck stuck several times creeping down the dark, treacherous road to the well, hanging up the ass end of the truck, jacking it up in the dark, rocking it free and then dropping down into the Growler Valley. We continued on for one more six-pack around the north end of the Granite Mountains, where we got stuck in the sand one last time, finally crawling into our sleeping bags shortly after midnight. At six in the morning a sheriff's search-and-rescue team roared up, looking for some high school kids that some criminal son-of-a-bitch had hired to collect 20- and 40-mm. brass military cartridges. When a helicopter flew over, this bastard drove off, ditching the kids. One of the kids, we later learned, died of thirst and exposure. The search

Ed Abbey in the Cabeza Prieta Wilderness. A caricature of Doug Peacock appears on Abbey's t-shirt. Abbey's Hayduke character was inspired by his friend.

team pulled us out of the sand and went on. Ed and I drove through Montrose Well west into the Mohawk Valley. At the low pass we found bighorn sheep tracks. Later, on New Year's Eve at Eagle Tank, it sleeted and snowed on us—an unusual occurrence. We stayed three days in the Sierra Pinta, then dropped south onto the black basalt of the Pinacate lava fields.

Years later, I followed the tracks of a desert sheep from the bottom of Temporal Pass in the Growler Mountains to the center of the Growler Wash, where I lost the trail. I had gotten out there by walking southwest from Ajo after I had taken the bus from Tucson. I had come on a one-way ticket purchased for me by Lisa, the woman I later married. The Greyhound Bus clerk had been reluctant to even sell her the ticket for me.

"Lady," the clerk had said to Lisa, "nobody buys a one-way ticket to Ajo."

From Ajo, I shouldered my backpack and disappeared over the mine tailings, passing the camp of the O'odham hermit, Chico Shunie, just before daylight. It was dark again the next night when I reached the bottom of the Growler valley. Even by the dim light of the moon I could see big pieces of Hohokam pottery and *Glycymeris* clamshells lying on the desert pavement—it was the "Lost City" of the Hohokam shell trekkers. From here in the Growler Valley, an ancient shell trail ran south to Bahia Adair on the Sea of Cortez and north to the Gila River near Picture Rocks, where desert sheep are the most common animal petroglyph motif. I lost the trail of the bighorn because of the darkness and because a rattlesnake nailed me in the calf that night, though the bite turned out to be a dry one.

The next day, with a story to tell, I walked 20 miles to Papago Well, where Clarke and Ed Abbey were waiting for me.

Shortly after Gage's death, a mutual friend of ours contacted me. He was one of the cofounders of the Sanctuary Movement for Central American refugees, and he asked me to consider "taking over the Southwest Sector." This meant that I might illegally lead small groups of refugees, mostly from El Salvador, from Highway 2 in Mexico, north through the Cabeza Prieta, and up toward Interstate 8 or some other point where they could be picked up by vehicle.

I agonized long and hard over this decision. I had already begun my work with grizzly bears and was immersed in it. I also knew a lot about myself from my exposure to the radical politics of the 1960s and my time in Vietnam. It was clear that this kind of effort was one where my talents did not lie. There was also the danger of overcommitting and exhausting myself. Nevertheless, this was something I could do, and it needed doing.

The dilemma tore at me and I couldn't sleep. Once again, I went into the Cabeza Prieta to slumber and to track the sign that would show me what to do. The bus dropped me on the Tacna off-ramp. I shouldered my backpack draped with three-gallon canteens and staggered into the creosote, headed toward Mexico. I skirted the Copper Mountains, passed Buck Mountain, and, at the mouth of A-1 Wash, I found the corrugated remains of a giant set of ram's horns. The next morning I followed another sheep's tracks south up the wash until I passed over the tiny divide into the inner valley north of the tanks where Gage had seen his ram.

Sooner or later everyone runs into death, and I ran into a lot of it early on. And so I have used this great desert to bargain with the departed and get a handle on my insomnia. It's true, I invent ceremonies when necessary, especially when my own culture provides none; I erect my own memorials and celebrate my own Day of the Dead. But mostly I just shoulder a backpack and walk beyond fatigue across the bajadas, maybe crossing a set of sheep tracks and following them up a wash, finding a perfect campsite. The story of this place is not of loss but renewal.

The Cabeza Prieta desert is the most important thing Ed Abbey, Ed Gage and I ever shared, and it is not coincidence that these two closest desert friends from the past two decades are out there now. Gage's death was a tough one because he was a suicide. I maintain a secret and no doubt illegal memorial for him on a hilltop in one of these desert valleys. Each year for the past seven years I have hiked to this monument and held a private ceremony.

The last time Ed Abbey smiled was when I told him where he was going to be buried. I smile too when I think of this small favor, this last simple task friends can do for one another—the rudimentary shovel work, the sweaty labor consummating trust, and finally testing the exact confirmation by lying down in the freshly dug grave to check out the view: the bronze patina of boulder behind limb of palo verde and turquoise sky, beyond branch of torote. It was then that I received a sign: seven buzzards soaring above, who were soon joined by three others, all 10 banking over the volcanic rubble and riding the thermal up the flank of the mountain, gliding out and over the distant valley.

Even now, years after his death, I grin when I crest the ridge above his grave. The earth falls away and mountain ranges stretch off into the gray distance as far as the eye can see; there is not a human sign or sound, only a faint desert breeze stirring the blossoms of brittle-bush. We should all be so lucky.

On the eve of March 16, I journeyed to the edge of this desert place. March 16 is a "Day of the Dead" for me, the anniversary of the My Lai massacre (I was 20 miles away in Vietnam that day) and also the day in 1989 that three friends and I buried Ed Abbey here, illegally, in accordance with his last wishes.

I had traveled out here alone to Ed's grave, bearing little gifts, including a bottle of mescal and a bowl of pozole verde I had made myself. I sat quietly on the black volcanic rocks listening to the desert silence, pouring mescal over the grave and down my throat until the moon came up an hour or so before midnight. Suddenly I heard a commotion to the south, the roar of basaltic scree thundering down the slope opposite me. A large, solitary animal was headed my way.

I got the hell out of there.

Two days later I told my story of the desert bighorn ram I heard but never saw to my poet friend Jim Harrison.

"Well, Doug," Jim said, "maybe it was old Ed."

This Is the Center of My World

CHARLES BOWDEN

excerpted from *Blood Orchid,* 2000

I can feel every bone in my feet, my face is swollen and red, the fingers on my hand seem half numb and I have carried the 70-pound pack for a hundred miles. I sit in the saddle between the burnt hills and eye the valley. Tucson is more than a hundred miles to the east, Yuma and the Colorado River a hundred or more to the west. No one is here. This is the center of my world. At night, I can see the glow of the lights of Phoenix in the night sky although the city is at least a hundred miles away.

I walk toward the aluminum forest. Technically, I am on a gunnery range where military aircraft practice hitting targets. Sometimes the targets are inscribed on the ground, and when I stumble across them I find various pieces of arsenal lying about the bull's-eye area. Often the targets have been drones, aluminum glides pulled by other planes. When these drones break loose from time to time, they often impale themselves in the desert floor: the aluminum forest. For years, nature lovers have fussed and demanded that someone remove the dead drones because they ruin the view of this particular valley, which happens to be in a National Wildlife Refuge. I don't want them taken away. They are a monument to what has happened to this dry ground. Here the Cold War was fought and lost, and, by God, I want some kind of memorial to this defeat.

The Border as My Ex-wife:
An Epilogue

One time I told a reporter from I don't know where
that the border was like my ex-wife and he furiously
wrote this down in his notebook, supposing that
I would tell him more. The only thing I added
was that I have a pact with my ex-wife: I don't
talk bad about her and she doesn't talk bad about me.
—Luis Humberto Crosthwaite

I Don't Talk about Her and She Doesn't Talk about Me

Luis Humberto Crosthwaite

Translated by John William Byrd & Antonio Garza

There are people who like to talk about the border. I've seen them in supermarkets, in bars, in taxis, on city buses, on television, in newspapers. They always do it very seriously, like they were talking about a relative who just died or gossiping about a dying man. There are also those who dedicate themselves to studying the border, who are very knowledgeable and talk about her like experts.

I, on the other hand, am one of those who don't like to talk about the border. Right now, I'm writing these lines with a certain discomfort.

People are all the time arriving in my city to ask me about the border. They call it "the border phenomenon." I respond with annoyance. They notice this, they've figured me out. I have this reputation as someone who doesn't like to talk about her. And I've earned it.

These foreigners see me on the street and say, "Look at him, his name is Luis Humberto Crosthwaite and he doesn't like to talk about the border. He's never said anything interesting to us. He is an envious man." And they point their fingers at me.

I've seen them pointing at me. Luckily for them, there is always someone else just around the corner who gets excited talking about this subject, and they always keep their pants' pockets full of clichés to satisfy the imagination of those who want to know more and more.

To me, the border is like an ex-wife. I really just don't want to talk about her; it's too personal. It doesn't make much sense to explain this to a reporter who has an interest in drug trafficking or illegal aliens. It would bore them. They would feel like I was yanking their chain.

One time I told a reporter from I don't know where that the border was like my ex-wife and he furiously wrote this down in his notebook, supposing that I would tell him more. The only thing I added was that I have a pact with my ex-wife: I don't talk bad about her and she doesn't talk bad about me.

Or even better, the border is like my girlfriend. There are girlfriends we are boastful about and there are girlfriends we guard like an expensive secret. This one I have locked away in my heart.

We never go out together, but at parties we exchange smiles from across the room, delighted in knowing that nobody has found us out. We get a kick out of friends introducing us to each other like strangers. She says: "Good to meet you." And I tell her, "Nice to meet you." Then we make small talk about the weather and sports. "Did you know that…?" And she acts like she doesn't know that, acts like we have never spoken.

The border and me.

She knows that a lot of people talk about her. She is on the lips and minds of lots of men and women. They want her to be a real person so that they can interview her. If she were, they would ask her useless questions like: "How does it feel to be the border?"

They would judge her to be a stupid person because she wouldn't give them the answers that they wanted. The reporters would print, "She is interesting but not very intelligent." They would ask her: "Why did you decide to be a border, why not something else?" And she would just stay quiet, stuttering, stammering. It would make her scared that she didn't know what to say or have anything to say. "I am the border because I don't know how to be anything else." Too simple, this isn't a response. "There are a whole series of social problems, Miss Frontera, that are connected to you and you say that you don't know why you exist?" The reporter would turn off his tape recorder and stomp off feeling annoyed, convinced that it's better for the other people to talk about her, those who know the rhymes and reasons. "I want to know about the violence, about the death, about the heavy stuff, stuff that you expect to find on the dividing line between two countries that are so different."

The border arrives sadly at my house, asking me for a hug, some soothing words. Unhappily, I don't always have these words that she hopes for; I can't always be gentle and understanding. Sometimes I have too much work. Sometimes I don't even lift my eyes to see her or say hello when she comes. She sits down close to me, or she throws herself on my bed and starts to cry. Sometimes, I don't even notice.

I confess this about myself (my cruelty, my inability to understand) and I feel that I am saying too much, that I should leave this page blank, that anything I write here could be used against me. However, I don't have any way to avoid the topic.

I can put some distance between an interviewer and myself. I can refuse to answer his questions. But I can't stop thinking about her.

The border is my life.

I look at the palm of my hand and discover in its lines the destiny and the loves of the border. I rejoice in the simple mention of her name: Frontera.

I can repeat this name for infinity: *frontera, frontera…*

Or I don't have to do it; I can keep my silence and still find her in this silence.

THE BORDER AS MY EX-WIFE: AN EPILOGUE

La frontera (girlfriend, ex-wife) has left my house now that she realizes I have all this to write and no time for her. In her infinite solitude, she will travel the streets of my city, feeling a weariness mixed with fatigue and desolation. When she is happy, she looks young and enthusiastic; when she is alone they can see in her face the years she carries, her old age. She is a beautiful woman, but she suddenly feels old. There are still some who consider her beautiful, but she knows well (or at least thinks it) that her best times are past.

José Guadalupe Posada

I am a pathetic case; I know it. I stop writing for a few moments to go out and look for her. It is too late. I don't find her. What's the use of asking her forgiveness? Am I really trying to find her?

She has always been with me. We are the same age. When I was a kid, she was a young border. We used to play together. Later we were great friends and at the moment when we began to need love and companionship, there was no other person for us but each other.

In our worst moments, we threw plates and vases, books and lamps. Our fights were memorable, legendary. We always make up, with big hugs and rivers of tears, because we knew (or we know) that there is nobody else for us, that we are the same person, one indivisible being.

I am the border.

I will not say anything more now. If these words make me feel that I have betrayed her, adding more would be the most terrible thing that I have done in my life. We have this pact, I have to remember it: I don't talk about her and she doesn't talk about me. At least, I abstain from saying another thing. That's the reason for this book. Let those who want to speak, speak. It is their right. I will excuse myself beforehand because I have to stop writing. There is someone outside my house who needs me, who continues cruising the streets of my city. If I find her, I will hug her and bring her to my house again. I will try to comfort her and when I do that I will be comforted too.

There will be many more who will attempt to talk about her, trying to decipher her mysteries. I will be here, sleeping at her side, trying to be a better person for her. How many times have I tried? I seriously doubt that I can do it.

But I won't go further. Excuse me. I should stop writing.

A United States / Mexico Border Partial Reading List

Bowden, Charles. *Down by the River: Drugs, Money, Murder and Family*. Simon & Schuster. New York. 2002.

Bowden, Charles. *Juárez: Laboratory of the Future*. Aperture Foundation. New York. 1998.

Burckhalter, David L., Gary Paul Nabhan, Thomas E. Sheridan. *La Vida Norteña: Photographs of Sonora Mexico*. University of New Mexico Press. Albuquerque. 1998.

Burciaga, José Antonio. *Drink Cultura: Chicanismo*. Capra Press: Joshua Odell Editions. Santa Barbara. 1993.

Byrd, Bobby and Susannah Mississippi Byrd. *The Late Great Mexican Border: Reports from a Disappearing Line*. Cinco Puntos Press. El Paso. 1996.

Crosthwaite, Luis Humberto. *Idos de la mente*. Editorial Joaquín Mortiz. 2001.

Crosthwaite, Luis Humberto. *Instrucciones para cruzar la frontera*. Editorial Joaquín Mortiz. 2002.

Davidson, Miriam. *Lives on the Line, Dispatches from the U.S.-Mexico Border*. University of Arizona Press. Tucson. 2000.

Islas, Arturo. *Rain God: A Desert Tale*. Alexandrian Press. Palo Alto. 1984.

Miller, Tom. *Writing on the Edge*. University of Arizona Press. Tucson. 2002.

Nabhan, Gary Paul. *Gathering the Desert*. University of Arizona Press. Tucson. 1995.

Nathan, Debbie. *Women and Other Aliens: Essays from the U.S. Mexico Border*. Cinco Puntos Press. El Paso. 1991.

Quinones, Sam. *True Tales from Another Mexico: The Lynch Mob, the Popsicle Kings, Chalino, and the Bronx*. University of New Mexico Press. Albuquerque. 2001.

Ross, John. *México Bárbaro*. E-mail newsletter: wnu@igc.apc.org.

Urrea, Luis Alberto. *Across the Wire: Life and Hard Times on the Mexican Border*. Anchor Books. New York. 1993.

Urrea, Luis Alberto. *By the Lake of Sleeping Children: The Secret Life of the Mexican Border*. Anchor Books. New York. 1996.

Wald, Elijah. *Narcocorrido: a journey into the music of drugs, guns, and guerrillas*. Rayo Books. New York. 2001.

Weisman, Alan. *La Frontera, The United States Border with Mexico*. Photographs by Jay Dusard. University of Arizona Press. Tucson. 1986.

Acknowledgments

Balli, Cecilia. "Ropa Usada." Copyright © 2002 by Cecilia Balli. Used by permission of the author.

Barajas, Rafael (El Fisgón). Artwork. "Wetbacks," "Crucified Illegal," and "Uncle Sam Shooting Up," from *Los Moneros de la Jornada,* published by La Jornada Ediciones in Mexico. Copyright © 1999 by Rafael Barajas. Used by permission of the artist.

Berman, Bruce. Photographs. "Our Lady of Ropa Usada" and "The Day Old Blue Eyes Died." Copyright © 2002 by Bruce Berman. Used by permission of the photographer.

Berman, Bruce. "Towers of Crap." Copyright © 2002 by Bruce Berman. Used by permission of the author.

Borden, Tessie. "Juárez Center Fights for Forgotten Women," from *The Arizona Republic* (February 26, 2002). Copyright © 2002 by *The Arizona Republic.* Used by permission of *The Arizona Republic.*

Bowden, Charles. "Camera of Dirt," from *Aperture Magazine 159* (Spring 2000). Copyright © 2000 by Charles Bowden. Used by permission of the author.

Bowden, Charles. Excerpt from *Blood Orchid* (North Point Press). Copyright © 2000 by Charles Bowden. Used by permission of the author.

Byrd, Bobby. "Introduction," and "Enrique Madrid." Copyright © 2002 by Bobby Byrd. Used by permission of the author.

Byrd, Lee. Photographs "Enrique and Ruby ," "Border Checkpoint," "Esther Chavez," and "Stop the Violence." Copyright © 2002 by Lee Byrd. Used by permission of the photographer.

Cardona, Julián. Photographs. Copyright © 2002 by Julián Cardona. Used by permission of the photographer.

Courtney, Heather. Photograph "Ramon Castillo," from the documentary *Los Trabajadores \ The Workers.* Copyright © 2002 Heather Courtney. Used by permission of the photographer.

Crosthwaite, Luis Humberto. "The Smooth Rhythm" and "Afterword." Copyright © 2002 by Luis Humberto Crosthwaite. Used by permission of the author.

Crosthwaite, Luis Humberto. "Ña'a ta'ka ani'mai: What Will Be in My Heart," from *Lo Que Estara en mi Corazón,* published by EDAMEX and the Instituto Nacional de Bellas Artes (INBA), 1994. Copyright © 1994 Luis Humberto Crosthwaite. Used by permission of the author.

Daily, Dennis. Photograph "Norteño Duet." Copyright © 2002 by Dennis Daily. Used by permission of the author.

Delgado, Francisco. Cover art "$26." Copyright © 2002 by Francisco Delgado. Used by permission of the artist.

Draper, Robert. "Soldiers of Misfortune," from *Texas Monthly* (August 1997). Copyright © 1997 by Robert Draper. Used by permission of the author.

Evans, James. Photograph "Man in Ghilli Suit," from *The Texas Monthly* (August 1997). Copyright © 1997 by James Evans. Used by permission of the author.

Ross, John. "Carnival of Blood," from *Mexican Barbaro* #305 (April 20, 2002).
Copyright © 2002 by John Ross. Used by permission of the author.

Silko, Leslie Marmon. "The Border Patrol State" from *The Nation* (Oct. 17, 1994).
Copyright © 1994 by Leslie Marmon Silko. Used by permission of the author.

Udiarte, Roberto Castillo. "Johnny Tecate," from Letras Libres, www.libres.com,
an e-zine no longer published. Copyright © 2001. Used by permission of the author.

Urrea, Luis Alberto. "Tijuana Wonderland," from *Nobody's Son*, the University of Arizona Press.
Copyright © 1998 University of Arizona Press. Used by permission of the University
of Arizona Press.

Valdez, Diana Washington. "A Lawyer for Suspect in Killings in Juárez Slain," from the *El Paso
Times* (February 7, 2002). Copyright © 2002 by the *El Paso Times.* Used by permission
of the *El Paso Times.*

Villoro, Juan. "Nothing to Declare: Welcome to Tijuana," from Letras Libres (May 2000).
Copyright © 2000 by Juan Villoro. Used by permission of the author.

Ybarra-Frausto, Tomas. "Rasquachismo," from *CARA Chicano Art: Resistance & Affirmation.
An interpretive exhibition of the Chicano Art Movement*, published by the Wight Art
Gallery, UCLA, Los Angeles. Copyright © 1991 by Tomas Ybarra Frausto.
Used by permission of the author.

Zepeda, Ofelia. "Where the Wilderness Begins" from *Isle: Interdisciplinary Studies in
Literature and Environment* 4.1 (Spring 1997) Copyright © 2002 by Ofelia Zepeda.
Used by permission of the author.

About the Contributors

CECILIA BALLÍ writes for *Texas Monthly* and is pursuing a PhD in cultural anthropology at Rice University. A native of Brownsville, her work explores culture and identity along the U.S./Mexico border, in the Tejano and norteño music scene. She has written for *Latina Magazine* and was a reporter for the *San Antonio Express-News*.

RAFAEL BARAJAS is the infamous "El Fisgón," the witty and acerbic political cartoonist for the newspaper *La Jornada* in Mexico City.

BRUCE BERMAN has long been recognized as one of the premier photographers along the U.S./Mexico Border. He is a regular contributor to *Texas Monthly*, among other publications.

TESSIE BORDEN writes for the *Arizona Republic*. She is the Mexico City correspondent.

CHARLES BOWDEN lives in Tucson, Arizona and writes about what matters to him. His most recent book is *Down by the River: Drugs, Money, Murder and Family.*

BOBBY BYRD, author of nine books of poetry including most recently *The Price of Doing Business in Mexico*, has received a fellowship in poetry from the National Endowment for the Arts; a D.H. Lawrence Fellowship; and an International Residency Fellowship to live in Mexico which was funded jointly by the NEA and the Instituto de Belles Artes de México. In 1985, he and his wife Lee founded Cinco Puntos Press. He co-edited *The Late Great Mexican Border, Reports from a Disappearing Line* with his daughter, Susannah Mississippi Byrd.

JOHN WILLIAM BYRD, writer and editor, grew up on the U.S./Mexico Border in El Paso, Texas. He graduated from UT Austin with dual degrees in Anthropology and Zoology, and spent six months studying at La Pontificia Universidad Catolica in Quito, Ecuador. *Puro Border* is his first book.

LEE BYRD, author of the award-winning collection of short stories, *My Sister Disappears* (SMU Press, 1993) and co-publisher of Cinco Puntos Press, possesses a remarkable talent with the visual arts, which she vents through photography and collage. She likes to spend her spare time with the children of the neighborhood where she has made her home for the last 25 years.

JULIÁN CARDONA was born in Zacatecas, México but was raised on the border where he went to school and, as an adult, worked as a technician in the maquiladora industry. Cardona's work was featured in the 1998 Aperture publication, *Juárez: The Laboratory of Our Future*, written by Charles Bowden; and in the book *Borders and Beyond*, published in 2001. He lives in Mexico City.

LUIS HUMBERTO CROSTHWAITE is a prize-winning novelist who is very much involved with the contemporary literature of his country and the frontera. He has written three novels, four collections of short stories, one non-fiction book and a play. His work has been honored with the National Award for Non-Fiction Books and the National Award for Short Stories. Recently, he has published *Estrella de la Calle Sexta*, a book of short stories; *Idos de la Mente*, a novel; and *Instrucciones para Cruzar la Frontera*, a collection of short stories. He lives in Tijuana with his wife Teresa and their two (very beautiful) children.

HEATHER COURTNEY is a documentary filmmaker based in Austin, Texas. Her film *Los Trabajadores/ The Workers* has screened at over 20 national and international venues and in 50 community-based settings in conjunction with immigrant rights groups all over Texas. It has won numerous awards, including the International Documentary Association's David Wolper Student Award and the Audience Award at the South by Southwest Film Festival. She recently received a Fulbright scholarship to start work on her next documentary in Guanajuato, Mexico. For more information on *Los Trabajadores*, please see www.daylabormovie.com.

DENNIS DAILY lives in Las Cruces, New Mexico with his wife Veronica. They spend several weeks a year in Veronica's hometown of Durango, Mexico, where Dennis has been photographing and making sound recordings of folk traditions in contemporary Mexican society.

FRANCISCO DELGADO grew up in Juárez, Chihuahua, but completed high school in El Paso. He earned his MFA in Painting, Drawing and Printmaking in May 2002 from Yale University. Francisco, who painted the cover *$26*, is becoming known nationally for his political paintings which satirize U.S. icons that are blind to the mestizo and immigrant communities of Mexico.

ROBERT DRAPER is writer at large for *GQ Magazine* and a former senior editor for *Texas Monthly*. He is the author of *Rolling Stone Magazine: The Uncensored History* and the novel *Hadrian's Walls*; he's at work on his second novel. He lives in Asheville, North Carolina.

JAMES H. EVANS is a photographer who moved to Marathon, Texas to dedicate his life to documenting the life and landscape of the Big Bend and its borders. His first book will be released by the University of Texas Press in the spring of 2003. You can learn more about his work at www.jameshevans.com.

TOMAS YBARRA-FRAUSTO says of his work as prominent archivist, scholar and critic of the Chicano art movement, "Papelitos (little bits of paper), whether rent receipts, paid bills, or piles of personal letters, can become layered bundles of personal history. I have always been a pepenador (a scavenger) and saver of paper scraps." His archives, collected between 1965 to 1997, are housed at the Smithsonian at the Archives of American Art where he serves as a fellow.

MARIE "LOUIE" GILOT is a reporter currently working the police beat for the *El Paso Times*. She was born and raised in France and went to college in New York City where she worked at the *Wall Street Journal*. She came to El Paso three years ago looking to cover border affairs, crime and the assorted oddities which make up life on the U.S./Mexico border.

JULIAN HERBERT was born in Acapulco in 1971. At the age of 10, he immigrated (without intending to illegally cross the border) to the north of Mexico. He studied Spanish literature at the Universidad Autónoma de Coahuila and majored in corridos norteños. He is the author of three books of poems: *Chili Hardcore* (1994); *El Nombre de Esta Casa* (1999); and *El Cielo es el Naipe* (2001). He has published articles, stories and poems in Mexico, Spain and Argentina. He is the vocalist in a rock and roll ensemble called Los Tigres de Borges.

MICHAEL JAMES is co-owner of the Heartland Cafe, The Redline Tap, and The No Exit Cafe in Chicago and publishes the *Heartland Journal*. His photography show, "Mexico 1962," has traveled on exhibit in the greater Chicago area.

MARK KLETT is currently the Regent's Professor of Art at Arizona State University. In his work, he focuses on landscape issues. He has published nine books, including *Second View: the Rephotographic Survey Project; Revealing Territory;* and *Desert Legends* (with Gary Paul Nabhan). He lives in Tempe, Arizona with his wife and two daughters.

PETER LAUFER, author and journalist, traveled through Mexico in 2001 and 2002 to research changes in the media under the Vicente Fox administration. He is the author of several books, including a bilingual children's book, *Made in Mexico/Hecho en Mexico*.

JACK LOEFFLER is a writer, ethno-musicologist, and radio producer in Santa Fe, New Mexico. His recent book, *adventures with ED: a portrait of Abbey*, was published by University of New Mexico Press.

TRACY LYNCH is a freelance photographer in the Big Bend area and long time resident of Terlingua.

FRANCISCO VAZQUEZ MENDOZA was born in Colotlán, Jalisco, México in 1969. He studied journalism at ITESO and has worked at the *Siglo 21* and *Público* newspapers in Guadalajara. He is the Opinion Editor at *Público*, responsible for editorial pages, letters to the editor and political cartoons. He also writes the political column "La Tremenda Corte" for the same paper.

GARY PAUL NABHAN's most recent book was *Coming Home to Eat: The Pleasures and Politics of Local Foods.* He is the recipient of a MacArthur Fellowship, a Lannan Literary Fellowship and the John Burroughs Medal for natural history writing. He directs the Center for Sustainable Environments in Flagstaff, Arizona.

DEBBIE NATHAN is a writer and translator whose work has appeared in *The Village Voice, Texas Observer, The Atlantic Monthly, Salon, www.mrbellersneighborhood.com* and other venues. She is author of *Women and Other Aliens: Essays from the U.S.-Mexico Border*; co-author of *Satan's Silence: Ritual Abuse and the Making of a Modern American Witch Hunt*; and one of the translators for a collection of Latin American short stories and essays, *Yiddish South of the Border* (in press). A native Texan, she spent most of the 1980s and 1990s writing, doing politics and raising her kids in El Paso. She and her family currently live in New York City.

RAMSES NORIEGA has been a visual artist since childhood in Mexicali. He now resides in Fresno, California. After 25 years of college teaching and international art exhibits, he is retired and volunteers as a mentor to college-age students from his church.

DOUG PEACOCK, author of the bestselling memoir *Grizzly Years: In Search of the American Wilderness,* says, "I tend to like the animals that can kill and eat me."

TERRENCE POPPA is a Pulitzer-Prize finalist for his journalistic work regarding Mexico's old regime. His book, *Druglord, the Life and Death of a Mexican Kingpin*, offers keen insights into the involvement of the recently defeated PRI in drug trafficking and other organized crime. He currently owns and operates a private investigation agency in Seattle, Washington, and is working on a novel.

JESSICA POWERS is a writer and historian. She is the senior editor and collaborator for *Puro Border.* Her first book, a guide to hiking with dogs in southern New Mexico and West Texas, will be published by Cruden Bay Books in 2003.

SAM QUINONES is a freelance writer who has lived in Mexico City since 1994. A recipient of a 1998 Alicia Patterson Fellowship, he has written for numerous publications. He is the author of *True Tales from Another Mexico: the Lynch Mob, the Popsicle Kings, Chalino and the Bronx* (University of New Mexico), from which the piece *The Murdered Women of Juárez* was taken. He can be contacted at www.samquinones.com.

RUBÉN RAMIREZ is a writer and photographer for the *El Paso Times.*

DAVID ROMO is a free-lance writer, musician and linguist who, with his father, operates a Chevron service station six blocks from the border. Romo currently is editor of *El Bridge*, a cultural newspaper that emphasizes the relationship between art and political and social issues; and he is coordinating a multi-media project, *Somos Fronterizos,* which will document grassroots artistic expression in El Paso and Juárez. After two years of study at the Hebrew University in Israel, he received his degree in Judaic Studies from Stanford University.

JOHN ROSS was born in New York City in 1938. For many years, he has served as a foreign correspondent in Mexico and was one of the first to report on the Chiapas uprising. Most recently, he published a work of nonfiction, *The War Against Oblivion – Zapatista Chronicles 1994-2000* and a chapbook of poetry, *Against Amnesia.* He writes the weekly on-line newsletter "México Bárbaro."

LOU RUTIGLIANO, a freelance journalist for print, radio, and film media and most recently a reporter at the *El Paso Times*, is working on his Masters of Journalism at the University of Texas at Austin, where his focus is on journalism on the Internet and in Latin America.

LESLIE MARMON SILKO grew up in the Laguna Pueblo, fifty miles from Albuquerque. A prolific writer, she is the author of several books of poetry, fiction, and non-fiction, including *Ceremony, Storyteller* and *Yellow Woman and a Beauty of the Spirit*.

ROBERTO CASTILLO UDIARTE, alias Johnny Tecate, was born in the town of Tecate, Baja California in 1951. He is currently a professor of literature at the Universidad Autónoma de Baja California and at the Universidad Iberoamerican in Tijuana. His most recent books are *Elamoros guaguaguá, Banquete de podioseros, menu roquero para compass y compitas* and *La passion de Angélica según el Johnny Tecate*.

LUIS ALBERTO URREA has published several books, including a collection of border volumes. He is temporarily exiled to Chicago, but plans to vanish into the West. He has won The American Book Award, and the Western States Book Award. His latest book is *Six Kinds of Sky* (Cinco Puntos Press).

DIANA WASHINGTON VALDEZ, who has dual citizenship in the U.S. and Mexico, writes for the *El Paso Times*, covering Juárez. She is currently at work on a book concerning the women of Juárez.

JUAN VILLORO was born in Mexico City in 1956. He has been a professor at the Universidad Nacional Autónoma de México (UNAM) and a visiting professor at Yale. He is the author of the novels *El Disparo de Argón* and *Materia Dispuesta*; stories for children; and magazine articles and reports. His book of stories, *La Casa Pierde,* received the Premio Villaurrutia award in 1999 and his book of essays, *Efectos Personales*, won the Premio Mazatlán award in 2000. He now lives in Barcelona.

OFELIA ZEPEDA, PhD, is a member of the Tohono O'odham Nation and is a professor in the department of linguistics at the University of Arizona. Her work involves training native speakers of American Indian languages as teachers and researchers of their own languages. Ofelia is a published poet; her books include *Ocean Power: Poems from the Desert* and *Jewed 'I-Hoi/Earth Movements*, a bilingual collection.

Postscript

September 14, 1847.
The American flag waved on top of the Palacio Nacional in Mexico City.
General Winfield Scott slept on the Mexican president's bed.

It was the beginning of the end.

But so many good things came out of that.
Tijuana was a ranch and became a city.
Paso del Norte became Juárez and El Paso, and —155 years later—
a few good friends made a book called *Puro Border*.

Let's not forget.

—lhc